PICTURE PERFECT

PICTURE PERFECT

THE ART AND ARTIFICE
OF
PUBLIC IMAGE MAKING

Kiku Adatto

BasicBooks
A Division of HarperCollinsPublishers

For Michael, with love

Designed by Ellen Levine

Library of Congress Cataloging-in-Publication Data
Adatto, Kiku. 1947–
    Picture perfect: the art and artifice of public image making/
Kiku Adatto.
        p.   cm.
    Includes bibliographical references and index.
    ISBN 0-465-08087-1 (cloth)
    ISBN 0-465-05754-3 (paper)
    1. Presidents—United States—Election—History—20th century.
2. Television in politics—United States.   I. Title.
JK524.A72   1993
324.7'3'09730904—dc20   92-53236
                                                          CIP

95 96 97 **RRD H**   9 8 7 6 5 4 3 2

Contents

Acknowledgments   vii

Introduction   1

1.   Picture Perfect   7

2.   The Rise of Image-Conscious Television Coverage   24

3.   Contesting Control of the Picture   61

4.   Exposed Images: Image-Consciousness in Art
Photography and Popular Culture   94

5.   Mythic Pictures: The Maverick Hero in
American Movies   124

Epilogue   167

Notes   177

Index   189

Acknowledgments

THE MARKLE FOUNDATION PROVIDED A GENEROUS GRANT FOR THE research and writing of this book. I want to thank Lloyd Morrisett, Dolores Miller, and Jocelyn Hidi for their gracious support throughout. A fellowship at the Shorenstein-Barone Center on Press, Politics and Public Policy at Harvard's Kennedy School of Government enabled me to complete the research that formed the basis of chapter 2, on television news.

In order to learn the reactions of those involved in television coverage of presidential campaigns, I interviewed some sixty-five network reporters and producers, media consultants, and politicians. I am grateful to all of them for their patience in watching the videotaped excerpts I showed them, and for their willingness to share with me their insights. I am especially grateful to John Ellis, Esther Kartiganer, Bob Schieffer, Sanford Socolow, Sander Vanocur, and Bill Wheatley for helping me make my way in an unfamiliar world.

When it came to writing the book, I benefited greatly from the suggestions of my friend Pearl Bell, who read the entire manuscript with insight and care. I am also grateful to Moshe Halbertal, Gavin Lewis, Stephen Love, Barbara Norfleet, David Riesman, Matthew Sandel, Joy Sandel, and Judith Shklar for their many helpful comments and criticisms.

Joy Gragg, Russ Muirhead, Paula Nisbett, and Gloria Park provided invaluable research assistance, and Sue Wonderlee, John Jones,
and Wade Smith of Harvard's media services assisted in editing the
videotapes.

Gloria Loomis, more than an agent, was warm and helpful
throughout. At Basic Books, Martin Kessler believed in the book
from the start and encouraged me to pursue the connections I saw in
television news, art photography, and popular movies.

I would also like to acknowledge the role of family and friends, who
helped bring this project to fruition. My parents, Lily and Albert
Adatto, my sisters, Vicki and Debbie, my brother, Richard, and my
friends Denise Black, Michele Caplette, and Lynne Saner were a
constant source of encouragement. My two boys, Adam, age six, and
Aaron, age four, inspired by my example, were far more prolific than
I. As they watched me labor on a single book, they wrote and
illustrated dozens of their own, on topics ranging from ants to volca-
noes, guppies to dinosaurs. Kjerstin Salvesen, my friend and theirs,
gave me the security of knowing that my children were happy while I
was at my desk.

Above all, I am grateful to my husband, Michael Sandel, my
closest intellectual companion and my best and most sympathetic
critic. It is to him that I dedicate this book.

Introduction

I T WAS BITTER COLD IN WASHINGTON THE DAY OF RONALD REAGAN'S second inaugural. Like many Americans, I tuned in to see the ceremonies on television. But the parade was canceled, and the inauguration moved inside the Capitol. Outside, the television reporters stood amid icy reviewing stands, empty seats, and scaffolding. Bereft of the images they had come to record, they looked like displaced actors on a discarded set.

Over three years later, as I watched the 1988 presidential campaign unfold on television, I began to see that having the image before them posed its own problems for reporters. Much to my surprise, the political coverage of the Bush-Dukakis campaign focused as much on the process of image making as on the discourse of politics. I wondered whether it had always been that way.

I decided to compare the television coverage of the 1988 and 1968 campaigns. The campaign of 1968, between Richard Nixon and Hubert Humphrey, was the first to be waged—especially on the Republican's part—with careful attention to how it would play on the evening news. And so, with help from the Vanderbilt University archives of television news and the media services of Harvard University's Kennedy School of Government, I assembled and watched videotapes of the three major networks' weekday evening newscasts from

Labor Day to Election Day in 1968 and 1988, some 280 broadcasts.

Political reporting had indeed changed. There was a dramatic shift in focus from the speech of the candidates to their efforts at image making. I discovered that the average length of a "sound bite," or block of uninterrupted speech, fell from 42.3 seconds in 1968 to only 9.8 seconds in 1988.[1]

But despite all the attention my finding received, I was more interested in telling a larger story of which television is only a part. This is the story of the rise of a new image consciousness in American culture, which has been unfolding since the Second World War in photography, popular movies, and television.

When the photograph was first invented in the nineteenth century, people were fascinated by the realism of the camera even as they acknowledged the artifice of the pose. In contemporary American culture, our sensibility has shifted. Now we are alive as never before to the artifice of images. Today we pride ourselves on our knowledge that the camera can lie, that pictures can be fabricated, packaged, and manipulated.

We have even developed an affection for artifice, an appreciation of slick production values whether in political campaigns, beer commercials, or a favorite movie. A political cartoon that appeared during the 1992 presidential primaries captures this tendency well. Two rural Southerners sit on the front porch of a ramshackle general store called "Bubba's," talking politics. One says to the other, "I like Buchanan's sound bites, but Clinton and Tsongas have slicker production values."[2]

If one side of us appreciates, even celebrates, the image as an image, another side yearns for something more authentic. We still want the camera to fulfill its documentary promise, to provide us with insight, to be a record of our lives and the world around us. But because we are so alive to the pose, we wrestle with the reality and artifice of the image in a more self-conscious way than our forebears.

This tension is most vividly displayed in television coverage of presidential politics. As political campaigns mastered the art of television image making, reporters shifted from recording the words of candidates to exposing their images and revealing their contrivances. But in 1988 the networks did not succeed in avoiding manipulation by the politicians or in vindicating television's documentary promise. For all their attention to the pose behind the picture, the networks remained entangled in the artifice of the images they showed. By lavishing attention, even critical attention, on photo opportunities, media events, and political commercials, they gave yet more airtime to the candidates' potent pictures. And too often, no amount of reporting on their status as images diminished their impact.

Such television coverage conveyed, in effect, the paradoxical message: "Behold these striking pictures. But as you behold them, beware of them, for they are not real. They are fake, the products of media consultants and spin-control artists who are trying to move you or deceive you or persuade you. So do not take these pictures at face value. They are setups, contrived for the sake of our television cameras, and in this sense, our cameras lie."

But if these pictures were mere contrivances, why did the networks persist in airing them? Why not simply refuse to show them? Some network reporters and producers replied that their job is to show what happens each day in the presidential campaign; since modern campaigns consist largely of contrived media events and ads, that is what they must show on the evening news. Others, including politicians, media advisers, and some television journalists, observed that given competitive pressures for ratings and profits, the networks cannot resist showing the visually arresting pictures that the campaigns produce.

There is truth, no doubt, in the various explanations—economic, political, and technological—of the transformation of television news. But what intrigued me most in watching the 1988 coverage and talking to the participants was something else. Whatever the causes of the image-conscious style of television news, it created a tension or dilemma for television journalists. On the one hand, the growing entertainment orientation of network news compelled reporters and producers to get the best possible picture, even if this made them accomplices in artifice; on the other hand, the traditional documentary ambition of television journalism compelled them to puncture the picture, to expose the image as an image. Although network reporters and producers did not think of their job in these terms, they found themselves engaged in the paradoxical role of first perfecting and then puncturing the picture, by calling attention to its self-conscious design. In 1992, the networks devoted less coverage to image-making, but the fast-paced, entertainment-driven style of coverage, with its impatience for political speech, persisted.

Although we often blame television for all that is wrong with contemporary politics, the preoccupation with political image making is not unique to our time. Since long before the advent of television, politicians have sought to manipulate the power of images, and journalists have struggled with the realism and artifice that pictures convey.

Those who despair at the triviality of modern campaigns often complain that Abraham Lincoln would never have triumphed in the television age. But Lincoln was far from innocent of the political use of pictures. When he became president he wryly thanked his photographer Mathew Brady for providing him with the dignified image that helped him win the White House. His presidential campaign was the first to distribute mass-produced portraits of the candidate. Their popular appeal led one of Lincoln's advisers to conclude, "I am coming to believe that likenesses broad cast, are excellent means of electioneering."[3]

More broadly still, the potential of the camera for both realism and artifice has a significance beyond its political expression. Over two decades before television news became preoccupied with the construction of political images, art photographers and moviemakers began saying through their work, "Behold the image. See how it is made and manipulated."

Photographers in the 1950s and 1960s called attention to the way in which the camera "frames" reality. They not only looked with an ironic eye at the images the media asks us to take for granted, but they drew attention to how the image was constructed in their own photographs. Moviemakers also made television's power to fabricate images the subject of their stories. Popular movies self-consciously called attention to their own image making—sometimes in the form of genre spoofs, and sometimes breaking out of the story to call attention to the movie as a movie.

This self-consciousness in movies is an important strain, but not the dominant one. When most movies ask us to "behold the image," they do not want us to see the image as an image. They want us to relax, sit back, and suspend our disbelief. While we do just that, movies tell us stories about our lives. Although the movies do not claim to be presenting facts, we often believe and are moved by what we see, sometimes more so than by what we see or hear in schools, lecture halls, or on the evening news. As a result, they form a common frame of reference. We all quote the movies—politicians, newscasters, people at parties, kids playing. After watching the top ten most popular movies from 1968 through 1991, and most of the critically acclaimed films during this period (over three hundred movies in all), I found that, for all their different stories, they display a common pattern.[4] In contrast to the image-conscious, myth-debunking sensibility that now dominates other realms of our culture, most movies ask us to believe in the image and are the bearers of traditional American myths and ideals.

Thus, what began as a study of television news and presidential politics led me to a larger story about the images the camera holds up to society—the still camera, the television camera, and the movie camera. These images, which often seem to have little to do with each other, fit together in ways we do not expect.

Thinking about American photography and the movies made me more alert than I might otherwise have been to the image-conscious character of television news. In turn, observing the changes in television news led me to see photography and the movies in a different perspective, as sources of insight into the forces that shape our political culture. In particular, the resonant, mythic images that persist in the movies helped me understand that certain images resist unraveling no matter how much attention is called to their self-conscious design.

In telling the story of the rise of a new image consciousness in American culture, I make no claim to explaining causes and effects. Although the image-conscious sensibility became prominent first in art photography and later in television news and popular culture, this does not imply that television reporters took their cue from the art photographers. The photographers were more interested in television than television reporters and producers were interested in (or even aware of) developments in the art world. My aim is not to explain, in causal terms, the developments I describe. It is rather to explore the expressions and limitations of the image-conscious sensibility, and to consider its consequences for our understanding of ourselves. Since I hope to show that our image-conscious culture plays out, in heightened form, tendencies as old as the photograph itself, my story begins with the invention of the photograph a century and a half ago.

Picture Perfect

JUST BEFORE NOON ON MARCH 8, 1839, LOUIS DAGUERRE, A FRENCH painter and inventor, traveled through the streets of Paris to an appointment with a visitor from America. For over seventeen years, Daguerre had been the proprietor of one of the most popular spectacles in Paris. It was a theater of illusions called the Diorama.

No actors performed in Daguerre's Diorama theater. It consisted of a revolving floor that presented views of three stages. On each stage was an enormous canvas (72 by 48 feet) with scenes painted on both sides. Through the clever play of light, Daguerre could make one scene dissolve into another. Parisians were treated to the sight of an Alpine village before and after an avalanche, or Midnight Mass from inside and outside the cathedral accompanied by candles and the smell of incense.

The realism of these illusions was so compelling that an art student once set up an easel and began to paint one of the scenes. Daguerre was quick to set him straight. "Young man, come as often as you want to, but don't work here, because you will be making nothing but a copy of a copy. If you want to study seriously, go out of doors."[1]

The illusions of the Diorama were no doubt far from Daguerre's mind as he walked up the three flights of steps to the apartment where his American colleague was waiting. He had come to see Samuel

Morse and his new invention, the telegraph. The two men talked for an hour. As they talked, Daguerre's Diorama was engulfed in flames. It burned to the ground before he returned, destroying years of work.

Fortunately, for Daguerre all was not lost. He had recently completed work on another invention, already secured beyond the reach of the flames. Two years earlier, in 1837, Daguerre had found a way to preserve chemically, on silver-plated copper, an image of reality. He had invented the photograph.

Photography as Document and Artifice

Since the sixteenth century, artists had used a device called a "camera obscura" to enhance the perspective of their paintings. The camera obscura (literally, "dark room") was a box with a lens that formed an image on ground glass that the artist could trace. Daguerre had used this device to draw the lifelike paintings for his theater of illusion.

Many artists had dreamed of preserving the image rather than tracing it, but until the 1830s, no one had succeeded.[2] Daguerre's invention of the photograph—known then as the "daguerreotype"—would transform the way people saw the world and themselves. But in the day of its invention, the photograph seemed to offer a simpler triumph—of reality over illusion, of accuracy over art.

Photography seemed to promise a picture more perfect than art could produce. At last it would be possible to document the world objectively, free of the vagaries of the artist's eye. They called the photograph "the pencil of nature." Samuel Morse, who became a photographer himself, observed that photographs were not "copies of nature, but portions of nature herself."[3] Oliver Wendell Holmes, father of the noted jurist, called the daguerreotype "the mirror with a memory."[4]

The new photographs were so true to life that people examined them as scientists would examine a specimen. Edgar Allan Poe was struck by the photograph's perfect correspondence to nature. "If we examine a work of ordinary art by means of a powerful microscope, all traces or resemblance to nature will disappear—but the closest scrutiny of the photographic drawing discloses only a more absolute truth, a more perfect identity of aspect with the thing represented."[5]

Quite apart from its scientific interest, the daguerreotype won instant popularity in America as a means of portraiture. Traditionally, only the wealthy could afford to commission portraits. With the invention of photography, portraiture became democratic. People from every walk of life could afford one. Every town had a portrait studio. Photographers floated down rivers in houseboat studios, and traveled in covered wagons through the countryside.

Drawn to photography for its realism, its "absolute truth," Americans soon confronted a puzzling feature of the new invention. Not all daguerreotypes succeeded in capturing the truth of their subjects. Ralph Waldo Emerson, for example, once lauded the photograph for its authenticity. "No man quarrels with his shadow, nor will he with his miniature when the sun was the painter."[6] When he saw his own portraits, however, he was dissatisfied, noting that his family called them "supremely ridiculous."[7]

A successful daguerreotype was more than a mechanically produced representation; it required collaboration between photographer and subject. Since the exposure time was about thirty seconds, the subject had to sit perfectly still, aided by a brace behind him. The photographer had carefully to arrange the light, the lenses, and the composition of the frame. But the great portrait photographers knew that rendering the reality of their subject required more than technical mastery. It demanded of the photographer the insight and imagination to draw the person out, to capture the revealing moment. And it demanded of the subject the art of being natural, of being himself before the camera.

For all their fascination with the realism of the photograph, Americans grasped from the start that portrait photography was an art, the art of rendering an image that tells the truth about its subject. More than mere physical depiction, the daguerreotype sought to express "the subject's internal reality—the spirit of fact that transcends mere appearance."[8] As a nineteenth-century historian of photography observed, "a portrait is worse than worthless if the pictured face does not show the soul of the original—the individuality of self-hood, which differentiates him from all beings, past, present or future."[9]

The famous Boston daguerreotypist Albert Southworth described the art of making someone look real. "Nature is not at all to be represented as it is, but as it ought to be, and might possibly have been. . . . The aim of the artistic photographer [is] to produce in the likeness the best possible character and finest expression of which the particular face or figure could ever have been capable. But in the result there is to be no departure from truth."[10]

If photography aspired to the "spirit of fact," rather than brute representation, there was always the possibility that the camera could lie. The need to pose, to look good before the camera, meant that even the "pencil of nature" could sometimes deceive. A photograph could fail to do justice to its subject, or on the other hand, make people look better than they really were. "Hurrah for the camera," said Emerson sarcastically. "The less we are the better we look"; and the novelist N. P. Willis observed, "Some of us know better than others how to put on the best look."[11] Mark Twain poked fun at idealized family portraits for showing people in uncustomary poses, "too much combed, too much fixed up."[12] Nadar, a noted French portrait photographer, could not resist recording the truth about a French police official who looked all too distinguished in the photograph he had taken. On the back of the photo, he wrote "spy, parasite."[13]

Boss Tweed, the corrupt head of the New York City political machine of the 1860s, looked the picture of probity in his official photograph, taken by the famous Civil War photographer Mathew Brady. Tweed, like other politicians of his day, had great control over his photographic image, since the slow shutter speed of cameras prevented any candid photography. The truer pictures of Boss Tweed were the unflattering Thomas Nast cartoon caricatures that appeared in *Harper's Weekly* in the early 1870s. "Stop those damn pictures," Tweed is said to have demanded of his men. "I don't care so much what the papers write about me. My constituents can't read. But damn it, they can see pictures."[14]

Here, then, was a paradox of picture taking that appeared from the start. Despite its promise of the ultimate document, of a picture more realistic than art could achieve, the camera was also an instrument of artifice and posing, even fakery and deceit. The invention that enabled people to write with the sun would blur the distinction between appearance and reality, between the image and the event. Daguerre's two inventions—photography and the theater of illusions—thus had more in common than at first appeared.

Contesting Control of the Picture

The era of the unique photographic image, the daguerreotype, ended near the time of the Civil War. New types of photography superseded it based on the use of negatives allowing the easy reproduction of photographic images. Yet, photographs could not be reproduced in magazines and newspapers, and the photograph was simply used as a model for drawings and etchings. It was not until the turn of the century that photography became a form of mass communication.

By 1900 photographs were readily reproduced in newspapers, inaugurating a new era of photojournalism. Kodak's small, hand-held camera, invented in 1888, gave everyone the opportunity to take snapshots. The catchy advertising slogan, "You press the button, we do the rest," boasted of how easy and automatic photography had become. The Kodak became an immediate success, providing a simple way of recording personal and family life. Because of its faster film and ease of use, Kodak's new camera also made it possible to photograph subjects who had not posed or consented to be photographed.

The turn of the century also marked the rise of the movies. In 1896 large-screen motion picture projection was invented. Movies began in vaudeville theaters appealing to the working and immigrant classes, but soon widened their appeal across class lines. The cultural dominance of movies would extend until the mid-1940s.

In the movies, fantasy and document were merged right from the start. During the 1898 war with Spain, audiences craved news from the front, but there was no documentary newsreel footage. That did not prevent Thomas Edison's movie company from fabricating flag raisings against painted backdrops or reenacting executions for a public eager for information. [15]

By the third decade of the twentieth century, pictures became even more defining of American popular and political culture. With the invention of sound, movies became still more realistic in presenting their fanciful pictures. Whether mocking social conventions or fueling hopes of social success, movies like It Happened One Night (with Clark Gable and Claudette Colbert) and Top Hat (with Ginger Rogers and Fred Astaire) shaped the popular imagination during the Depression years.

The drama inherent in pictures was also exploited by the new picture magazines of the late 1930s. The first issue of *Life* magazine in 1936 trumpeted its pictures of news events, novelties, human-interest stories and public-relations stunts. An advertisement for *Time* magazine, carried in *Life*, bore the headline, "There is no drama like reality," succinctly summarizing the blending of drama and documentation in popular picture magazines.

The new medium of television, introduced in the 1940s, was thus the inheritor of a potent visual culture in which the camera played many roles. Like radio in the 1920s and 1930s, television first succeeded as an entertainment medium and then developed strong news divisions, recruiting reporters from print and radio. The news began as only a fifteen-minute program, expanding to the half-hour format in 1963.

By the 1950s television became the dominant visual medium, effacing the picture magazines and the movies. The perfect picture of the television age could be presented "live" in people's living rooms. In 1950, only 9 percent of American households had a television set; by 1960, the figure was 87 percent.

The realism of the television image has been enhanced by a series of technological innovations; color, portable cameras, and satellite hook-ups and electronic editing which permit an instant image from around the world. Cable television provided a host of channels and choices of entertainment and news, from reruns of movies and old television shows to round-the-clock news on CNN and unedited coverage of major news events on C-SPAN.

As photography, then the movies, and finally television became mass forms of image creation, both the promise and the paradox reverberated through American culture. Given the prominence of images in mass democracies like ours, the paradox assumed increasing political importance. Boss Tweed could only complain about those "damn pictures." His successors adopted sophisticated media strategies to control them.

At least since Machiavelli, political consultants have urged politicians to worry more about appearance than reality. "Everyone can see what you appear to be," Machiavelli wrote, "whereas few have direct experience of what you really are."[16] Four centuries later, American politics is largely a contest for control of television images.

As the American triumph in the Persian Gulf war became tarnished by the spectacle of abandoned and victimized Kurdish refugees, a Doonesbury cartoon depicted President Bush's political predicament. "So what happened? What happened to my perfect little victory?" the President asks. His aides reply: "We lost control of the pictures, sir. . . . During the war, we killed 100,000 Iraqis, but we controlled the media, so no one saw the bodies. With the Kurds, it's a different situation. Every baby burial makes the evening news. . . . I'm afraid we are just going to have to tough it out. At least until we can get the pictures back on our side."[17]

A few years earlier, during the Iran-Contra hearings that made Oliver North a national celebrity, Democrats learned what it meant to "lose control of the pictures." Steven Spielberg, the Hollywood director, was visiting Washington during the televised hearings. As he watched the hearings with some Democratic congressmen, he offered them a lesson in camera angles. "Watch this," Spielberg said, as he turned down the sound and directed the congressmen's attention to North's image on the screen. "The camera on North is shooting up, from about four inches below his eyes. This is the way they shot Gary Cooper in the western, *High Noon,* to make him look like a hero." When the camera panned to the committee members questioning North, Spielberg pointed out, the lighting was dim. Seen at a distance, they looked sinister. Spielberg told the assembled Democrats, "It doesn't matter what Oliver North says. He has already won the battle, because he looks like the hero and everyone else looks like the villain." This realization shocked the congressmen. They knew they could not change the camera angles without being criticized. As one Democratic congressman remarked, "We knew we were in trouble."[18]

A short time later, when it came to the hearings for Supreme Court nominee Robert Bork, Democrats had learned their lesson. This time they focused attention on the setting and stagecraft. The television cameras would look directly at the controversial nominee, not up from the well of the committee room. There would be no more heroic camera angles. As a Democratic political adviser observed, "This time, we wanted to make sure that the playing field was fair."[19] Although ideological and constitutional disputes led to his defeat, Bork did come across badly on television, and failed to win confirmation to the Supreme Court.

The contest for the control of television images, now a familiar feature of American politics, is on most vivid display in presidential campaigns. Since 1960, when Richard Nixon lost narrowly to John Kennedy after refusing to use makeup in their televised debate, presidential candidates have sought carefully to cultivate their television image. By the 1980s, staged photo opportunities, contrived media events, carefully crafted sound bites, and highly coordinated spin-control efforts had become standard tactics in the battle to control the image that appears on the evening news.

But the contest over images was not only a contest between Democrats and Republicans. As media consultants became increasingly sophisticated at manipulating television on behalf of their candidates, the contest for control of television images was joined by the networks themselves. By 1988, network reporters and producers, seeking to resist manipulation by the campaigns, struck back. Rather than report simply on the statements and activities of the candidates, the networks made image making itself the focus of their coverage, calling frequent attention to the campaigns' efforts to construct images for television.

When covering candidate Bush witnessing the destruction of a missile under an arms control treaty, for example, Brit Hume of ABC reported the event as a photo opportunity and told his viewers how the army had bulldozed acres of trees to provide the proper camera angles for television. The language of political reporting was filled with accounts of staging and backdrops, camera angles and scripts, sound bites and spin control, photo opportunities and media gurus. So attentive was television news to the way the campaigns constructed images for television that political reporters began to sound like theater critics, reporting more on the stagecraft than the substance of politics.

This image-conscious style of coverage is now so familiar that it is difficult to recall the transformation it represents. The heightened attention to the construction of images for television, so prominent in 1988 coverage, was all but absent only twenty years earlier. Only 6 percent of reports in 1968 were devoted to theater criticism, compared to 52 percent in 1988. In 1968, the term photo opportunity, now a well-worn phrase of political reporting, was used only once. [20]

The turn to image-conscious coverage by the television networks was an attempt—ultimately unsuccessful—to avoid manipulation by the campaigns, and wrest control of television images from the politicians. But it also reflected the emergence in television of a cultural tendency that had earlier found expression in art and photography: the striving, mostly dormant in the first century of American photography, to draw attention to the image as image, as artifice, as act of construction.

The Image-Conscious Culture

In the decades after World War II, artists and photographers began self-consciously to explore their role in the image-making process. For example, in 1970 Lee Friedlander published a book of photography called *Self Portrait*, in which his own shadow or reflection appeared in every frame. As one critic observed, "by indicating the photographer is also a performer whose hand is impossible to hide, Friedlander set a precedent for disrupting the normal rules of photography."[21]

Perhaps the most famous example is the pop art of Andy Warhol, including his paintings of Campbell's soup cans, Brillo pads, Marilyn Monroe, and other icons of popular culture. By making products like soup the subject of art, Warhol changes our way of seeing them. Where an actual ad for Campbell's soup would direct our attention to the product, a Warhol painting of the same soup can, however realistic, directs our attention less to the product than to the packaging of the product. It makes us aware of the image as an image.

Warhol took as his subjects not only the fabricated images of advertising and the movies, but the documentary images of television and newspapers. He made multiple silk screen images of the Kennedy assassination, car crashes, and the front pages of tabloids.

In this way, Warhol recapitulated in art the paradox that had attended photography since its inception. On the one hand, he reproduced the images that he depicted with almost perfect accuracy; his Campbell's soup can was almost indistinguishable from the real thing. At the same time, the very act of reproducing, rearranging, and repeating the images makes us see them differently—ironically, or humorously, or critically.

Warhol once remarked, "I don't know where the artificial stops and the real starts. The artificial fascinates me, the bright and shiny."[22] Like the young artist who set up his easel in Daguerre's theater of illusions, Warhol created "a copy of a copy," an image of an image. But for Warhol, unlike the nineteenth-century artist, that was just the point. In our highly commercialized, media-saturated society, appearance had become reality; the boundary between reality and illusion, Warhol insisted, is less secure than we think.

Social commentators took up the new image-conscious sensibility of the 1950s and 1960s, some with alarm, some with praise. In *The Image* (1961), Daniel Boorstin complained that Americans were being increasingly beguiled by "pseudo-events"—scripted performances by corporations and politicians designed to "make news"—rather than engaged in real events. Marshall McLuhan wrote of the power of television to transform reality, and declared that, "the medium is the message." And Joseph McGinniss described the sophisticated construction of television images by Richard Nixon's 1968 campaign in *The Selling of the President* (1969).

Despite the hyperconsciousness of image-making that developed in the art, photography, and social criticism of the 1950s and 1960s, television news did not partake of this sensibility until two or three decades later. Television coverage of the 1968 presidential campaign scarcely mentioned the image-making apparatus of the candidates. Even as they reported the first presidential campaign "made for the evening news," reporters in 1968 continued to reflect the print-journalism traditions from which they had descended. They covered the media events of the day—mostly rallies and press conferences— as political events, not as exercises in impression management. Reporters covered what the candidates said, not the image they sought to create on the evening news. It was not until the 1980s that television displaced politics as the focus of coverage, and political reporting became theater criticism.

The preoccupation with the self-conscious construction of television images also found its way into entertainment programming, and at roughly the same time. One of the most popular television shows of 1990 was "America's Funniest Home Videos." Americans tuned in to watch and laugh at scenes of people getting stuck in dishwashers, having their pants fall down, or finding a hand reaching out of their soup pot.

It was not the first time that a television program made a hit comedy of the surprises and misfortunes that befall people in their everyday life. In the 1960s, the popular program "Candid Camera" had a similar appeal. There, too, viewers were regaled by the spectacle of ordinary people encountering unexpected circumstances. But there was a difference, which marks an important shift in American popular culture from the 1960s to the 1990s.

In "Candid Camera," the subjects were innocent, unaware of the television camera. Only the punch line, "Smile, you're on Candid Camera," revealed that others were watching. In "America's Funniest Home Videos," by contrast, the presence of the camera is no surprise. The participants hold the camera in their hands. Many episodes are not candid but posed, home videos self-consciously constructed to play before a national audience on television. While "Candid Camera" has enjoyed a revival in the 1990s, the far more popular "America's Funniest Home Videos" exemplifies the new image-consciousness.

Like Warhol's art three decades earlier, "America's Funniest Home Videos" draws our attention to the image as an image. In the opening of the show, the camera focuses on the upper tier of the television studio, where a family watches television in a staged living room. A variation of this theme is played out in the studio below. A huge screen displays the home videos competing for the prizes. The stars of the program are the contestants themselves, now in the studio audience, shown watching their videos on television.

By 1990, the image-conscious sensibility also found expression in the changing style of television news documentaries. The title of Edward R. Murrow's "See It Now" (1951) conveyed the traditional documentary ambition—to portray an event whose reality is independent of the camera's eye. Its title gestured toward the events it documented. By contrast, a newsmagazine program of the late 1980s played out television's new self-referential tendency. "West 57th" took its title from the street address of the CBS studios where the program was produced. The title of the program referred not to its subject matter but to the fact and circumstances of its production. As if to reinforce the point, its opening sequences showed reporters and producers amid videotape machines and editing equipment, directing viewers' attention to the production as a production.

A similar shift in emphasis—drawing the viewer's attention away from the event and toward the apparatus of television's coverage of the event—can be seen in the way the networks photograph their anchormen on the evening news. In 1968, the images of the candidates or other newsmakers virtually filled the screen, with the anchormen occupying a corner of the screen. By 1988, it was the anchormen who filled the frame, while photographs of the candidates had shrunk to cameo size. Like the photographer in Lee Friedlander's photos, the television anchorman's image became a looming presence in the frame, as if inseparable from the event he reported.

The Flight from Substance: The Self Deformed

The image-conscious sensibility that has emerged in American popular culture in recent decades is not limited to art and photography, television and film. It also carries consequences for our understanding of ourselves. Much as image-conscious coverage of political campaigns directs our attention away from the substance toward the packaging and stagecraft, recent accounts of identity emphasize the sense in which we construct, even fabricate ourselves. Traditional notions of fixed selves, defined by character or soul, give way to the modern notion of a centerless self, always in the process of forming or reforming itself.

Even as Boorstin bemoaned the dominance of images and pseudo-events and Warhol proclaimed his fascination with the artificial, the sociologist Erving Goffman described the fabricated self in his influential book, *The Presentation of Self in Everyday Life* (1958). For Goffman, the self is defined by its "performances," consisting of "fronts," "settings," "dramatic realizations and misrepresentation," and "the art of impression management." Sincerity is no longer a matter of conscience or faithful adherence to one's truest self, but a quality of "individuals who believe in the impression fostered by their own performance."[23]

The fabricated self, like the image-conscious culture it shapes and reflects, takes flight from substance and focuses instead on its own constructed status. Some see this way of viewing ourselves as liberating. If the self is not fixed by a character or soul or historically given identity, it is unburdened by the past, open to a wider range of possibilities. As one defender of the fabricated self has written, "Positing identity as a mutable fabrication rather than a stable 'truth,' is one way to resist the coercive agendas these representations can come to perpetuate."[24]

But there is also a dark side to the fabricated self, which the modern history of photography vividly portrays. From the time of the daguerreotype to the documentary photography of the 1930s and 1940s, American photography celebrated individuality, and ennobled it. The highest goal of the portrait was to reveal the character and inner life of the subject portrayed. But beginning in the 1950s and 1960s, the individual was no longer presented as distinct and whole.

The photography of Robert Frank, for example, explores the perplexities, the dissonances, the moral ambiguity of American life in the 1950s. In Frank's images, we find dark and empty highways, an out-of-focus starlet at a movie premiere, a television set left on in an empty room, a poster of Eisenhower askew in a store window displaying formal wear.

In the "social landscape" of the 1960s, the individual is shown exposed, obscured, fragmented, and deformed. The relation between self and society is askew, oblique. Neither the individual nor the environment that he or she inhabits appears harmonious or whole. The photographer defines the individual by his or her lack of fit. In this new social landscape there is little sense of privacy; even in the private sphere of family and home the individual is exposed.

Diane Arbus, for example, made freaks, deviants, and outcasts the subject of her photographs. Even ordinary people—a baby crying or a child playing in Central Park—are made to look deformed, freakish. In the 1960s, photographers are less concerned with the inner life of their subjects than the incongruities of their outward appearance. Garry Winogrand, for example, did a series of photographs of people at the Central Park Zoo in which the people look like the animals. The images are amusing but the individuals are objectified. They have no identity beyond Winogrand's humorous typology.

The pop art of Andy Warhol displays a similar stance toward the self. Warhol had no interest in the soul of his subjects, but was fascinated by the surface. He chose celebrities as his subjects—Marilyn Monroe, Elizabeth Taylor, and Elvis Presley—and reproduced multiple silk-screen images of them drawn from their publicity photographs. When Warhol himself became a celebrity, he deliberately fabricated details of his biography, telling different interviewers different "facts" about his life.

A century earlier, in a whimsical commentary on the new invention of photography, Oliver Wendell Holmes presciently anticipated the image-conscious sensibility that Warhol came to represent. "Matter as a visible object is of no great use any longer," Holmes mused,

> except as the mould on which form is shaped. Give us a few negatives of a thing worth seeing, taken from different points of view, and that is all we want of it. . . . There is only one Coliseum or Pantheon; but how many millions of negatives have they shed. . . . Matter in large masses must always be fixed and dear; form is cheap and transportable. We have got the fruit of creation now, and need not trouble ourselves with the core. Every conceivable object of Nature and Art will soon scale off its surface for us. Men will hunt all curious, beautiful, grand objects, as they hunt the cattle in South America, for their *skins*, and leave the carcasses as of little worth.[25]

As if to confirm Holmes's lament, Warhol entitled his multiple reproductions of the Mona Lisa, "Thirty are Better than One."

The Persistence of Tradition

As great as the transformation in sensibility produced by the rise of image consciousness has been, it is far from total. Alive as we are to the pose, to the artifice of imagery, we retain, in settings private and public alike, a large measure of the traditional aspiration that the photograph can create an authentic document of our lives.

In everyday life, photographs still serve a documentary ambition apart from the image-conscious sensibility. In wallets and on mantlepieces, in family albums, boxes, envelopes, and drawers, on home movies and more recently, home videos, we show and save pictures. When we look at the photographs that document our lives—baby pictures, wedding pictures, family reunions—we see ourselves in much the same way as our nineteenth-century forebears did at the time the photograph was invented. Good or bad, in or out of focus, perfect or pedestrian, each photo is a document, a record, a tangible reminder of the way we really were, of the things we actually did.

The power of the photograph to affirm identity is dramatically revealed when lost photographs are recovered, as happened with the lost work of Richard Samuel Roberts. In the 1920s and 1930s, Roberts was the portrait photographer for the black community of Columbia, South Carolina. In large letters outside his studio stood the sign, "PERFECT PICTURES." Roberts offered his clients a "true likeness" which he claimed was "just as necessary as every other necessity of life." He chronicled the typical activities of American community life—weddings, graduations, men in business suits and baseball uniforms, mothers and babies, club women and town leaders. [26]

But these photographs were lost for decades. The town directory of Columbia, South Carolina, for 1920 listed Roberts in the "Colored Dept." as a janitor. The newspapers of the day were likely to recognize blacks only in reporting crimes. The rediscovery of the portraits in 1977 prompted an oral history project to identify the individuals in the photographs. The exhibition in 1986 gave both blacks and whites the opportunity to see the black community as it once saw itself. The photographs were critical documents of lives once lost to public view.

The documentary power of the photograph has been heightened by the widespread use of the video camera. Since the 1980s, the video camera has enabled not only reporters but ordinary people to document public events, to bear witness to otherwise dark or incredible occurrences, to prove with pictures what words alone seem powerless to prove.

In 1991, when Los Angeles police officers brutally beat a suspect, Rodney King, an amateur photographer recorded it with his video camera. This video document, broadcast on television news programs across the country, led to a public outcry, an indictment of the officers, and an investigation of the department's practices. Although civil-rights lawyers and citizens had long complained of police brutality and mistreatment in the black community, the pictures spoke louder than the complaints. The riots and protests that followed the jury's refusal to convict the defendants stemmed largely from the fact that few believed that any evidence presented in the trial could have contradicted the brutal scene the video document displayed.

In the world of sports, videotaped replays became more than a way of letting television viewers see again a touchdown pass or a stolen base. They also became ways of confirming or refuting the calls of umpires and referees, of getting at the truth. In the 1980s, the National Football League changed its rules to allow referees to consult instant replays to authenticate controversial calls. The NFL ceased the practice in 1992, but other sports, such as horse racing and track, continued to rely on the camera's eye to determine winners in "photo finishes."

Implicit in the widespread use of the video camera to bear witness, to render an objective picture of reality, is the traditional conviction, born with the daguerreotype, that the camera does not lie. Even in the video culture of the 1990s, awash as it is with image making and manipulation, celebrity and contrivance, photo opportunities and media events, the documentary aspiration persists; our search for the authentic document coexists with our self-conscious preoccupation with the image as an image.

Traditional understandings also persist in our view of the selves that images portray. The posing, centerless, fabricated self has not fully displaced our stubborn belief that individual agents can master events and vindicate noble ideals. This can be seen in the difficulty of unraveling or deconstructing the hold that some images, especially mythic or heroic ones, have on our imagination.

During the 1984 Republican convention, NBC tried to expose Ronald Reagan's manipulation of television imagery by highlighting the contrivances of the video that was used by the Republicans to introduce Reagan at the convention. Anchorman Tom Brokaw took care to prepare his audience for the fabrications to follow: "This will be an evening of scripted, colorful pageantry, kind of like an old-fashioned MGM musical, in which thousands of people and bands and balloons and confetti will move right on cue directed by an unseen hand. And at the climactic moment, Ronald Reagan, just like his good old friend Fred Astaire, will glide into view."[27]

But NBC's effort to expose the image-making apparatus of the slickly produced Reagan video misses a deeper truth about the meaning of political images. Reagan's images, posed though they were, derived their potency from the cultural themes they conveyed, from the meanings they evoked. They resonated with the public because they tapped genuine ideals that continue to run deep in American culture—ideals about the capacity of self-reliant individuals to shape their destiny, about the power of patriotism and faith, family and community to infuse our lives with larger meanings.

Laying bare the constructed character of Reagan's potent visuals did not dissolve their hold any more than a tour of a movie set lessens the pleasure we take in a favorite film. Exposing Reagan as the president from the movies did little to diminish his appeal, because Reagan was more than the sum of the parts he played. He was an actor in a larger sense, fusing his politics with the myths and ideals that popular movies still affirm.

These themes find expression in the heroes of American movies from James Stewart as the idealistic senator in *Mr. Smith Goes to Washington* (1939), to Spencer Tracy as the incorruptible presidential candidate in *State of the Union* (1948), to John Wayne as patriot and rugged individualist in *The Alamo* (1960) and *The Green Berets* (1968), to Luke Skywalker, Han Solo, and Indiana Jones in the more recent movies of George Lucas and Steven Spielberg. Popular movies make no claim to being real, yet they are part of how we see ourselves. They embody the "spirit of fact," as surely as the idealized photographs that mark the rituals of our daily lives.

Over a century and a half after its invention, the promise and the paradox of photography are with us still. From video cameras mounted on Air Force jets, we record smart bombs descending upon their targets in the Persian Gulf and watch a war on television. At the same time, suspicious of the pose, we wonder whether, for all the satellite hookups and video wizardry, we are really witnessing the truth of the war.

The modern revolution in the technology of picture-making has extended the potential of the camera for authentic documentation, but has also created the potential for the image to subvert reality on an unprecedented scale. We have played out the paradox of the artifice of imagery to a degree unimaginable to those who called the camera the "pencil of nature." They aspired to the "perfect picture," and judged the image by its fit with the world. In our image-conscious culture, we have reversed the words. We seek moments or events that are "picture perfect," and judge the world for its fitness as an image.

The Rise of Image-Conscious Television Coverage

Sound-Bite Democracy

Standing before a campaign rally in Pennsylvania in October 1968, the Democratic vice presidential candidate Edmund Muskie tried to speak, but a group of antiwar protesters drowned him out. Muskie offered the hecklers a deal. He would give the platform to one of their representatives if he could then speak without interruption.

Rick Brody, the students' choice, stepped to the microphone where, cigarette in hand, he delivered an impassioned if disjointed case against the establishment. Those who saw the demonstrators as "commie pinko rads" were wrong. "We're here as Americans." To cheers from the crowd, he denounced the candidates the 1968 presidential campaign had to offer. "Wallace is no answer. Nixon's no answer and Humphrey's no answer. Sit out this election!"

When Brody finished, Muskie made his case for the Democratic ticket. That night, Muskie's confrontation with the demonstrators played prominently on the network news. NBC showed fifty-seven seconds of Brody's speech and over a minute of Muskie's.

Twenty years later, things had changed. Throughout the entire 1988 campaign, no network allowed either presidential candidate to speak uninterrupted on the evening news for as long as Rick Brody spoke in 1968.

By 1988, television's tolerance for the languid pace of political discourse, never great, had all but vanished. Not only had the average sound bite for presidential candidates dropped from 42.3 seconds to 9.8 seconds, but in 1968 almost half of all sound bites were 40 seconds or more, compared to less than 1 percent in 1988. In fact, it was not uncommon in 1968 for candidates to speak uninterrupted for over a minute on the evening news (21 percent of sound bites); in 1988, it never happened.[1]

The 1968 style of coverage enabled not only the candidates but partisans and advocates from across the political spectrum to speak in their own voice, to develop an argument on the nightly news. Lou Smith, a black activist from Watts, spoke for almost two minutes without interruption on NBC (Chancellor, October 22). Another network newscast aired over two uninterrupted minutes of Chicago Mayor Richard Daley's attack on media coverage of riots outside the Democratic convention. In 1988, George Bush and Michael Dukakis sometimes spoke less in an entire week of sound bites than Lou Smith or Mayor Daley or Rick Brody spoke on a single night in 1968.

While the time the networks devoted to the candidates' words sharply declined between the two elections, the time they devoted to visuals of the candidates unaccompanied by their words increased by over 300 percent.

In 1968, most of the time we saw the candidates on the evening news, we also heard them speaking. In 1988, the reverse was true; most of the time we saw the candidates, someone else, usually a reporter, was doing the talking. In a three-week period in the midst of the 1968 campaign, for example, the candidates spoke for 84 percent of the time their images were on the screen. In a comparable three-week period in 1988, the candidates spoke only 37 percent of the time. During the other 63 percent, we saw their pictures—not only posing in media events, but delivering speeches—without hearing their words.

Television's growing impatience with political speech raises serious questions about the democratic prospect in a television age: What becomes of democracy when political discourse is reduced to sound bites, one-liners, and potent visuals? And to what extent is television responsible for this development?

Since the Kennedy-Nixon debates of 1960, television has played a pivotal role in presidential politics. The Nixon campaign of 1968 was the first to be managed and orchestrated to play on the evening news. With the decline of political parties and the rise of media-savvy political consultants, presidential campaigns became more adept at conveying their messages through visual images, not only in political commercials but also in elaborately staged media events.[2] By the time of Ronald Reagan, the actor turned president, Michael Deaver had perfected the techniques of the video presidency.[3]

For television news, the mastery of television imagery by the politicians posed a temptation and a challenge. The temptation was to show the pictures. What network producer could resist the footage of Reagan overlooking a Normandy beach, or of Bush on Boston Harbor? Indeed, the networks showed not only the media events that the campaigns staged, but even their commercials. The most striking of these, such as Bush's "revolving door" prison commercial, appeared repeatedly in network newscasts throughout the campaign. At the same time, the networks sought to retain their objectivity by exposing the artifice of the images they showed, by calling constant attention to their self-conscious design.

Preoccupied with the pictures, they often forgot about the facts. Whether the pictures came from media events or political commercials, the networks covered them as news, often with little attempt to correct the distortions they contained. Alerting the viewer to the construction of television images proved no substitute for fact correction, no way back to reality.

A superficial "balance" became the measure of fairness, a balance consisting of equal time for opposing media events, and equal time for opposing commercials. Rather than confront the image with the facts, or with the candidates' actual records on the issue at stake, the networks simply balanced perceptions, setting one contrived image alongside another. Bush posed with his policemen; Dukakis posed with his. The candidates' actual records on crime did not necessarily figure in the story.

To be sure, image-conscious coverage was not the only kind of political reporting to appear on network newscasts in 1988. Some notable "fact correction" pieces, especially following the presidential debates, offered admirable exceptions. But the turn of television news to theater criticism set the tone of the 1988 coverage, and defined a new and complex relation between politics and the press.

This new relation, between image-conscious coverage and media-driven campaigns, raises with special urgency the deepest danger for politics in a television age. This is the danger of the loss of objectivity—not in the sense of bias, but in the literal sense of losing contact with the truth. It is the danger that the politicians and the press could become caught up in a cycle that leaves the substance of politics behind, that takes appearance for reality, perception for fact, the artificial for the actual, the image for the event.

Media Events: Constructing and Deconstructing Television Images

One morning in September 1968, Hubert Humphrey took a walk on the beach in Sea Girt, New Jersey. Shoes off, pants rolled up to avoid the surf, he paused to pluck a shell from the sand and toss it into the ocean.

This being a presidential campaign, Humphrey's stroll was no solitary idyll. The candidate was soon surrounded by a swarm of reporters and camera crews, who invited him to hold forth on Nixon, the Supreme Court, crime, and education. Humphrey was happy to oblige.

That night on the evening news, the story played in two different ways. Don Oliver of NBC (September 13) played it straight, as a news conference by the sea. The beach was in the background, but the story was the substance, what Humphrey said. Oliver showed the crowd of reporters and cameras, but made no mention of television's presence.

For David Schoumacher of CBS (September 13), the story was less the substance than the setting. He covered Humphrey's appearance by the sea as an exercise in image making, a way of posing for television. "It used to be kissing babies," Schoumacher began, "now candidates like to have their pictures taken walking alone on the beach. Apparently it is intended to show the subject at peace with himself and in tune with the tides."

In Schoumacher's report, Humphrey's statements scarcely mattered.

The story was the media event itself. "Reporters struggled through the sand trying to keep up and hear over the sound of the surf. Hours later they were still comparing notes to figure out what the Vice President had said. Mostly they said his campaign was going well."

These two versions of Humphrey's walk on the beach hint at the transformation that network campaign coverage would undergo over the next two decades. Oliver's version, which focused on the candidate and what he said, was traditional political reporting that in 1968 was still the norm for television news. Schoumacher's version, which focused on the construction of images for television, was a novelty in 1968, but an intimation of things to come.

Looking back on his report, Don Oliver recalls that, in 1968, both the campaigns and the reporters were less image-driven than today. "I focused on Humphrey's speech because I believed the candidates were still saying things of interest and not merely spouting slogans some advertising man had dreamed up. In 1968 it was still rather innocent. So when a candidate appeared at an event, you didn't really look for who manipulated it."[4]

Reviewing his report, Schoumacher acknowledges, "I was doing some 'show-bizzy' stuff with that piece." He explains that, "in 1968, the campaigns were making their first successful attempts to manipulate reporters, and we were trying to fight as best we could." Not all campaigns were equally adept at the art of manipulating television, Schoumacher recalls. "Although Wallace and Nixon were quite sophisticated, the Humphrey campaign wasn't. They would often stick you in a corner so you wouldn't get in the way of the people who were attending the event. They never advised us on setting up camera angles. They didn't realize that the people in attendance were a stage set."[5]

The idea that campaign stops were media events, and the participants a stage set, only gradually emerged. The 1968 campaign was just the beginning of the battle to control the pictures that would play on the evening news. The presidential candidates had not yet acquired the habit of speaking in carefully crafted sound bites for easy television consumption. Humphrey's garrulousness was legendary. As reporter Jack Perkins quipped, "It would have been impossible to extract a short sound bite from one of his speeches."

Frank Shakespeare, one of Nixon's media advisers, recalls that

Nixon did not speak in explicitly fabricated sound bites either. Given the style of reporting, such speech was not required as a condition of coverage on the network news. Despite the Nixon campaign's worries about press hostility to their candidate, Shakespeare observes, "We were always confident that if Nixon broke new ground or addressed an issue in a serious way, you had a reasonable shot of getting a direct portrayal on television."[6]

By the 1970s, the campaigns and the networks had grown more sophisticated in the creation and use of television images. Still, the networks were ambivalent about making television itself the focus of political coverage. This ambivalence was reflected in a 1976 dispute between Walter Cronkite and Roger Mudd over whether to air a piece focusing on candidates' attempts to manipulate television news.

During the primary campaign, Mudd and producer Brian Healy prepared a report revealing how Senator Frank Church, Governor Edmund G. Brown, Jr., and Ronald Reagan used media events in California. The five-minute report was an extended piece of image-conscious coverage, designed to highlight the growing ability of the campaigns to contrive events to play on television. "Reagan had spent three hours and five minutes talking to not more than 2,000 people in the flesh," Mudd reported. "He took no new positions, he broke no new ground; but that night in Los Angeles' three early-evening news-casts, he was seen by an audience of 1,071,000 people for five minutes and fifty-one seconds. And that night on the three network news-casts, he was seen for four minutes, four seconds by 37 million people." At the end of the segment, a political consultant commented, "The return is very small in terms of astute judgments on the candidate. The return is high in terms of just plain exposure. I like it the way it is because it makes my job easier. But I'm not sure the voters are getting a straight deal on it."[7]

Walter Cronkite refused to air the piece on the "CBS Evening News," fearing it cast television news in a negative light for allowing itself to be manipulated. Mudd's report, which ran the next day on the "CBS Morning News," was a hard-hitting version of the image-conscious reporting that would soon become standard fare. Mudd now thinks such reporting is overdone. "When we did the piece in 1976, we thought we were being very courageous. That kind of reporting was not a staple in the 1970s. By the 1980s, those were standard pieces to put on the plate. By 1988, we had had too much."[8]

By 1988, presidential campaigns had become adept at crafting images for television, and the networks covered them with frequent reference to this fact. They often portrayed the candidates as rival image makers, competing to control the picture of the campaign that would play on the evening news. The traditional focus on the candidates' statements and strategies gave way to a style of reporting that focused on the candidates' success or failure at constructing images for television.

When Bush kicked off his 1988 campaign with a Labor Day appearance at Disneyland, the networks covered the event as a performance for television. "In the war of the Labor Day visuals," Bob Schieffer reported (CBS, September 5), "George Bush pulled out the heavy artillery. A Disneyland backdrop and lots of pictures with the Disney Gang." Dukakis' appearance that day in a Philadelphia neighborhood did not play as well. His maneuver in the "war of the Labor Day visuals" was marred by a squealing microphone, an incident highlighted in the image-conscious coverage of all three networks.

Likewise, when Bruce Morton (CBS, September 13) showed Dukakis riding in a tank, the image was the story. "In the trade of politics, it's called a visual," Morton observed. "The idea is pictures are symbols that tell the voter important things about the candidate. If your candidate is seen in the polls as weak on defense, put him in a tank." Even when Morton turned to the speech that followed the ride, it was with an eye to the television image the candidate sought to project. "Dukakis, against a backdrop of tanks and flags, used the word 'strong' eight times."

In 1988, the networks covered even the presidential debates as occasions for television image making. Two days before the first debate, Peter Jennings (September 23) began ABC's coverage by noting, "Today, Bush and Dukakis have been preparing, read rehearsing." There followed a report by Brit Hume, describing a Bush meeting with Soviet Foreign Minister Eduard Shevardnadze as "unquestionably a campaign photo opportunity." Hume alerted his viewers to listen as the television microphones picked up the sound of Bush whispering to Shevardnadze, "Shall we turn around and get one of those pictures in?"

Jennings then announced that Dukakis too had found time for "a carefully staged photo opportunity." In the report that followed, Sam Donaldson drove home the point again. Showing Dukakis playing catch with a Boston Red Sox outfielder, Donaldson described the event as "this morning's made-for-television, predebate photo op-portunity."

The hyperconsciousness of television image making on the part of networks and campaigns alike, so pervasive in 1988, was scarcely present only twenty years earlier. While Nixon and Humphrey both sought to use television to their advantage in 1968—Nixon with considerable sophistication—their media events consisted for the most part of traditional rallies, parades, and press conferences. The networks, for their part, rarely drew attention to the image-making apparatus of "visuals" or "backdrops."

Throughout the entire 1968 general election campaign, only once did a network reporter use the term "photo opportunity" on the evening news. Reporting on Nixon's appearance with television star Jackie Gleason on a Florida golf course, CBS reporter John Hart used the term with derision. "Nearly everything Nixon does these days is programmed," Hart reported. He then described Nixon's "deliber-ately casual moments, moments his programmers have labelled 'photo opportunities' " (CBS, October 15). Hart finds it troubling that the term he used sarcastically has today become a commonplace of media jargon that lacks any critical edge.

"In 1968, I thought it was a joke," Hart recalls. "I thought if you said the campaign is calling this a 'photo opportunity,' people would laugh, and photo opportunities would be disgraced. People would say, 'Oh, we see through it now.' But over the years, I've seen reporters use it in a neutral sense without the irony. It was created cynically, in a manipulative sense. And suddenly the act and what it represents is accepted."[9]

By 1988, the politicians, assisted by a growing legion of media advisers, had become more sophisticated at producing pictures that would play on television. The networks, meanwhile, were unable to resist the temptation to show the pictures. Vivid visuals made good television, and besides, some network producers argued that if the candidate goes to Disneyland or rides in a tank, does not covering the campaign mean covering those events? "We were dying to deal with the issues," complained one network producer. "We were pleading with these guys to do more substance, to give us the opportunity to do more substantive pieces. In the end, we just covered what was out there. If what is out there is theater, then that is what we cover."[10]

Even as they tape the media events and show them on the evening news, however, television journalists acknowledge the danger of falling prey to manipulation, of becoming accessories to the candidates' stagecraft. One way of distancing themselves from the scenes they show is to turn to theater criticism, to comment on the scenes as a performance made for television, to lay bare the artifice behind the images.

Given limited access to the candidates, image making becomes one of the few subjects of coverage available. "The press plane was the decoy, where they took all the reporters off and fed them pablum," observes Tom Bettag, executive producer of the CBS evening news during the 1988 campaign. "The manipulation is the only thing the reporters were allowed to get their hands on, and the image making became one legitimate way of looking at the candidates."[11] CBS producer Susan Zirinsky adds that revealing the artifice is one way that journalists try to avoid being manipulated. "I think very often when you feel snookered you feel you've done a service if you point it out. It's your own moral conscience as a journalist speaking. You say, 'Hey, we did not just go and cover this event. There is more to this. You wouldn't believe what happened.' "[12]

However critical its intent, image-conscious coverage often has the opposite effect. One of the problems with theater criticism as a style of political reporting is that it involves showing the potent visuals the campaigns contrive. Reporters become conduits for the very images they criticize. Lisa Myers's report on Bush's use of television (NBC, September 19) is a case in point. "It is a campaign of carefully staged events and carefully crafted images," Myers began. A sequence of Bush images then appeared on the scene. "George Bush, friend of the working man" (Bush wearing a hard hat). "Bush the patriot" (Bush saying the Pledge of Allegiance). "Bush the peacemaker" (Bush watching the Pershing missile destruction).

Even as Myers described the artifice of Bush's political theater, she provided additional airtime for some of his most flattering images. Furthermore, the political message the pictures were intended to convey was presented uncritically. Myers focused on the effectiveness, not the truthfulness of the images. The photo of Bush in a hard hat, for example, was simply presented as a testimonial to Bush's image-making skill. There was no mention of the fact that Bush's labor policies were unpopular with workers, or that he had been booed by workers at an earlier campaign stop, as all three networks reported at the time (September 6).

Myers concluded by observing that the Bush campaign, by limiting reporters' access and "carefully scripting each event" was skillfully "managing the news." But in giving Bush's "carefully crafted images" another television run, her own report fell prey to the manipulation she documented.

In the hands of network producers, the campaigns' media events generated visuals as flattering as paid political advertisements. It is no wonder that even sophisticated observers could fail to distinguish them. When Leonard Garment, Nixon's media director in 1968, was shown a videotape of Myers's report, he asked in genuine confusion, "Is this a Bush commercial?"[13] By 1988, it was hard to tell the difference.

"In 1988, the media events turned out to look like paid ads," comments Joe Napolitan, who in 1968 was in charge of Humphrey's media. "The press let the campaigns structure 'commercials,' and they produced them and ran them on the evening news."[14]

Some reporters acknowledge that their attempts to be critical of campaign contrivances may sometimes be lost on the viewer. Reviewing his report on Bush's campaign kickoff in Disneyland, CBS correspondent Bob Schieffer is unsure the piece comes across the way he had intended. "When I used the phrase, 'the war of the Labor Day visuals,' I was being satirical. It just reminds me that you can't be too subtle on television. I thought it was ridiculous. Here Bush is with the balloons, Snow White, and Goofy. I was doing it to show how hollow it was, but I'm not sure it came across that way."[15]

Jeff Greenfield, an ABC correspondent, suggests that image-conscious coverage can be a distraction from genuinely critical reporting. Reporters "become stylistically skeptical, but not substantively. You score great points if you show how the campaigns move a tree to make the picture look better. But frankly, it's the frustration of feeling so manipulated."[16]

Although theater criticism seeks to alert the viewer to the artifice of the images that the campaigns contrive, even critical versions of image-conscious coverage can fail to puncture the pictures they show. When Bush visited a flag factory in hopes of making patriotism a campaign issue, Brit Hume (ABC, September 20) reported with some cynicism that Bush was wrapping himself in the flag. "This campaign strives to match its pictures with its points. Today and for much of the past week, the pictures have been of George Bush with the American flag. If the point wasn't to make an issue of patriotism, then the question arises, what was it?"

Though he showed Bush's potent visuals, Hume reminded viewers that Bush's purpose was implicitly to question the patriotism of Dukakis, who had vetoed a law mandating the Pledge of Allegiance. But the very pictures that Hume tried to debunk would live to run again on the evening news, as file footage, or stock imagery illustrating Bush's campaign.

Only three days later, the staged image of Bush at the flag factory appeared without comment as background footage for a report (ABC, September 23) on independent voters in New Jersey. The media event that Hume reported with derision was quickly transformed into a visual document of Bush. The criticism forgotten, the image played on.

Political Ads as News: Free Time for Paid Media

In the final week of the 1968 campaign, the Nixon campaign aired a television commercial showing a smiling Hubert Humphrey superimposed on scenes of war and riots. The Democrats cried foul, and the Nixon campaign agreed to withdraw the ad. The next night on the evening news, Walter Cronkite (CBS, October 29) and Chet Huntley (NBC) reported briefly on the withdrawal, though neither showed any part of the ad.

It was one of the few times that a political commercial received even passing mention on the network news that year. Political ads were not considered news in 1968. Although both Nixon and Humphrey spent heavily on television commercials, only two clips from paid political ads appeared on the evening news, both from a staged Nixon "panel show" in which the candidate answered questions from a preselected group of citizens. [17] Not once did the network newscasts run excerpts from the candidates' thirty- or sixty-second commercials.

Twenty years later, political commercials were a staple of television news campaign coverage. Network newscasts showed 125 excerpts of campaign commercials in 1988, and ran some so repeatedly that they became visual motifs, recurring video stand-ins for the candidates themselves.

The attention the networks gave political ads in 1988 illustrates their growing preoccupation with imagery made for television. As with their coverage of media events, so with political ads, the danger is that reporters become unwitting conduits of the television images the campaigns dispense. No matter how critical the narrative, to show commercials on the news runs the risk of giving free time to paid media, of letting the visuals send the message they were designed to convey.

Most of the time, the narrative was not critical. For all their use of commercial footage, the networks rarely corrected the distortions or misstatements the ads contained. The reporter addressed the veracity of the commercials' claims less than 8 percent of the time.

The few cases where reporters corrected the facts illustrate how the networks might have covered political commercials but rarely did. When Richard Threlkeld (ABC, October 19) ran excerpts from a Bush ad attacking Dukakis's defense stand, he froze the frame at each mistaken or distorted claim.

BUSH AD: Michael Dukakis has opposed virtually every defense system we've developed.

THRELKELD: In fact, he supports a range of new weapons systems, including the Trident 2 missile.

BUSH AD: He opposed antisatellite weapons.

THRELKELD: In fact, Dukakis would ban those weapons only if the Soviets did the same. The same principle is incorporated in the INF Treaty which George Bush supports.

BUSH AD: He opposed four missile systems including the Pershing 2 missile deployment.

THRELKELD: In fact Dukakis opposes not four missile systems but two as expensive and impractical and never opposed deploying Pershing 2s.

In another notable case of fact correction, Lesley Stahl (CBS, October 25) corrected a deceptive statistic in Bush's revolving-door furlough ad. The ad showed criminals entering and leaving a prison through a revolving door as the narrator said: "[Dukakis's] revolving-door prison policy gave weekend passes to first-degree murderers not eligible for parole." The words "268 escaped" then appeared on the screen.

Stahl pointed out that "part of the ad is false. . . . 268 murderers did not escape. . . . The truth is only four first-degree murderers escaped while on parole." She concluded by observing, "Dukakis left the Bush attack ads unanswered for six weeks. Today campaign aides are engaged in a round of finger pointing at who is to blame."

But the networks were also guilty of letting the Bush commercial run without challenge or correction. Only four days earlier, Stahl's CBS colleague Bruce Morton had shown the revolving-door ad and the deceptive statistic without correction. Even after her report, CBS and ABC ran excerpts of the ad without correction, just days before the election. In all, network newscasts ran excerpts from the revolving door ad ten times throughout the campaign, only once correcting the deceptive statistic.

It might be argued, in defense of the networks, that it is up to the candidate to reply to his opponent's charges, not the press. But this argument is open to two objections. First, if the job of the press is to report the truth, then airing misleading commercials without challenge or correction does not amount to objective reporting. Second, the networks' frequent use of political ads on the evening news creates a strong disincentive for a candidate to challenge his opponent's ads. As Dukakis found to his misfortune, to attack a television ad as unfair or untrue is to invite the networks to run it again.

Two weeks before the election, the Dukakis campaign accused the Republicans of lying about his record on defense, and of using racist tactics in ads featuring Willie Horton, a black convict who committed rape and murder while on furlough from a Massachusetts prison. In reporting Dukakis's complaint, all three networks ran excerpts of the ads in question, including the highly charged pictures of Horton and the revolving door of convicts. Dukakis's response thus gave Bush's potent visuals another free run on the evening news.

As they appeared on the evening news, the Bush ads on crime enjoyed a heightened impact due to the networks' readiness to combine them with material from the Willie Horton ad produced by a group not formally tied to the Bush campaign. This link was so seamless that many viewers thought the revolving-door furlough commercial featured Willie Horton, when in fact it never mentioned him. Bruce Morton (CBS, October 21), for example, showed the pictures of the revolving-door furlough ad while recalling the Horton story as a voice-over. "The Bush campaign has scored big on television ads on crime, especially on the Massachusetts furlough program under which Willie Horton on furlough committed rape and assault."

Even as he reported the Bush campaign's disavowal of the Horton ad, Brit Hume (ABC, October 25) highlighted the racial dimension of the Horton story as images from the revolving-door ad filled the screen. "They also denied any racial intent in television spots about black murder convict Willie Horton who raped a Maryland woman and stabbed her husband, both white, while on prison furlough from Massachusetts." Likewise, a special report by Jackie Judd on crime (ABC, September 22) opened with a photograph of Willie Horton filling the screen. Even though her report tried to provide some perspective on the furlough issue, her images reinforced the Willie Horton ad. Although Bush campaign ads never showed him, Willie Horton's picture appeared nine times on the evening news, five times in juxtaposition to official Bush commercials. Horton's victims also were shown holding a press conference by all three networks (October 7) in addition to their appearance in commercials broadcast on the evening news on other occasions. In these ways, the networks contributed to the massive media exposure of Willie Horton.

The networks' coverage of campaign commercials reached its greatest intensity on October 25, when Dukakis attacked Bush's negative ads, and Bush replied. That night on the evening news, the networks not only reported the candidates' charges and countercharges, but showed no fewer than twenty excerpts of campaign commercials to dramatize the dispute. Although the story of the day concerned competing claims about the veracity of the ads, the networks focused on the effectiveness not the truthfulness of the ads they showed.

In defense of their ads, Bush campaign officials called a press conference that day to offer evidence to back their claims. All three networks covered the press conference, but none bothered to assess or even to report any of the evidence the Bush campaign offered. Instead, they treated the press conference as one more media event, with sound bites from John Sununu—"The data speaks for itself"—and Dan Quayle—"Every statement is accurate and can be documented"—and supporting charts and documents as backdrops to yet another exercise in image making.

The networks became in effect electronic billboards for the candidates. Not only were Bush's furlough ads featured, but so were Dukakis's "handlers ads," attacking Bush as a packaged candidate. Political commercials that were not even aired on network television nonetheless reached a national audience via the evening news. The Willie Horton ad, for example, was shown on cable television but not on the networks, according to its producer, Larry McCarthy.

"In 1968, reporters just did not think ads were the story,"[18] notes Joseph Napolitan, Humphrey's media director. Frank Shakespeare, Nixon's media adviser, agrees. "The press was not interested in somebody making a commercial. That was like going into a newspaper and asking if you could go into the print shop. An ad can be very effective, but it is peripheral. What's central is the candidate, what he says, what he stands for."[19]

Reporters who covered the Humphrey-Nixon campaign, are today hard put to recall any of the 1968 commercials. According to Roger Ailes, who has been making commercials for Republicans from Nixon to Bush, campaign ads have not suddenly become more important in presidential politics, or more effective. He attributes the current preoccupation with ads to a decline in journalistic standards, and a shift in emphasis from political substance to compelling pictures. "I'm sure somebody suggested showing ads in 1968, and someone said, 'Why would we want to give them free air time?' Reporters then were busy trying to figure out what the campaign was about from an issues standpoint and report it. I think they were actually still doing journalism in those days. Today people build their whole newscast around these ads because they haven't done any real reporting."[20]

Network producers offer different explanations for the increased attention to political ads in campaign coverage. CBS producer Jill

Rosenbaum argues, "To ask us not to use [political commercials] is to ignore a huge part of the political environment. You can't make a distinction in the campaign between what's on television because it's news and what's on television because it's a commercial."[21]

Yet it was precisely this blurring of the distinction between news and commercials that the campaigns exploited. By 1988, the campaigns actively promoted upcoming commercials to network producers and reporters. "It used to be that we would struggle to get a copy of an ad," notes Andy Franklin, director of political coverage for NBC during the 1988 campaign. "Now, if you want an ad, you get it, sometimes before the stations that are going to air them as commercials."[22] Brian Healy, who directed CBS's 1988 campaign coverage, adds that campaigns now actively promote upcoming ads to network reporters and producers. "They'll say, 'We are going to start running some ads next week that are going to be devastating.' Because it is videotape, they can put it into a computer and knock it over to you. And you look at it and decide whether it will fit into the stories you're doing. It's that easy."[23]

Campaigns eased access to political commercials as they limited access to the candidates themselves. Presidential campaigns now call press conferences where the candidate does not appear, but a video presentation of new television ads does. Sanford Socolow, senior producer for the "CBS Evening News" with Walter Cronkite in 1968, is scornful of the networks' widespread use of political commercials. "In 1988, an ad agency staging a glamorous opening was enough to get their political ads on the evening news. In 1968, we would have turned our backs on it."[24]

Ted Koppel, who covered Nixon's campaign in 1968 for ABC, did one of the few reports that year to focus on political advertising. Koppel's report, on Nixon's staged "man in the arena" citizen panel show, was an early instance of image-conscious coverage that differs in some ways from the theater criticism now prevalent in campaign reporting. The piece begins by revealing the artifice of Nixon's staged television show. A polished master of ceremonies is shown warming up the audience, urging them to applaud on cue, to "sound like ten thousand people." Koppel reports, "Across the country . . . the same jovial emcee warms up one studio audience after another for the most successful television personality since Ronald Reagan washed his hands of 'Twenty Mule Team Borax.' In 1960, television was a prime factor in defeating Nixon. This year it may be his most effective vehicle on the road to the White House" (ABC, September 25, 1968).

Koppel's coverage of the Nixon commercial differs from the 1988 style of ad coverage in that the commercial never fills the screen. We see it only from afar, displayed on television monitors as people are shown watching it in different settings. Far from giving free air time to the Nixon ad, the report focuses on how the images were made and what Nixon was trying to achieve. A telling image in the Koppel report is a picture of reporters isolated in a screening room, barred not only from the panel of questioners, but even from the studio audience. This isolation of the press was a harbinger of things to come.

Agreeing in part with Ailes, Koppel thinks the current prominence of ads as news has something to do with television's appetite for gripping visuals. "Part of the problem is that we are becoming trapped again and again by enhanced production values." He also suggests that the preoccupation with ads in 1988 reflected the emptiness of the campaign itself. "In 1968 you had two very interesting candidates facing major issues. In 1988 you had two very boring candidates. The television ads were it in 1988."[25]

Reuven Frank, former president of NBC news, was the producer who guided the "Huntley-Brinkley Report" in the 1960s. He states the traditionalist's objection to broadcasting commercials as news. "The trap is making the ad the story by showing it on the news." Frank opposed showing even Lyndon Johnson's famous "Daisy ad" on the evening news during the 1964 presidential campaign. The ad, now part of the lore of negative campaign advertising, implied that Barry Goldwater, Johnson's Republican opponent, might be quick to use nuclear weapons. It never mentioned Goldwater by name. Instead it showed a little girl pulling petals off a daisy. Her voice merged with a countdown for an atomic explosion that then filled the screen.

The Democrats withdrew the ad after one showing. "It was not a story. It was not news," Frank insists. "But one of the networks showed the ad and that inflated its importance. It made the ad the story. That's the trap."[26]

By 1988, the networks had succumbed to the trap that Frank describes. The campaigns, meanwhile, had become highly adept at generating controversies about ads to attract network coverage. As Larry McCarthy, producer of the Willie Horton ad observed, "I have known campaigns that have made ads and only bought one spot, but released them in major press conferences to get it into the news. It's become a fairly common tactic."[27]

And controversy or not, by repeatedly showing ads, the networks risked being conduits for the campaigns' contrivances. Oddly enough, the networks were alive to this danger when confronted with the question of whether to air the videos the campaigns produced for their conventions. "I am not into tone poems," said Lane Venardos, the executive producer in charge of convention coverage at CBS. "We are not in the business of being propaganda arms of the political parties."[28] But they seemed blind to the same danger during the campaign itself.

The networks' use of commercial footage on the evening news was not restricted to days when ads were an issue in the campaign itself. From Labor Day to election day, network newscasts drew freely on commercial images to illustrate an issue or to represent the candidates themselves. Commercial images became part of television's stock of background visuals, or file footage, aired interchangeably with news footage of the candidates. As CBS producer Bill Crawford explains, "Television is a picture medium. When you are 'picture poor'—and that's a term—you go back to your reels of good pictures. That's the nature of the business."[29]

To illustrate the candidates' appeals to Hispanic voters, for example, Peter Jennings (ABC, October 28) juxtaposed a clip of Dukakis speaking to a Hispanic audience in Texas with an excerpt from a commercial showing Bush with his Hispanic grandchildren. A John Cochran (NBC, October 18) report comparing Bush and Dukakis's foreign policy stands included sound bites from the presidential debates along with an image from a commercial showing Bush shaking hands with Gorbachev.

Tom Brokaw (NBC, September 30), reporting on the political leanings of blue-collar workers in the industrial Midwest, interspersed interviews with actual workers with an excerpt from a Dukakis commercial showing actors playing workers saying, "I voted for the Republicans but that doesn't make me a Republican." Following the sound bite from the workers in the ad, and while the images from the

Dukakis ad were still on the screen, Brokaw reported, "They blame the administration for the loss of more than half the steel jobs in the district." Whether "they" referred to the actual workers or the ones depicted in the ad seemed almost beside the point, so seamless was the movement between real speech and commercial image.

So successful was the Bush campaign at getting free time for its ads on the evening news that, after the campaign, commercial advertisers adopted a similar strategy. In 1989, a pharmaceutical company used unauthorized footage of presidents Bush and Gorbachev to advertise a cold medication. "In the new year," the slogan ran, "may the only cold war in the world be the one being fought by us." Although two of the three networks refused to carry the commercial, dozens of network and local television news programs showed excerpts from the ad, generating millions of dollars of free airtime.

"I realized I started a trend," said Bush media consultant Roger Ailes. "Now guys are out there trying to produce commercials for the evening news."[30] When Humphrey and Nixon hired Madison Avenue experts to help in their campaigns, thoughtful observers worried that, in the television age, presidents would be sold like products. Little did they imagine that, twenty years later, products would be sold like presidents.

Media Advisers as Celebrities

As a young reporter covering the Nixon campaign in 1968, Ted Koppel always kept a copy of Theodore White's *The Making of the President, 1960*, by his side. It was the book that revolutionized presidential campaign reporting. Before White, reporters focused on political speeches, parades, and rallies. White took the public behind the scenes, revealing the strategies and struggles that traditional political reporters had missed.

In 1968, Joe McGinniss took behind-the-scenes reporting one step further. While White had valorized politics, McGinniss debunked it. In *The Selling of the President*, published shortly after the 1968 campaign, he demystified politics in the television age, showing how public-relations people and admen sold presidents like soap and cigarettes. Koppel recalls its impact on reporters. "All of a sudden everybody said, 'Oh I get it. They're trying to sell candidates the way they sell soap.' And from that moment on, we had emerged from the Garden of Eden. We were never able to see candidates or campaigns quite the same way again."[31]

Twenty years later, television reporters had learned the lessons of McGinniss too well. Along with the attention to stagecraft in 1988 came an unprecedented focus on the stage managers themselves, the "media gurus," "handlers," and "spin-control artists." The media advisers McGinniss exposed with a critical eye became celebrities on the evening news.

A week before the first 1988 presidential debate, ABC led its nightly newscast with a story about the 1984 campaign. The network had acquired an audiotape of a meeting of Reagan's image makers, and though the tape contained no significant revelations, ABC made it the lead story of the day.

Noting that the 1988 campaign consisted of "carefully crafted speeches, staged events, and expensive commercials," anchor Barry Serafin (September 19) announced, "Tonight we have a rare look behind the scenes, where the image shaping begins." The story that followed played audio excerpts of a meeting four years earlier, in which Reagan media advisers cynically discussed the dearth of ideas coming from the White House, their hopes for a small audience for the presidential debates, and Reagan's ability to run against government. "He just believes that he's above it all," said one participant to general laughter. "He believes it, that's why they believe it. I can't believe it but they do."

Although the report contained scarcely any news, its prominent place on the evening news aptly reflected the networks' preoccupation with image making. In 1968, neither political advertisements nor the men who made them were news. There were a few references to "advance men," fewer still to "communications experts," and reporters rarely interviewed them or sought their "expert" opinion on the campaign itself. Only three reports featured media advisers in 1968, compared to twenty-six in 1988.

In addition, the stance reporters took toward media advisers had changed dramatically. In *The Selling of the President*, McGinniss exposed the growing role of media advisers with a sense of disillusion and outrage. By 1988, television reporters covered image makers with deference, even admiration. Media advisers and advertising professionals, some partisan, some independent, frequently appeared on the evening news as authorities in their own right. Sought out by reporters to analyze the effectiveness of campaign commercials, they became "media gurus" not only for the candidates but for the networks as well.

By 1988, Roger Ailes, as media adviser to Bush, was a featured figure on the news, credited with crafting Bush's television image. One flattering report, for example, showed Ailes watching Bush on a television set as Lisa Myers (NBC, September 23) reported that the celebrated "media guru" supplied Bush his best one-liners.

As if reveling in the spotlight, the image makers dispensed with the traditional pretense of concealing their role. In one of the rare 1968 reports on television image making, Nixon television adviser Frank Shakespeare denied managing his candidate's image. "We don't advise him at all what to do. We put the cameras on him close and that's it" (Kaplow, NBC, October 25).

In 1988, by contrast, media experts described their manipulative craft without embarrassment or evasion. Before the first presidential debate, Republican consultant Ed Rollins told Lesley Stahl (CBS, September 23), "These are very staged events, and anyone who says they're not is kidding themselves." He told Lisa Myers (NBC, September 23), "I think the image and how he (Bush) looks is as important as the words he says." Recalling the preparations for Walter Mondale's debate with Reagan, Democrat Bob Beckel told Stahl, "We spent more time talking about ties than East-West relations."

Like the reporting of media events and political commercials, coverage of media advisers focused on theater over politics, perceptions over facts. Rather than correct the facts in the political ads they showed, reporters sometimes solicited the "testimony" of rival media advisers instead. For example, Jim Wooten (ABC, October 10) did an entire report on negative campaign advertising without ever assessing the veracity of the commercials. Instead, he interviewed media advisers from both sides who insisted their ads were accurate. In a practice unheard of twenty years ago, reporters also aired the opinions of media experts not associated with either campaign to evaluate the candidates' political ads. Wooten (ABC, October 10) reported that the Dukakis commercials had not "impressed the advertising community." Stan Bernard (NBC, October 25) interviewed an "impartial" advertising professional who testified that Dukakis was a "crybaby" for complaining about negative ads, and that his advertising campaign in general left voters "totally confused and totally turned off." Another media expert pronounced Dukakis's "advertising ineptitude almost unparalleled," and suggested this was a reason to doubt his ability to "manage the country" if elected.

So prominently did media advisers figure in network campaign coverage that their role became the subject of interviews with the candidates themselves. Interviewing Dukakis, Dan Rather (CBS, October 27) wanted to know which image maker was to blame for arranging a media event that backfired. "Governor, who put that helmet on you and put you in that army tank?" When Dukakis sought to deflect the query, Rather persisted. "But who put you in?" Dukakis replied, "Michael Dukakis put me in."

Even as the press bemoaned the influence of media advisers, it made celebrities of them. A *Time* magazine cover story proclaimed 1988 the "Year of the Handlers." The story condemned the candidates for their

> passive and uncritical acceptance of the premises of modern political manipulation. Bush flogs patriotism at a flag factory, the far more restrained Dukakis joyrides in a tank, and neither seems embarrassed by the prearranged artifice. There is a cynical edge to it all, as the backstage puppeteers pull the strings, and Bush and Dukakis dangle before the TV cameras obediently reciting their memorized themes for the day.

But even as it criticized the media-managed campaigns, *Time* celebrated the handlers, featuring Republican James Baker and Democrat John Sasso on the cover of the magazine.[32]

Political and media advisers themselves argue that their newfound celebrity is misplaced. Speaking of his appearance on the cover of *Time*, Sasso says, "My family was thrilled, but I thought it was absurd. I refused to be interviewed. What I thought or said was not that important. It was irrelevant to the everyday concerns of people. The press's obsession with handlers distorts the political process."[33]

In 1968, Roger Ailes labored in obscurity as Nixon media man, his name never mentioned on the evening news. By 1988, he was a celebrity. "We have grown too big because the media has focused laser-like attention on us for six or eight years," Ailes observes. "It's always the story of 'What is the commercial?' On one commercial alone, I turned down about 85 percent of the requests from the press for interviews. I could be out in the public eye far more than I am."[34]

Among those critical of the amount of coverage now devoted to media advisers and spin doctors is former CBS anchorman Walter Cronkite. "I was dumbfounded at the attention given to them after the [1988 presidential] debates," Cronkite states.

> I was amazed at the time they gave to it. I thought it was ridiculous to listen to those fellows for any great length of time. It was interesting to find out how really far out they would reach to try to make their point on how poorly the opposition did each time. It had a kind of fascination, like a snake coming up out of a basket. I was not offended by the way the correspondents handled those things; I was offended by the amount of time they gave to it.[35]

In addition to devoting airtime to the testimony of media advisers and spin doctors, the networks focused sometimes admiring attention on their manipulative craft. For example, in an exchange with CBS anchor Dan Rather on Bush's debate performance, correspondent Lesley Stahl lavished praise on the techniques of Bush's media advisers:

DAN RATHER: What about this perception, the extraordinary jump in the perception that George Bush has very human qualities?

LESLEY STAHL: Well, last night in the debate that was a very calculated tactic and strategy on the part of his handlers. They told him not to look into the camera. [*She gestures towards the camera as she speaks.*] You know when you look directly into a camera you are cold, apparently they have determined.

RATHER [*laughing*]: Bad news for anchormen I'd say.

STAHL: We have a lot to learn from this. They told him to relate to the questioner, to relate to the audience if he could get an opportunity to deal with them, to relate to the opponent. And that would warm him up. Michael Dukakis kept talking right into the camera. [*Stahl talks directly into her own camera to demonstrate.*] And according to the Bush people that makes you look programmed, Dan [*Stahl laughs*]. And they're very adept at these television symbols and television imagery. And according to our poll it worked.

RATHER: Do you believe it?

STAHL: Yes, I think I do actually.

The celebrity status of media and political consultants reflected something the public could not see—a new and disturbingly close relationship between the press and the political consultants. The press was increasingly depending on consultants as their primary sources. As David Broder, political columnist for the *Washington Post*, observes, "You put two things together; reporting the campaigns from the inside, and the emergence of a new set of inside players, who are devoid of any responsibility for government past or future, and you change the definition of political reporting."[36]

"It was a deal with the devil," states a network producer. "If you can't talk to George Bush, then you talk to Roger Ailes and Bob Teeter. And if they are giving you information, then you protect them. Roger Ailes is a vindictive man, and you have to say good things about him in order for him to continue to feed you information. The public has no idea how much reporters depend on handlers as sources."[37]

Failed Images as News: Gaffes and Gutter Balls

Early in the 1988 campaign, George Bush delivered a speech to a sympathetic audience of the American Legion, attacking his opponent's defense policies. In a momentary slip, he referred to September 7, rather than December 7, as the anniversary of Pearl Harbor. Murmurs and chuckles from the audience alerted him to his error, and he quickly corrected himself.

The audience was forgiving but the networks were not. Despite the irrelevance of the slip to the contest for the presidency, all three network anchors highlighted it on the evening news. Dan Rather introduced CBS's report on Bush by declaring solemnly: "Bush's talk to audiences in Louisville was overshadowed by a strange happening." On NBC, Tom Brokaw reported: "he departed from his prepared script and left his listeners mystified." Peter Jennings introduced ABC's report by mentioning Bush's attack on Dukakis, adding, "What's more likely to be remembered about today's speech is a slip of the tongue."

So hypersensitive were the networks to television image making in 1988 that minor mishaps—gaffes, slips of the tongue, even faulty microphones and flat tires—became big news. In all, no less than twenty-nine reports made mention of failed images. The networks' disproportionate attention to incidental campaign slips reflects the more general turn of campaign coverage to theater criticism. Their heavy focus on the construction of images for television led naturally to a focus on images that went awry.

As with the turn to theater criticism in general, the emphasis on failed images reflected a kind of guerilla warfare between the networks and the campaigns, an attempt by the networks to resist manipulation by puncturing the images the campaigns dispensed. The more the campaigns sought to control the images that appeared on the nightly news, the more the reporters tried to beat them at their own game, to deflate their media events by magnifying a minor mishap into a central feature of the event itself.

In 1968, before the preoccupation with television imagery had taken hold, such mishaps were rarely considered newsworthy. Only once in 1968 did a network insert a negative image into a report unrelated to the content of the campaign, when David Schoumacher (CBS, September 13) noted that Humphrey lost a foot race on the beach "to an out-of-shape reporter."

Yet it was hardly the case that politicians were without mishaps in 1968. Rather, the trivial slips they made did not count as news. For example, vice presidential candidate Spiro Agnew, addressing a Washington press conference, made a slip at least as embarrassing as Bush's Pearl Harbor remark. Accusing the Democrats of being soft on defense, Agnew accidentally attacked his own running mate, saying,

"Mr. Nixon is trying to cast himself in the role of a Neville Chamberlain." Like Bush, Agnew quickly corrected himself, saying that it was Humphrey who reminded him of Chamberlain. "Mr. Nixon, of course, would play the opposite role, that of Winston Churchill."

On the evening news that night, Agnew's slip of the tongue went without mention. The networks showed his remarks, including his misstatement and correction, but focused on the substance of his attack on the Democrats. None of the anchors or reporters made the slip itself the story, nor for that matter even took note of it.

Some of the slips the networks highlighted in 1988 were not even verbal gaffes or misstatements, but simply failures on the part of candidates to cater to the cameras. In a report on the travails of the Dukakis campaign, Sam Donaldson (ABC, October 17) seized on Dukakis's failure to play to ABC's television camera as evidence of his campaign's ineffectiveness. Showing Dukakis playing a trumpet with a marching band, Donaldson chided, "He played the trumpet with his back to the camera." As Dukakis played "Happy Days Are Here Again," Donaldson's voice was heard from off-camera calling, "We're over here, Governor." Donaldson completed the picture of futility by showing Dukakis at a bowling alley throwing a gutter ball.

Interestingly, the other networks also covered the bowling alley, but without showing the gutter ball. Chris Wallace (NBC, October 17) showed a more successful Dukakis ball, greeted by cheers from the crowd. "In these tough times," he concluded, "it's the kind of encouragement that keeps the candidate going." Bruce Morton's (October 17) report for CBS split the difference. "When you're losing, everything is a symbol," he said, "whether you throw a gutter ball or knock down some pins."

The campaigns and the networks blame each other for the atmosphere that rivets media attention on gaffes. Roger Ailes says, "Let's face it, there are three things that the media are interested in: pictures, mistakes, and attacks. It's my orchestra-pit theory of politics. If you have two guys on a stage and one guy says, 'I have a solution to the Middle East problem,' and the other guy falls in the orchestra pit, who do you think is going to be on the evening news?"[38]

Andrew Savitz, a Dukakis campaign aide in 1988, argues that the media's focus on gaffes forces candidates to avoid spontaneity and the risks that go with it. "Nobody does anything spontaneously with a bunch of cameras around now. One of the real driving forces is a sense of fear. A mistake made before the national cameras is a mistake forever."[39] Even the most careful attempts by candidates to present a favorable image for the cameras can go wrong. John Sasso recalls a photo opportunity in which Dukakis played catch with a Boston Red Sox baseball player: "Dukakis threw twenty balls and dropped one, and that's what ended up on television."[40]

Reporters and producers argue that a gutter ball or a muffed catch can serve as a visual metaphor of an inept campaign. They also point out that modern media-driven campaigns invite the focus on gaffes. "In 1988, the campaigns were so highly crafted, so manipulative, so much trying to control the coverage, that when a mistake was made, it really stood out," observes NBC producer Bill Wheatley. "We would be less than human in not reporting it."[41]

Richard Salant, former president of CBS News, attributes television's coverage of gaffes and slips to the growing influence of entertainment values in network news. He recalls the repeated pictures of President Ford stumbling on the steps while getting off airplanes. "They used to do this in vaudeville with banana peels. It runs very deep in the nature of entertainment. People bought televisions not to watch the news but to see Milton Berle."[42]

Perhaps the most memorable media event that failed in 1988 was Dukakis's tank ride. In one form or another, the much-ridiculed image of Dukakis in an M-1 tank appeared eighteen times on network newscasts during the 1988 campaign. It appeared so often that it became a symbol of Dukakis's failure to be the master of his image as a presidential candidate—so much so that the Bush campaign even used it in one of its own campaign commercials.

Memorable though the tank ride became as a media event that backfired, it is striking to recall that initial television coverage of the event was not wholly negative. Both Bruce Morton (CBS, September 13) and Chris Wallace (NBC, September 13) covered the event with light-hearted humor. "Biff, bang, powee!" Morton began, over pictures of a helmeted Dukakis riding in the tank. "It's not a bird. It's not a plane. It's presidential candidate Michael Dukakis in an M-1 tank as staff and reporters whoop it up" [*From off camera come voices calling*, "*Go Duke!*" "*That a boy, Duke!*"]. On NBC, Chris Wallace began, "Don't call Michael Dukakis soft on defense. Today he rolled across the Michigan plains like General Patton on his way to Berlin."

Only eight days later, in another report, Morton (CBS, September 21) aired the visual of Dukakis in the tank again, this time portraying it as a failed image. "Sometimes, even in sophisticated 1988, the visuals fail. Reporters hooted when Dukakis drove up in a tank." The picture was the same, but the interpretation had changed. So had the audio track. This time, sounds of laughter accompanied the visuals of the tank ride, replacing the cheers that were heard the first time the event was aired.

Several days later, a CBS report on an unrelated issue aired the Dukakis tank ride again, also with a negative audio track. Reporting the candidate's views on the budget deficit, Bill Whitaker (September 27) opened with a shot of Dukakis in the tank, accompanied by a barely audible voice saying, "Put 'em up!" followed by laughter.

As the treatment of the tank ride illustrates, the networks' focus on failed images not only exaggerates trivial aspects of the campaign; it also invites editorializing with images.

Campaign officials from both sides see in this tendency an unhealthy entanglement between politicians and the press. "The press is fascinated by the frequency of faux pas," notes Kathryn Murphy, director of communications for the Republican Party during the campaign. "The response of the campaigns is to minimize mistakes. Then reporters complain that the campaigns are too tightly controlled."[43] Dayton Duncan, press secretary to Dukakis, agrees. "Public officials have to be error-free actors. Many reporters view an interview as their chance to have a politician make a mistake. A mistake is viewed as one way of stripping away the artifice."[44]

Balancing Pictures and Perceptions: The Problem of False Symmetry

The focus of television news on media events, political commercials, media advisers, and failed imagery did not succeed in avoiding manipulation by the campaigns. Instead, it shifted attention from the substance to the stagecraft of politics, and eroded the objectivity of political reporting.

Rather than report the facts, or the actual records of the candidates, there was a tendency simply to balance perceptions, or to air an opposing image. Fairness came to mean equal time for media events, equal time for political commercials. But this left the media hostage to the play of perceptions that the campaigns dispensed.

The problem is best defined by those few instances when reporters went beyond the play of perceptions to refer to the record or report the facts. For example, Robert Bazell, reporting on the issue of the environment (NBC, October 21), began by showing how Bush and Dukakis used media events and contrived backdrops to portray themselves as ardent environmentalists. Rather than simply juxtaposing pictures of Bush riding a boat in Boston Harbor and Dukakis posing against backdrops of mountains and beaches, Bazell related their actual records and positions on such issues as global warming, acid rain, offshore drilling, and pesticide use.

In another notable example, ABC's Jim Wooten (September 26), assessed the validity of each candidate's claims in the first presidential debate. He interspersed clips of the candidates' statements with a correction of their facts:

DUKAKIS: I was a leader in the civil-rights movement in my state and in my legislature.

WOOTEN: Well, he did propose an antidiscrimination commission once, but that was about it.

BUSH: I want to be the one to banish chemical and biological weapons from the face of the earth.

WOOTEN: But he was the man who cast three tie-breaking Senate votes for new chemical weapons.

BUSH: The Governor raised taxes five different times.

WOOTEN: The Governor also cut taxes eight times, and people in thirty-three other states pay a greater part of their income in taxes than citizens of Massachusetts.

BUSH: I am proud to have been part of an administration that passed the first catastrophic health bill.

WOOTEN: In fact, the administration opposed some of the key provisions in that bill, and the president signed it reluctantly.

Unlike Wooten's reports after the first and subsequent debates, most coverage did not attempt to assess or correct the facts, but rested instead with the play of perceptions. In setting the pictures or the claims of each campaign side by side, the networks sought fairness in balance, without breaking through the images to report the facts.

After ABC (September 22) showed a Bush media event with Boston police, Peter Jennings made explicit what the networks often did reflexively, equating fairness with a balancing of images. "In the interest of fairness," he announced, viewers would now see a scene of Dukakis posing with police officers too. In the piece that followed, Sam Donaldson reported that Dukakis "surrounded himself with his own sea of blue today . . . in a made-for-television appearance." To its credit, ABC followed this juxtaposition of media events with an issue-oriented report on the candidates' positions on crime. Much of the time, however, the networks settled for a balance of campaign imagery alone.

The most flagrant instance of this tendency was in the presentation of the candidates' political ads. Reports were balanced in that they showed commercials from both sides. But setting the candidates' ads side by side, however balanced, does not necessarily make for objective reporting. It simply trades off the images the campaigns dispense. This leaves the viewer victim to the distortions the images may contain.

Furthermore, even when the reports did make some attempt to evaluate the candidates' rhetoric and imagery, the concern for "balance" (in the sense of not taking sides) led reporters to equate different orders of distortions or mistakes. In the name of balance, the reports created a false symmetry.

For example, in the final weeks of the 1988 campaign, the nightly newscasts often cast both campaigns as "dirty," even though the false accusations and smear tactics they actually reported were mostly perpetrated by Republicans (including some not formally tied to the Bush campaign). By showing excerpts from commercials such as the Willie Horton ad, the networks gave national exposure to inflammatory ads produced by local Republican groups, ads the Bush campaign could claim to renounce.

When Dukakis attacked these ads, the networks treated his attacks as one more chapter in a dirty campaign, as if Dukakis's criticisms were on a par with the smears themselves. "We begin with a presidential campaign that is going through an especially mean phase," said Peter Jennings (October 24), opening an ABC newscast. Tom Brokaw

(October 24) began NBC's nightly news in a similar vein: "Election day, two weeks from tomorrow, and it's getting very nasty again." The next night, Jennings (October 25) declared, "It's becoming difficult in this campaign to keep abreast of the accusations. . . . There are certainly some who wonder what all this has to do with running the country in the 1990s, but whatever happens, this kind of charge and countercharge is the hallmark of the campaigns at this point."

Introducing one newscast that week, Brokaw (October 25) seemed to promise the kind of reporting that would examine the content of the accusations and sort fact from falsehood: "Campaign commercial wars: Who's lying and who's not?" But the coverage that followed failed to answer this question. It focused instead on the effectiveness of the candidates' ads, and on the way they were perceived by voters and media experts.

In 1968, by contrast, fairness took a different form. Rather than seek symmetry within each broadcast, the networks sought fairness over the course of the campaign by covering a wide range of views, and allowing people to speak for themselves in sustained segments. This was true not only for candidates but also for critics drawn from across the political spectrum.

When a candidate made a major statement, the networks showed his opponent's reply. For example, when Humphrey gave an important speech on Vietnam, the networks aired Nixon's response. But they showed no similar compulsion to balance media events and images. When Humphrey took a walk on the beach, or when Nixon rode a hydroplane, the networks made no effort to show a rival image. Often, they ignored the gimmick altogether. And since they did not show excerpts from political commercials, the problem of balancing advertising images did not arise. They avoided entanglement with the candidates' image making, and so avoided the need to "balance" coverage of their respective gimmicks.

The Blurring of Commentary and Political Reporting

It might seem that reporters' reluctance to answer Brokaw's question, "Who's lying and who's not?," reflects a healthy instinct for the sidelines, a refusal to take sides. But notwithstanding their penchant for "balance" in 1988, reporters intervened more frequently in the stories they covered, and injected their opinions more freely, than did their predecessors twenty years earlier.

In 1968, reporters on the whole allowed the candidates and their critics to speak for themselves. The newscasts themselves distinguished sharply between reporting and commentary. Looking back twenty years later at the 1968 coverage, one is struck by how detached and dispassionate anchormen and reporters alike were in presenting the daily story. Coverage still partook of an unadorned "wire service" style of reporting, emphasizing description not interpretation. Opinions and analysis were reserved for explicitly designated commentary segments, which resembled spoken op-ed pieces. Two of the three networks offered campaign commentary in 1968, with Eric Sevareid on CBS, and Frank Reynolds and various guest commentators on ABC. In all, the networks broadcast some fifty-seven political commentaries during the general election campaign.

In this way, the treatment of fact and opinion reflected the practice of print journalism, with news and editorials at least nominally on separate pages. This demarcation had the effect of enhancing the credibility of the television journalist in both realms. In the role of reporter, the journalist enjoyed the credibility that goes with detached, straightforward reporting. In the role of commentator, the journalist was able to offer analysis and opinion at sufficient length to develop an argument, as in a traditional newspaper column or op-ed piece.

In 1988, by contrast, explicit political commentary had all but vanished from the networks' evening newscasts. In 1988, only eight commentary segments appeared, all by John Chancellor of NBC.

Of course, the rarity of explicit commentary in 1988 did not mean that anchors and reporters refrained from offering their views—far from it. They inserted them freely in their reporting, blurring the line between fact and opinion. This in turn diminished their authority, in two ways. On the one hand, their reliability as witnesses diminished as they departed from the unadorned narrative style of traditional reporting. At the same time, their impact as commentators was blunted as their occasion for commentary became cramped, reduced to a kind of sniping at the sidelines. In 1968, commentary segments averaged two minutes in length; by 1988, the shift from explicit to injected commentary had reduced the reporter's critical voice to a tag line, a passing snide remark. The compressed pace of 1988 coverage forced not only the candidates but also the reporters to deliver their opinions in sound bites and one-liners.

In 1968, for example, Frank Reynolds devoted two minutes and fifteen seconds to a hard-hitting commentary on how Nixon, Humphrey, and Wallace were all exploiting the theme of "law and order." When, twenty years later, Brit Hume sought to make a similar point, he was reduced to a twelve-second tag line at the end of a report on a Bush campaign stop in New York: "Bush is running for president, not sheriff, but some days it is hard to tell. His polls show he's hurt Dukakis on crime. And if he can use the issue to hurt him in a state Dukakis once thought was his, so much the better."

The explicit commentaries of 1968 typically addressed large themes —the Vietnam War, protest and dissent, law and order, the condition of American cities. The "injected commentaries" of 1988, by contrast, compressed as they were into a few seconds in the daily story, often amounted to little more than fleeting jibes or ad hominem remarks.

For example, after covering a speech in which Dukakis attacked his opponent in strong terms, Sam Donaldson shifted suddenly from reporting Dukakis's words to undercutting them. "Unless you're Harry Truman—and Dukakis is not—the strategy of giving them hell runs the risk of sounding shrill and unpresidential. But Dukakis figures Bush started it, and he has no choice but to join in" (ABC, September 12). Ten days later, Donaldson (September 20) criticized Dukakis again in a tag-line commentary, this time for sticking to the issues: "Thirty-six years ago, Adlai Stevenson insisted he was talking sense to the American people, and Ike won in a landslide."

Words and Images at War

In 1968, the reporter spoke from the sidelines, allowing the candidates time to tell their story. By 1988, the narrative structure of political reporting had become more complex, consisting of a tension, even a struggle, between the stories the campaigns and the reporters sought to tell.

The candidates sought to construct their story through the use of media events and catchy one-liners. The networks used their own juxtaposition of images, sound bites, and reporting. On both sides, the staccato language of sound bites and fast-paced visuals had replaced the familiar pace of ordinary speech. As a result, the presidential campaign on the nightly news came to look and sound less like traditional political discourse and more like commercial advertising.

This change can be seen in the contrast between Charles Quinn's report on Muskie's encounter with antiwar demonstrators in 1968 (NBC, October 25) and Bruce Morton's coverage of Dukakis's similar encounter with antiabortion demonstrators in 1988 (CBS, September 9).

In Quinn's coverage, there are few cuts in either the pictures or the words. Quinn speaks only at the beginning and end of the report, briefly and off-screen. He sets the context for the drama—"It was the worst heckling Senator Muskie has faced so far in the campaign"—then backs off to show it unfold. The camera lingers at a medium distance on both Muskie and the demonstrators, later moving in for close-ups of Muskie and student spokesman Rick Brody. The words of candidate and protester are the heart of the story. Over half of the report is devoted to Muskie's or Brody's speech.

In the case of Dukakis and the antiabortion protesters, by contrast, the story on the evening news was not about what the candidate or the protesters said, but about the television image the confrontation produced. "Most of what candidates do is aimed at your television screen," began Bruce Morton in his report on the confrontation. "The Dukakis campaign would have liked to have these pictures of his appearance before a mostly Polish audience today, but there were these pictures too." As Morton speaks, the report cuts quickly from favorable pictures of Dukakis to a woman sitting on the floor with her children yelling, "Do we have to destroy our children?"

In contrast to the coverage of the Muskie-Brody confrontation, the focus of Morton's report was not political speech, but the disruption of speech, and the television image the disruption created. Dukakis was relegated to a two-second sound bite addressing the protesters, and a seven-second sound bite delivering his economic message. An antiabortion demonstrator shouted for four seconds, and a National Right to Life representative interviewed later spoke for seven. Morton concluded the report by talking about television, and the balance of images that television conveyed. "What happened today was that the camera saw both realities. The few demonstrators with their issue, the vast majority of the crowd applauding Dukakis."

But the "reality" the camera "saw" was one in which no one spoke for more than nine seconds. It was a "reality" consisting of fast-moving images but little political discourse.

The same could be said of the 1988 coverage as a whole. The 9.8 second sound bite was one measure of this change. The decline of total candidate speaking time was another. The speaking time of presidential candidates on the nightly news was 56 percent greater in 1968 than in 1988, even without counting third-party candidate George Wallace.

The tendency to detach the candidates' pictures from their words is a characteristic feature of the theater-criticism style of reporting. While this style of coverage might seem to give the reporter the upper hand in the contest for control of television words and images, it does not always work this way.

In order to play the role of theater critic, the reporter has to show the theater, to put the potent images on television. Moreover, reporters are put in the paradoxical position of criticizing the very theater they help produce. The campaigns stage the media events, but the networks take the pictures—and the more dramatic the pictures, the more likely the story will run on the evening news. Reporters thus have a stake in the power of the visuals they go on to criticize. The networks are more than mere conduits; they help produce and promote the political theater they cover. The networks' stake in potent visuals is also what draws them to run the most vivid imagery of the candidates' commercials, as recurring motifs throughout the campaign.

Campaign coverage under these conditions is beset by conflicting impulses. This conflict is reflected in a tension between the visual and the narrative elements of the report. The visuals offer the most arresting images the campaigns dispense, while the narrative attempts to deconstruct these images, to reveal their artifice. This sets the reporter's narrative in competition with the campaign pictures, a competition the pictures are likely to win.

This competition was illustrated in a 1984 piece on Ronald Reagan by Lesley Stahl (CBS, October 4), which criticized at length Reagan's manipulation of television imagery during the campaign. Stahl was surprised to find that the Reagan White House loved the story. Grateful that the piece included almost five minutes of potent Reagan visuals, a presidential aide seemed oblivious to Stahl's critical narrative. "They don't listen to you if you are contradicting great pictures," the aide told Stahl. "They don't hear what you are saying if the pictures are saying something different."[45]

Stahl concluded from her experience that television images swamp words, that pictures speak louder than the reporter's critical voice. But Stahl's lament, which is often recited in complaints about the 1988 campaign, overlooks a deeper lesson about the use of words and images in political reporting.

Like many examples of theater criticism, Stahl's words often reinforced the images she intended to undercut. The opening of her piece was a paean to Reagan's image-making skills: "How does Ronald Reagan use television? Brilliantly." Aside from a few instances of fact correction, most of Stahl's report illustrated her opening statement. Far from being critical, her words were captions for the images she showed.

Stahl's conclusion, like her opening, was less critical than congratulatory. "President Reagan is accused of running a campaign in which he highlights the images and hides from the issues. But there is no evidence that the charge will hurt him, because when people see the president on television, he makes them feel good, about America, about themselves, and about him."

Unlike most examples of theater criticism, Stahl's report did, to its credit, make some attempt to confront Reagan's imagery with his record. In this respect, her narrative offered a critical counterpoint to his pictures. But her counterpoint lacked force because it spoke in no images of its own. While Stahl noted that Reagan used backdrops that contradicted his own policies on aid to the disabled and elderly, she showed no pictures depicting the consequences, only Reagan's visuals. Similarly, while she observed that Reagan distracted public attention from the bombing of the U.S. Marine headquarters in Beirut by offering patriotic images of the Grenada invasion, Stahl showed no images of Beirut, focusing instead on Reagan's pictures celebrating Grenada.

It might be argued that for reporters to use pictures to dramatize their points risks violating the line between reporting and editorializing. But this argument ignores the visual language of television, a language the campaigns have mastered to a highly sophisticated degree. It also ignores what is already a familiar practice in television reporting. Some of the best reporting on the facts and issues of the 1988 campaign—Jim Wooten's fact-correction pieces after the debates, Robert Bazell's report on the environment, and Lesley Stahl's piece on the forgotten issue of homelessness—made effective use of counterimages, illustrating discrepancies between candidates' rhetoric and records in ways that words alone might not have conveyed.

Most of the time, reporters rested with the campaigns' pictures. They revealed the artifice behind the images, but reproduced them nonetheless. So skillful were they in documenting the theater that it became difficult to distinguish the play from the real thing.

Contesting Control of the Picture

Picture Perfect News:
For and Against

Some of the most thoughtful critics of network coverage of presidential campaigns can be found at the networks themselves. Bill Wheatley was in charge of NBC's campaign coverage for 1992. In 1988, he was the executive producer of the "NBC Nightly News." He spent much of the time in between thinking of ways to overcome such problems as manipulation by campaign image makers and the compression of speech on the evening news.

Wheatley views the turn to theater criticism in the 1970s and 1980s as an attempt by reporters to reveal the campaigns' manipulation of images for television. Given the traditional obligation to report what happened on the campaign trail, the networks found themselves reporting constantly on their own manipulation. How could the networks break out of this pattern? "At some point," states Wheatley, "we need to say that the fact that we're being manipulated is no longer news. And at some point, we should do something to stop being victims. We should stop and say, 'Let's get rid of the manipulation and concentrate more on the themes.' "[1]

One way of doing this, Wheatley suggests, is to stop the practice of airing excerpts from campaign commercials as general file footage. Only when the story focuses on the ads themselves should the commercial video appear on the screen. "I think we fell into a trap with the ads [in 1988]. We used them too often, and as general footage. Not using the ads as part of general coverage would cut down on the candidates' ability to manipulate us."[2]

Wheatley is also critical of the trend toward short sound bites that appear at a rapid-fire pace. Reviewing taped excerpts of his network's 1988 coverage, Wheatley finds "discombobulated sound bites, sound bites that come out of nowhere. There is no setup, no introduction of the person who is about to speak." Identification of the speaker by a superimposed label at the bottom of the screen, Wheatley comments, is often insufficient. He points out that the bewildering pace is a symptom of the attempt to pack reports with as much information as possible, sometimes more than the viewer can absorb.[3]

At CBS, senior political correspondent Bob Schieffer agrees. "We are all agreed that we have squeezed sound bites too short." The reason is that "we have tried to put too many elements into our pieces," which has "often resulted in pieces that are superficial at best and often downright frivolous. This is a problem we can change by making the simple declaration, 'we are going to stop doing it that way,' and then sticking to it."

Schieffer would also return to a more traditional style of reporting, using pictures to document events rather than to grab and hold viewers' attention. In his view, network newscasts should strive to become "information-driven rather than picture-driven. This is not to say that we should stop using pictures. But we should use the pictures to impart information." Schieffer argues that a piece for the evening news should "be judged on what information it imparts, not on how it 'looks.' "[4]

Ted Koppel of ABC's "Nightline" is also critical of today's picture-driven network newscasts. The enhanced production values of recent years have made it more difficult, he believes, for reporters and politicians to convey substance on television. Looking back on his own coverage of Nixon in the 1968 campaign, Koppel is struck by the contrast.

There is a real irony when I look at the 1968 coverage. The real paradox is I got to say a lot more and got to be more analytical in those pieces precisely because the pictures were lousy. . . .

The brilliance of our production values today, the extraordinary technological leaps that we have made since 1968, are our own biggest hurdle. They are our biggest handicap. We have become so good at making it look slick, we have become so good at enhancing the visual elements, that you would have to be Robert Lowell, Mark Twain, or Thomas Jefferson to say something that is going to get through all that television noise. No one is that good. Nothing anyone says is profound enough to get past the hurdle of extraordinary production values we have put in our path. [5]

Some of those responsible for the evening news in the 1960s see today's fast-paced, picture-driven coverage as a product of pressures for ratings that they did not confront. Sanford Socolow, executive producer for the "CBS Evening News" with Walter Cronkite, describes the unwritten rules on pacing that now govern network newscasts.

Producers and reporters are charged with getting an exciting, enticing piece on the air, even if it means breaking up the candidate's train of thought. The correspondent is not allowed to talk more than twelve or fifteen seconds before there is some intermediate sound. It's called pacing. If in the heat of the battle to get on the air, if the substance gets in the way of the pace of the piece, then damn the substance. [6]

Walter Cronkite recalls that in his day, entertainment values did not play a part in campaign coverage.

We never thought that way at all. We were out after substance. We did not go for "sound bites." I think there were nights when [the candidates spoke] for forty seconds, and I was disappointed that we didn't have more. . . . We were not under the pressure to make everything as short as possible. The attitude today is that you have to hold them every second of that half-hour that you're on the air. We were not under that pressure. Part of that was because there were only two competitive networks—ABC wasn't that important. People hung in there. Maybe they didn't want to watch what they were watching, but they didn't turn us off."

Cronkite faults the current picture-driven style of coverage for crowding out speech. "The problem today is this absolute fear of having the anchor or a correspondent on the air as opposed to having pictures. It's the reason for the sound bite being as short as it is. It's just the form of television news today. It's the attitude of the producers, it's the entire ethic of the business."[7]

Shad Northshield, who in 1968 produced NBC's "Huntley-Brinkley Report," thinks the quality of network coverage has declined because of the intense pressure for ratings. "I think the political coverage in 1988 was basically not as good as the political coverage in 1968. It wasn't as good journalistically. It was much better technically, of course. But that's all it was." Today's network producers have turned to short sound bites and attention-grabbing visuals because of pressures imposed by the corporations who now own the networks. "They are doing it because of this goddamn, evil, bottom-line mentality. This business is a business. Television news is more television than news."[8]

Some of those responsible for coverage of the 1988 presidential campaign offer a spirited rejoinder to their critics inside and outside television news. They argue that the quality of coverage has improved, not declined, since 1968. More sophisticated technology enables faster, more flexible editing of pictures and words. And more sophisticated, image-conscious reporting does more to pierce the veil of campaign manipulation.

Tom Bettag was the executive producer of Dan Rather's "CBS Evening News" during the 1988 campaign. The 1968 campaign was before his time. Hearing of criticisms by his predecessors of the 1988 coverage, Bettag offers a vigorous reply. He argues that there is something to be said for the image-conscious turn of television news, and also for its faster pace. "I think that '68 coverage was remarkably naive about the images they put on. With time, we became more sophisticated in realizing that we were being used in the images. I think that is a positive step. Maybe it's not being done right. But the packaging is important, and Joe McGinniss's book was the first time a lot of us thought about that. What you're seeing is people still coming to grips with it."

Bettag resents what he sees as the old-timers denigrating the present to enhance the past. "I don't think the past was that good. I think there is a glorification of '68. One of the problems in '68 was that it was the 'just-the-facts-ma'am' wire service reporting. The time was very different. I would attribute the [longer sound bites] to the idea that they were trying to fill up a broadcast. The problem at that time was how to fill up a half-hour broadcast."

Far from being a model of objectivity, the 1968 style of coverage "was a sterility," Bettag argues. "It just laid out what the politicians said. It was a broadcast dominated by reports from beat correspondents in and around Washington. So much of the agenda was just filling it up with Washington stuff. You could let sound bites run for two minutes because it helped fill out the broadcast."

Today "the problem is one of massive compression," Bettag continues. "You're trying to stuff in more information from many other places. The compression [is an attempt] to give viewers as much information as they can quickly absorb. You get a much broader feel for what's going on." Bettag maintains that the faster pace of television news is a reflection of viewers' expectations. Over the past two decades, "people became used to a much faster pace of information. Madison Avenue was much slower paced in '68 than in '88. People's ability to receive visual information has speeded up. Just because television news has speeded up doesn't mean it's all bad. It means the people have changed. It's not just that television news has gone showbiz. Politics has changed too."[9]

Bill Crawford, a senior producer for CBS in 1988, was a field producer during the 1968 campaign. He attributes shorter sound bites to improved editing techniques. Like Bettag, Crawford claims that the politicians' speeches ran longer in the old days because the networks lacked the technical means to cut it easily, and in any case needed to fill airtime. "I think '88 sound bites were too short. Everybody in the business does; that's kind of a given. I also think that in '68 they were way too long and self-indulgent and done to fill the time. It was also the result of the kind of editing we had to do then."

Reviewing videotapes of the 1968 coverage, Crawford comments that, given the generous time devoted to the candidates' speeches, "these pieces have a nice, musty, antique feel about them." This is due, he suggests, to the difficulty of editing film, which was used in 1968, compared to the ease of editing videotape, which by the 1980s had replaced film in television news. "That's why the sound bites [in

1968] were so long, because you didn't have the ability to go 'pop, pop, pop.' The mechanics drove it then, as the mechanics drive it now."

Like Bettag, Susan Zirinsky was not yet in television in 1968. By the 1980s, she was one of CBS's leading political producers, covering the Reagan presidency and the 1988 campaign. She argues that modern video editing techniques have improved coverage by enabling producers to package pictures and words from different campaigns and different events in a single report. "As the technology changed, I think the product got better, not worse. You can give people things later, meet deadlines with greater proficiency, and [have] a greater hand editorially. The candidates and the process may have become warped. I don't think our technical expertise warped it."

Zirinsky does not defend the short sound bites of 1988. "Yes, I think sound got too short. Absolutely. We're moving the other way now." But she argues that those who complain about short snippets of political speech often confuse two different things—sound bites and "natural sound." Natural sound, she explains, is an editing technique that employs a few words of a candidate's speech without intending to convey information.

> "It's an effective editing tool when you're cutting a piece and want to break up the pacing or want to hear the candidate just for his rhythm and his mood or whatever you're trying to achieve. It's not really a sound bite. It is just a burst of natural sound.
>
> "It's part of the editing. It breaks the track up and gives pacing to a piece. It's a television technique. Everybody I've read misconstrues sound bites as averaging four seconds. Of course they are, if you take these bursts of sound that aren't really sound bites. If you showed me three scripts, I could tell you, that's a sound bite, that's a sound bite, that's a burst of natural sound.' "[10]

Dan Rather, anchor of the "CBS Evening News," makes a similar point. He does not defend the short sound bite the networks now employ, stating, "I am firmly committed to lengthening sound bites, extending them to at least twenty to twenty-five seconds." But like Zirinsky, he worries that "researchers count 'natural sound' as sound bites and thus their statistics are wrong. . . . A producer or reporter may show a candidate speaking for three or four seconds and use it as an opener and consider it natural sound." Rather acknowledges, however, that "the public might not see it that way. When people see the candidate they may expect they are going to hear part of his speech. . . . The natural undertow in this business is detrimental to length. I think a lot of this is wrong."[11]

That not all snippets of candidates' speech are genuine sound bites is small comfort to those concerned with the devaluation of political discourse on television news. That the networks sometimes use the words of presidential candidates as "bursts of natural sound" to improve the pacing of reports is further evidence of the growing emphasis on production values. In any case, the fact remains that Bush and Dukakis got to speak for thirty seconds or more only 15 times during the 1988 general election campaign, compared to 162 times for Nixon and Humphrey in 1968.

As for the argument that the networks ran long sound bites in 1968 because they needed to fill airtime, Walter Cronkite insists that it is simply untrue.

"That's personal revisionism on the part of people who weren't there. I don't think any of the old timers would tell you that. It's true, of course, that we didn't have as much material available, but it's not true at all that we couldn't have filled up the broadcast. There was never any problem of not having material for a broadcast, never. We were in a terrible time bind from the very beginning of getting in everything that was important."[12]

While no one would dispute the notion that video is easier to edit than film, the change in technology is not a sufficient explanation for the change in the style of political coverage. The ease of editing videotape does not by itself dictate short sound bites. Mechanics drive the coverage only to the extent that reporters and producers can use the new mechanics to achieve the effects they want. What effects do they want? Given growing pressures to win ratings by holding audiences all too ready to change the channel, the networks have used the new technology to produce fast-paced, visually arresting newscasts that are strong on pictures, short on words.

Some argue that, even as a way of winning high ratings, the 1988 style of campaign coverage was misconceived. Don Hewitt is no stranger to high ratings. The executive producer of "60 Minutes," the highly popular newsmagazine program, Hewitt has been in television news since 1948. He speaks bluntly and disdainfully of the fast-paced style of today's network newscasts. Hewitt says that producers began to worry about the pace of the broadcast in the 1980s. "By that time, the news had become so much a part of the entertainment business and razzle-dazzle. It wasn't just politics. Everything got charged up and there is no chance to think about anything."

But Hewitt thinks that the "razzle-dazzle" production techniques the producers have adopted are the wrong way to hold an audience. "Most of the people who work in television news are misguided. They don't understand." The key to the enormous success of "60 Minutes," he argues, is not pictures but words.

> "I don't use sound bites. I'd fire anybody who talks about sound bites. . . . "60 Minutes," which is one of the most popular broadcasts in the history of television, lives on talking heads and on people getting a chance to say what they have to say.
>
> "What [most network news producers] don't know is that you use your ear more than your eye. Your ear keeps you focused on the television set. I believe that. That's how I built this broadcast. They just don't know how to do it. We've been on the air since 1968. We're the longest running show on television because words are sacred to us. What we say is much more important than what we show you. We don't show you that much anyway, but we tell you a lot.
>
> "The success of this broadcast is built on audio and words. I can live with an out-of-focus picture, but I can't live with an out-of-focus sentence. What I don't want, in the middle of a "60 Minutes" story, is for some guy to say, 'Hey Mildred, do you understand what that guy is saying?' "[13]

For good or ill, the last quarter century has witnessed a transformation in the way television news covers presidential politics. Those who welcome it and those who deplore it agree that the transformation is due to changes in politics, economics, and technology. With the rise of media consultants, campaigns improve their ability to manipulate images for television. Reporters, seeking to resist manipulation, focus increasing attention on the image-making apparatus of the campaigns. Meanwhile, mounting pressures on network news divisions to boost ratings lead to fast-paced, visually compelling broadcasts, which heighten the networks' appetites for the pictures the campaigns dispense. Reporters and producers seek the best possible picture, whether from media events or political ads, then try to puncture the picture by revealing its artifice, by highlighting its contrived nature. Finally, the technologies of video editing enable the networks to deliver the perfect pictures and the reporting that would expose them in a slickly packaged collage of fast-moving images and words.

But the significance of this transformation goes beyond the political, commercial, and technological factors that brought it about. The new interplay of television and politics has brought with it a growing public disillusion with the media and the politicians alike. This disillusion, which found widespread expression in the aftermath of the 1988 campaign, was directed both at the campaign and at the coverage of the campaign. In ways that defied a precise fixing of blame, both the campaigns and the networks seemed entangled in a politics of imagery and artifice that left the substance of politics behind.

Some of the frustration may be connected to the failure of the democratic promise of television. On the one hand, television news promised a kind of ultimate document. Like photography itself, but with greater boldness, television offered—indeed at moments still offers—a direct access to reality, the tantalizing prospect of being there, of seeing the person or the event with our own eyes, of judging for ourselves. And yet, as coverage of the Reagan presidency and the Bush-Dukakis campaign displayed, television is also a powerful instrument of artifice, at once victim and accomplice of the sophisticated illusions that politicians and their media experts are able to spin.

For all that is new in the way television covers presidential politics, its predicament might best be understood as the modern expression of a paradox as old as the camera. By considering some earlier contests for the control of political images, we can shed light on the struggle that television news still confronts. The "picture perfect" mentality that informs television coverage of presidential politics plays out, in heightened form, tensions that have been present in photography from the start. Does the camera document reality or subvert it, by promising realism but producing a pose? When politicians are doing the posing, the stakes have always been high. When the camera became a television lens, the stakes grew higher still.

Not all that is troubling about "picture perfect" presidential campaigns is without precedent in American politics. Long before television, journalists struggled with the realism and the artifice that pictures convey. And from the earliest days of the republic, politicians have engaged in image making while critics have bemoaned the triumph of appearance over reality, of style over substance.

Presidential Image Making: Past and Present

Some months after the 1988 election, Michael Dukakis assailed "the increasingly shallow nature of electoral campaigns that trivialize important issues in the service of image making." Given the role of television, the 1988 election was about neither ideology nor competence. "It was about phraseology. It was about ten-second sound bites. And made-for-TV backdrops. And going negative." His biggest mistake, Dukakis said, was his failure to understand the phenomenon of television image-making.[14]

But political image-making and the "selling of the president" have a history almost as old as that of the republic itself. "A man will soon, without the imputation of indelicacy, be able to hawk himself in the highways as an excellent candidate for the highest promotion," declared Federalist Thomas Dwight in 1789, "with as much freedom and vociferation as your market men now cry codfish and lobsters."[15] Two years later, after losing the election of 1800 to Jefferson, Federalists responded in a fashion strikingly similar to that of Dukakis in 1988. They too blamed their opponents' skillful if scurrilous use of a new medium of communication that threatened to debase politics— the press. "The newspapers are an overmatch for any government," wrote Federalist Fisher Ames. "They will first overawe and then usurp it. This has been done, and the jacobins owe their triumph to the unceasing use of this engine."[16]

Federalists of the old school resisted the notion of popular electioneering, and opposed recourse to the printing press. "We can do infinitely more by private letters than by newspaper publications," argued one.[17] But in time, they had little choice but to take up the techniques of their opponents. In an age when newspapers and journals were published and written to win political adherents, the Federalists began newspapers of their own. Before long, Federalist electioneering sheets abandoned traditional scruples and appealed without embarrassment to popular sentiment. In the first stirrings of sound-bite democracy, "much was made of slogans and catch-words. . . . Intricate issues were summarized in a few phrases or reduced to a line of wretched verse. . . . Political problems which might have stymied Solomon were resolved in a pun or an epigram. . . . Editors ran the same cant words and phrases in their columns over and over again," as Federalists learned "to rely upon the effect of repetition."[18]

At least where the presidency was concerned, however, the new techniques of electioneering were held in check. As historian Gil Troy has written, the founders thought that presidential candidates should stand, not run, for office. While seekers of lesser offices might engage in the fray of campaigning, presidential candidates, true to the republican ideal of disinterested public service, would remain aloof and stand on their character and record. John Adams and Thomas Jefferson spent the 1796 and 1800 campaigns away from public view on their respective farms.[19] Prior to his 1832 reelection campaign, Andrew Jackson declared: "I meddle not with elections, I leave the people to make their own President."[20]

By 1840, the Whig and Democratic parties organized the masses with songs, slogans, and revival-like meetings in the first popular presidential campaign. Still, William Henry Harrison, the Whig candidate for president, presented himself as the humble embodiment of republican restraint. In his letter of acceptance to the Whig nominating convention, he stated that he would not "declare the principles upon which the Administration would be conducted." Stating a view of the presidency similar to today's view of Supreme Court justices, Harrison argued that the Constitution made the president an "impartial umpire" who should not make promises or policy statements as a condition of election. He decried the tendency of ambition to make "men of the fairest characters" act like "auctioneers selling . . . linen."[21]

As party politics displaced the eighteenth-century ideal of disinterested politics, the dignified silence of presidential candidates became less an expression of republican virtue, and more a strategy of political caution. Democratic opponents charged that Harrison's silence was a pose, a way of avoiding the issues. They attacked the "correspondence committee" that answered his mail as a group of handlers in effect, dubbing it "General Harrison's Thinking Committee." The Democrats "dismissed 'General Mum' as a 'caged' simpleton forced to rely on his 'conscience keepers.' "[22]

Four years later, the Democrats urged the strategy of silence upon their own candidate, the obscure James Polk. "If you could avoid reading or speaking or writing from now until the election, our success would be certain," a friend advised him. His opponent, Henry Clay, observed no such restraint. Although declaring that the people "should be free, impartial and wholly unbiased by the conduct of a candidate himself," Clay did not hesitate to pronounce upon a wide range of controversial issues. Refusing to heed the advice of handlers who insisted that he be "caged," Clay lost the election.[23]

If 1988 was, as *Time* declared, the "Year of the Handlers," James Baker and Roger Ailes were engaged in a practice that had fueled controversy and outrage for over a century. An 1852 political cartoon titled "Managing the Candidate" offers an early instance of an attack on handlers and image makers. The cartoon shows the Whig nominee, General Winfield Scott, trying to step over a controversial plank in the Whig's platform ratifying the Great Compromise of 1850 between the North and the South. Perched on Scott's shoulders, the Whig politician William Henry Seward covers Scott's mouth and holds his arm, preventing him from speaking or writing. "Never mind your tongue or your pen, I'll manage them," Seward says. "But . . . stretch your legs, as I do my conscience, and you can get over anything."[24]

When Nancy Reagan, on stage at the 1984 Republican convention, blew a kiss to an image of her husband, Ronald Reagan, portrayed on a video screen above the podium, the delegates applauded wildly. But for all its technological novelty, the scene recalled an earlier celebration of a presidential likeness at the dawn of the photographic age. As the Republican convention of 1860 nominated Abraham Lincoln, supporters in the balcony showered the delegates with portrait prints of the candidate, which they greeted with "perfectly deafening applause, the shouts swelling into a perfect roar."

When Lincoln was declared the nominee, his life-size portrait was exhibited from the platform, to further cheers.[25]

The Lincoln likenesses distributed at the 1860 convention and during the election campaign differ from the now-familiar Lincoln image that adorns the penny. Between his election and inauguration, Lincoln made an apparently image-conscious decision, encouraged by supporters who hoped to improve his appearance: he grew a beard. "[A]fter oft-repeated views of the daguerreotypes," a group of Republicans wrote Lincoln, "we have come to the candid determination that these medals would be much improved in appearance, provided you would cultivate whiskers and wear standing collars. Believe us nothing but an earnest desire that 'our candidate' should be the best looking as well as the best of the rival candidates, would induce us to trespass upon your valued time."[26]

Replying to a young girl who had written with similar advice, Lincoln seemed to resist the suggestion. "As to the whiskers, having never worn any, do you not think people would call it a piece of silly affect[at]ion if I were to begin it now?" But just as later politicians would overcome their distaste for wearing makeup on television, Lincoln overcame his fear of affectation. By the time he was inaugurated, the whiskers had appeared.[27]

The mass-communications revolution of the early twentieth century brought two new instruments of political image making, public relations and radio. As Republicans mounted a sleek advertising campaign to sell Warren Harding to the American people in 1920, critics protested the artifice of the modern campaign. "There is interposed between the voter and his final judgment the whole mechanism of modern publicity," wrote the *New Republic*. Another commentator worried that in this "new age of publicity," the publicity man had become the "president maker." The young Democrat named Franklin Roosevelt criticized Harding's campaign of contrived photo opportunities. "Photographs and carefully rehearsed moving picture films do not necessarily convey the truth."[28]

This did not prevent Calvin Coolidge, a man of few words, from making up for his taciturnity by "performing" for the cameras as tree chopper, hay pitcher, or host at the White House to such visitors as Henry Ford and Thomas Edison.[29] In 1932, Franklin Roosevelt himself easily prevailed over Herbert Hoover in that year's version of "the

war of the Labor Day visuals." Roosevelt projected a "picture personality," the *New York Sun* observed, while Hoover looked unhappy
even when photographed fishing.[30]

The 1936 campaign between Roosevelt and Republican Alfred E.
Landon was the first to be professionally choreographed for radio. The
Republicans hired a voice coach for Landon, and Roosevelt adopted a
calmer, more intimate speaking voice, even when addressing a live
audience, in deference to his radio listeners. As with television a
generation later, the new medium inspired politicians to dramatize
their message to hold the attention of a mass audience.[31]

At first, the broadcasting companies refused on principle to mix
politics with entertainment. When the Republicans produced a dramatic skit portraying the dire effects of the New Deal on an average
American couple, the networks refused to air the program. Edward
Klauber, a CBS official, explained that if the networks aired political
dramatizations, "the turn of national issues might well depend on the
skill of warring dramatists rather than on the merits of the issues
debated."[32]

The nominating conventions of that year were the first to be staged
for radio. The proceedings were reduced in length, Roosevelt's speech
was moved to the evening for prime listening time, and applause was
abbreviated to "short staccato cheers that ended quickly so that no
word would be lost."[33] Analyzing the 1968 presidential campaign,
Eric Sevareid would observe, "the important figure in the crowd is the
television cameraman. He provides the significant audience."[34] A
delegate to the 1936 Democratic convention said much the same of
the new mass medium of his day: The "real presiding officer was the
microphone."[35]

As the parties perfected the image-making techniques of advertising and radio, the 1936 campaign added new fuel to the long-
standing fear that salesmanship and showmanship would crowd out
the substance of democratic politics. *Newsweek* wrote that the radio
professionals would sell the Republican line as if it were "toothpaste or
tomato juice."[36] Offering a different litany of commodities, another
reporter wrote that the advertising men would sell Landon and "tax
phobia as they have automobiles, shaving soap, [and] cigarettes."[37]
Attacking Roosevelt's facility with radio, William Randolph Hearst's
San Francisco Examiner exclaimed, "Do we want a showman or a

statesman?" Decades before Michael Deaver and Ronald Reagan would perfect the video presidency, the journalist Marquis Childs concluded that campaigning in this "era of the news reel and the radio calls for a technique as deliberate as that of a Hollywood star."[38]

The Problem with Pictures: Past and Present

Like the long-standing worry about political image making, concerns about picture-centered journalism found expression long before the age of television. For over a century, Americans have vacillated between celebrating pictures and worrying about their contrived nature, their association with commercialism, and their tendency to crowd out words. In the mid-nineteenth century, journalists thought of pictures "as clutter on the page and a waste of space." As late as the 1880s, some reporters still protested that "pictorial reporting" or "illustrated journalism," as they called it, "betrayed us into making our eyes do the work of our brains."[39]

Prior to the 1880s, newspapers even resisted pictures in paid advertisements, penalizing advertisers who used illustrations. James Gordon Bennett, founder and editor of the *New York Herald*, "held that the advertiser should gain advantage from what he said, but not from how the advertisement was printed or displayed."[40]

Beginning in the 1880s, however, the relationship between newspapers and advertisers changed. As Michael Schudson points out, advertisements, which before this time had occupied less than a third of newspaper space, began to take up half the paper or more.[41] At about the same time, the development of the halftone engraving process enabled American newspapers, magazines, and books to reproduce photographs on the same paper that accepted type.[42] Photographs and words could now appear together on the printed page; spectacle, entertainment, and advertising would henceforth commingle with the news.

The mass reproduction of photographic images in newspapers and magazines led Americans living between 1885 and 1910 to experience a "visual reorientation" that historian Neil Harris compares to the transformation brought by the invention of the printing press four centuries earlier. For good and ill, the visual reorientation of the late nineteenth century anticipated the one brought by television in our time.

The printing of photographs in mass publications offered viewers a direct contact with reality, unmediated (or so it seemed) by the mind and hand of an artist. For the first time, Americans could actually see what important people, such as presidential candidates, looked like. The lack of such pictures explains the intense public interest in the mass-produced prints of Abraham Lincoln in the 1860s. In 1864, after Ulysses S. Grant's victories had made him the highest-ranking general officer in the army, even the Washington press corps did not know what he looked like. "The identification of the hero at Union Station was made on the basis of one man's memory of a faded photograph that had shown a corner of the general's face."[43]

As with television, so with the halftone photograph, the documentary promise coexisted with the dangers of distortion, fabrication, and simplification. Social critics of the late nineteenth and early twentieth centuries, responding to the sudden prominence of mass-produced pictures and photographs, gave early expression to many of the worries that television raises in our time. Writing of the "decadence of illustration," a critic wrote in 1899 "that illustrators of fiction were exaggerating the purely pictorial aspects of stories and failing to supplement the plots."[44] Another critic argued that deceptive and misleading illustrations of nonfiction should be subject to the same critical assessment as words. In a complaint similar to recent worries about media events and political ads on the evening news, C. F. Tucker Brooker wrote in 1911: "Has not the time come to demand that the pictures introduced into works on social and cultural conditions be subjected to the same investigation which is given to other testimony?" In virtue of their capacity to command attention, "pictures irresponsibly selected, and inserted without adequate investigation, can easily lead to more serious misapprehension than would result from glaring error in the letter-press."[45]

Critics also argued that pictures threatened to overwhelm words, to crowd out serious reflection with titillation, sensation, and distraction. In 1893, the Nation wrote that newspaper pictures had come to prominence as words lost their significance. "The childish view of the world is, so to speak, 'on top.' "[46] A 1911 editorial in Harper's Weekly railed against "over-illustration." "We can scarce get the sense of what we read for the pictures," the editorial argued. "We can't see the ideas for the illustrations. Our world is simply flooded with them. They lurk in almost every form of printed matter." Properly subordinated, illustrations aided thought, but improperly used, they became "a mental drug" that posed a threat to the development of young minds. "[I]t would be safe to say that a young mind, overfed pictorially, will scarcely be likely to do any original thinking."[47]

As the critics feared, the growing prominence of pictures coincided with pressures for the compression of speech. Bemoaning the nine-second sound bite of the 1990s, Walter Cronkite recently stated that "[d]istortion by compression may be the single biggest problem with television news." He called on network news departments to "show a little more responsibility by dropping the contrived photo opportunities and the planted sound bites in favor of longer interviews and statements by the politicians dealing with the issues."[48] The shrinking sound bite that Cronkite decried, however, is the ultimate expression of tendencies in American culture that appeared early in the twentieth century.

The founding of the *Reader's Digest* in 1922 ushered in what historian Daniel Boorstin has called "a new era of abridgments." When the magazine's founder, De Witt Wallace, went to his dubious father to borrow money for the new venture, he confidently told him, "We are living in a fast-moving world. People are anxious to get at the nub of matters."[49] Wallace produced his first issue by going to the New York Public Library and copying by hand from other magazines abridged versions of their articles. Most of the editors of the original magazines gave Wallace permission to reprint the articles, thinking it would bring them free publicity.[50]

Wallace's digest soon outsold all the magazines it digested. In time, it published more copies than the Bible. As one testimonial featured in the *Reader's Digest* put it, "I don't have time to read *all* the magazines, so I just read the best from all of them in the little magazine that fits right into my pocket."[51]

At about the same time, the modern impulse to compress found expression half way across the globe, where the Russian novelist Eugene Zamyatin glimpsed the sensibility that would later issue in the sound bite. "The old, slow, soporific descriptions are no more. The order of the day is laconicism—but every word must be supercharged, high voltage. Into one second must be compressed what formerly went into a sixty-second mixture."[52]

In America, the quickened pace of life formed the premise of the burgeoning advertising business of the twenties and thirties. A columnist for an advertising publication declared that speed had become an imperative of everyday life: "Quick lunches at soda fountains . . . quick cooking recipes . . . quick tabloid newspapers . . . quick news summaries." Another writer told of a "new American tempo" that gave American life "the turbulence of shallow water." Advertisers had to be quick to spot trends and change with them to keep pace with the American public.[53]

Like the publishers and advertisers, politicians also learned to compress their speech to keep pace with the public. Even in the days of the campaign whistle-stop, long before the advent of the thirty-second television spot, candidates chafed at the need to compress their message. "I have tried discussing the big questions of this campaign from the rear end of a train," Woodrow Wilson complained in 1912. "It can't be done. They are too big. . . . By the time you get started and begin to explain yourself the train moves off."[54]

The advent of radio as a campaign device imposed further pressures on politicians to compress their speech, though in retrospect the constraints hardly seem severe. Radio coverage of the 1932 campaign brought complaints from listeners and broadcasters, who objected that the speeches were too long and tedious. The radio editor of the *New York Times* explained that henceforth, politicians would have to reduce their speech to keep their audience. "It requires a highly interesting speaker and a sparkling topic to hold an invisible audience [for fifteen minutes] . . . [candidates] must learn to discard hour-and-a-half speeches and condense their thoughts to fit in a half-hour at the most."[55]

The 1930s also brought the birth of the popular picture magazines, such as *Life* and *Look*, which critics thought would contribute to the modern tendency of pictures to crowd out words. Walter Lippmann, for example, wrote of the "rivulet of text" that trickled between the imposing advertising photographs of the new magazines.[56]

In their lavish use of pictures, the new magazines were not burdened by worries about the fate of words or the risk of blurring news and entertainment, document and drama. For *Life* magazine, pictures were a means of revealing the drama in events. Its unabashed celebration of photojournalism was uncomplicated by the image-conscious sensibility of today's television news. News was entertainment, and entertainment was news.

In *Life's* inaugural issue of 1936, its editors introduced two regular features with a wholly unselfconscious enthusiasm for photography. They described "Life on the American Newsfront" as "a selection of the most newsworthy snaps made anywhere in the United States by the mighty picture-taking organization of the U.S. press." The "President's Album" would be a "kind of picture diary—a special focus on the personality center of the nation's life. Luckily for *Life*, it can start its diary with a President [Franklin Roosevelt] who is a marvelous camera actor and is not above demonstrating his art."[57]

For the editors of *Life*, there was no worry about distinguishing the authentic from the staged, the document from the fabrication. *Life* reveled in pictures without the critical edge of the image-conscious 1980s and 1990s. Documentary news shots of the Depression and of the rise of fascism were featured with the same fanfare as novelty shots of a "one-legged man on a mountain," a huge close-up of Jimmy Durante's nose, and public-relations photographs from the latest movies.

The same merging of documentation and drama, of news and spectacle, characterized *Time* magazine's advertisements during this period. An ad for *Time* in 1936 promised would-be readers access to "The Greatest Show of All."

In all the world there is no drama like reality, . . . no spectacle so great and stirring as the tremendous, marching pageant of news. In the year to come . . . great actors like Mussolini and Hitler will march across the stage before you in what may prove their farewell appearance. New players, today unknown, will spring into fame. . . . Millions of people will never see more than the sideshows, never get to understand what the tremendous show is all about. To them all this is wasted, for they will lose the best lines and miss the plot. *Time* can make sure you get the full drama of every worthwhile act.[58]

The 1930s also gave powerful expression to the documentary impulse in photography, most notably in photographers such as Walker

Evans and Dorothea Lange, who were employed by the Farm Security Administration. Their classic photos of the ravages of the Depression were not vehicles of spectacle and entertainment, but a form of witness and record. Works such as Lange's memorable "Migrant Mother" acknowledged the drama in the document, not for the sake of spectacle but for the sake of presenting in vivid terms the reality of American life in the Depression. Likewise, the photographs in Paul Taylor and Dorothea Lange's *An American Exodus* constituted a compelling documentary record of the victims of the dust bowls.

Television news in its formative years took up the documentary tradition, and aspired to bring out the drama in the news without lapsing into spectacle or entertainment. When network newscasts went from fifteen minutes to a half-hour format in 1963, Reuven Frank, executive producer of NBC's "Huntley-Brinkley Report," wrote a long memorandum on television news as a guide for his staff, many of whom had experience with newspapers or radio but not television.

Frank's memo was a revealing meditation on the use of pictures in television. He acknowledged that the camera does not merely record reality, but conveys reality by dramatizing it. Still, the drama would be for the sake of conveying reality, not for the sake of entertainment.

> "Every news story should, without any sacrifice of probity or responsibility, display attributes of fiction, of drama. It should have structure and conflict, problem and denouement, rising action and falling action, a beginning, a middle and an end. These are not only the essentials of drama; they are the essentials of narrative. We are in the business of narrative because we are in the business of communications."

Frank acknowledged the impact of television pictures, but sought to deploy that impact for the sake of informing, not amusing the public. "There will be no tricks to gain or hold audiences we do not want."[59]

The documentary ambition of television news also found expression in emphatic rules against the "staging" of events for the camera, rules still invoked by network reporters and producers. A CBS code written during the 1970s states, "Staging is prohibited. . . . We report the facts *exactly* as they occur. We do *not* create or change them."[60]

Charles Quinn, a reporter for NBC in the 1960s, recalls emphatically resisting an attempt to improve the picture during a civil-rights march. "Toward the end of the Selma March, they wanted me to do a stand-up [report] in front of the statehouse, where it was all a mess. A guy comes along bringing extra placards and said they wanted more rubble around my feet. He said he was the producer, and I told him to get that crap out of there. I said, 'This ain't Hollywood.' "[61]

But even the principled resolve to avoid staging, to eschew entertainment, to convey a reality independent of the camera's eye, could not fully overcome the problem of the pose, endemic to photography and heightened by television. From its earliest days, television learned that its presence altered the event. Where political coverage was at stake, this alteration drew the networks and the politicians into a contest for the control of television images, a contest played out with increasing intensity in our time.

The power of television to alter the event first appeared when television began to cover the national political conventions. Don Hewitt, executive producer of "60 Minutes," recalls the innocence about the image that prevailed in 1948, when television covered its first conventions. "When I went for the first time, we were sort of there as observers. It was exciting. You'd get a good credentials committee fight going or a platform committee fight. A good fight today is if NBC has their sign an inch bigger than CBS's, now there's a fight! Political conventions today are true media events, programmed for the media."[62]

At first, Hewitt recalls, the politicians were naive about the ways of television, so CBS ran a class for politicians about how to act during a convention. He feared that inducing image consciousness would spoil the spontaneity. "I remember telling CBS news executive, Sig Michelson, 'You're going to ruin the convention if you tell them not to fall asleep or pick their nose, because that's half the fun of the damn thing.' " Hewitt remembers an earnest inquiry from Frank Clement, the keynote speaker at the 1956 Democratic convention. "Clement was governor of Tennessee, and he walked into the CBS facility with his Aunt Ida. He said, 'I've got a problem. When I speak I like to do that (he raised his arms in jubilation), and when I do that my tie jumps up. Is it okay to do that if my tie jumps up?' It was like something out of Li'l Abner."[63]

As Hewitt points out, television changed the event by being there. "We began to realize that the convention was a television show, and these guys were the extras. Walter Cronkite was the star, and all those guys on the floor and at the rostrum were the extras."[64]

It did not take long for the politicians to learn the consequences of television's powerful presence. Walter Cronkite tells of a problem that arose while he was covering Estes Kefauver's 1956 campaign for the Democratic presidential nomination. "There were only four of us on his bus. He was such a dark horse, he would stop at even the smallest crossroads. I'd get off the bus, and the people would surround me rather than the candidate. Kefauver finally said, 'Walter, would you please get off the bus last so the people at least have a chance to meet me?' "[65]

The televised debates between John Kennedy and Richard Nixon in 1960 marked a fateful moment in the advent of image-conscious politics. Theodore White reported that the candidates fared about equally well among those who listened to the first debate on radio, but that among television viewers, Kennedy was the clear winner over Nixon. Where Kennedy appeared rested and fit, Nixon, who refused to wear makeup, appeared drawn and ill-shaved. "It was the picture image that had done it," White concluded, "and in 1960 television had won the nation away from sound to images, and that was that."[66]

Daniel Boorstin saw the Kennedy-Nixon debates as part of a growing tendency for imagery to displace reality in American life. In his 1961 book *The Image*, Boorstin detected in the debates, and in their public reception, elements of the image-conscious sensibility that has since come to dominate television coverage of presidential campaigns. "Public interest centered around the pseudo-event itself: the lighting, make-up, ground rules, whether notes would be allowed, etc. Far more interest was shown in the performance than in what was said."[67]

Although the politics of media events and photo opportunities was only in its infancy, Boorstin glimpsed the allure of arresting visuals that would come to grip television news. "The pseudo-events which flood our consciousness are neither true nor false in the old familiar senses. The very same advances which have made them possible have also made the images—however planned, contrived, or distorted—

more vivid, more attractive, more impressive, and more persuasive than reality itself."[68]

Reflecting on his defeat, Richard Nixon, like Michael Dukakis some three decades later, faulted himself for failing to adapt to the imperatives of television image making. "I spent too much time in the last campaign on substance and too little time on appearance," Nixon concluded. "I paid too much attention to what I was going to say and too little on how I would look. . . . One bad camera angle on television can have far more effect on the election outcome than a major mistake in writing a speech."[69]

In 1968, Nixon and his advisers resolved not to repeat their mistakes of 1960. This time, they would mount a made-for-television campaign. "For the first time, a really sophisticated group of broadcast people came around a candidate, and did it for television," recalls Frank Shakespeare, one of Nixon's media advisers. "We didn't even care what Scottie Reston said [in his syndicated column for the New York Times]. We never even read it. That was minor heresy then, for most of the journalists were print journalists. They did not realize what we knew. We were talking to millions of Americans."[70]

But even Nixon's media-managed campaign was innocent by the standards of the eighties and nineties. While the campaign succeeded at staging confined events, like the televised programs showing Nixon answering questions from a "citizens" panel, most of the media events were traditional rallies and speeches, and the campaign was not yet adept at matching a "message of the day" with a carefully contrived visual image. "We were much less attentive to the backdrops, staging, and settings of events that would play on network evening newscasts than now," Shakespeare comments. "In a highly structured event like the convention, we were very conscious of it, because in a convention you can design the set and time the event. But when we thought of a photo opportunity, we were still thinking in terms of newspaper photographs, making sure Nixon was positioned well."[71]

For their part, the networks devoted little coverage to the politics of image making. With a few exceptions—Ted Koppel's report on Nixon's use of television, John Hart's piece on the advertising and media experts working for Nixon, David Schoumacher on Humphrey's press conference by the sea—television news did not report on the construction of images for television. Only about one report in twenty involved image-conscious coverage during the 1968 campaign, compared to over half of all reports two decades later.

Looking back, Russ Bensley, a producer for the "CBS Evening News" in 1968, thinks the networks should have paid greater attention than they did to political image making. "A Madison Avenue campaign was largely beyond our experience. We missed the boat. We should have covered it more fully. It was a sea change in our politics."[72]

But as John Hart points out, most network reporters in 1968, steeped as they were in the sober traditions of print journalism, focused by training and instinct on the substance, not the stagecraft, of presidential campaigns. "It was not a conscious choice" to emphasize politics rather than theater criticism, Hart explains. "That was the tradition we were in. It wouldn't have occurred to us to do a lot of self-conscious stuff. We would have been embarrassed to do it. It wasn't that we were especially wonderful. It was just that we believed the world happens for its own sake, not for television."[73]

Through the seventies and eighties, the networks began covering presidential campaigns as though they happened for the sake of television, which increasingly they did. By 1972, the networks began labeling appearances contrived for television as "media events," which then had a derisive tone that has faded with familiarity. When George McGovern's campaign took the press to a Midwest farm so the candidate could make a statement about the wheat scandal against a backdrop of grain silos, NBC's Cassie Mackin protested. "This is a Presidential campaign and we don't need pretty pictures to get on the air," she complained. "Why can't they just run their campaign and let us take the responsibility of finding something interesting to say about it? It would be fine with me if they did nothing for the media."[74]

Before long, however, the contrived "pretty pictures" that Mackin disdained would become a staple of television coverage of presidential campaigns. This was due primarily to two developments that coincided in the early eighties. With the coming of Ronald Reagan and media masters such as Michael Deaver and Roger Ailes, the campaigns (and the White House) became highly adept at producing compelling pictures for television. At the same time, a heightened concern with ratings and profits increased the networks' desire to show entertaining visuals on the evening news.

"We absolutely thought of ourselves when we got into the national campaigns as producers," said Michael Deaver. "We tried to create the most entertaining, visually attractive scene to fill that box, so that the cameras from the networks would have to use it. It would be so good that they'd say, 'Boy, this is going to make our show tonight.' . . . We became Hollywood producers."[75]

Richard Cohen, a senior political producer at CBS during Reagan's presidency, testifies to Deaver's success. "Do you know who was the real executive producer of the television network news? Michael Deaver was the executive producer of the evening news broadcasts. Michael Deaver decided what would be on the evening news each night. He laid it out there. I mean, he knew exactly who we were, what we went for. He suckered us."[76]

In an earlier era, when network news divisions were insulated from pressures for ratings and profits, reporters and producers would have been less tempted by arresting images unrelated to genuine news. Richard Salant, president of CBS News during the sixties and seventies, stated the traditional ethic in an introduction to the CBS *News Standards* handbook. Catering to viewers' interests and tastes was the role of entertainment programs like "The Beverly Hillbillies," where "it is entirely proper to give most of the people what most of them want most of the time," Salant wrote. "But we in broadcast journalism cannot, should not, and will not base our judgments on what we think the viewers and listeners are 'most interested' in."[77]

In a story well chronicled in works by Ken Auletta, Peter Boyer, Ben Bagdikian, and others, changes in the structure and economics of network news in the 1980s eroded the traditional distinction between news and entertainment. Network news operations came to be seen as profit centers for the large corporations that owned them, run by people drawn less from journalism than from advertising and entertainment backgrounds. As the media analyst Edwin Diamond observes, "The ABC, CBS, and NBC news organizations are now recasting themselves—not, as in the past, because of the imperatives of journalism, . . . but because the network's new owners demand it."[78]

In the early days of television, Edward R. Murrow described broadcast journalism as an "incompatible combination of show business, advertising and news."[79] But through the sixties and seventies, the competitive pressure for ratings was scarcely felt in the day-to-day life of network reporters and producers. Shad Northshield, who succeeded Reuven Frank as executive producer of the "Huntley-Brinkley Report," recalls, "We had been out of first place [displaced by CBS] for eleven weeks before anybody mentioned it. Today, you cannot have any fluctuations in ratings without having someone scream at you."[80]

Today, ratings consciousness permeates the networks. Former NBC producer John Ellis remarks, "Even as late as 1979 or 1980, it would have been inconceivable for the executive producer of the nightly news to discuss ratings. Then it got to where our executive producer had to explain to the press why NBC was in the position we were in the ratings."[81]

Commercialization led to further emphasis on entertainment values, which heightened the need for the dramatic visuals the campaigns contrived. Given new technological means to achieve these effects—portable video cameras, satellite hookups, and sophisticated video editing equipment—the networks were not only disposed but equipped to capture the staged media events of the campaigns. Reporters themselves became more oriented to performance. As Peter Boyer writes, "In the new CBS News, correspondents were told that it was no longer just what they said that mattered, but the way they said it; they were part of the message—performers, in a sense—and they were encouraged to affect a more casual and relaxed style."[82]

CBS political correspondent Bob Schieffer, who resists the turn to entertainment values in network news, notes that the networks themselves have "made a market" for the contrived images the campaigns dispense. "Perhaps it is time to realize that while we have been criticizing the candidates for trivializing the campaigns, our desire for more and more pictures and our willingness to use them has encouraged these silly photo sessions that have become the staple of the modern campaign."[83]

Those most successful at supplying the networks' demand for arresting visuals are keenly aware of the new focus on entertainment on the evening news. Michael Deaver says his job peddling flattering images of Ronald Reagan was made easy by the fact that "the media, while they won't admit it, are not in the news business; they're in entertainment."[84]

Roger Ailes sees an analogy between his aim as a media adviser and the aim of network producers.

> We're all worried about arithmetic. They're worried about their ratings; I'm worried about the number of voters that are going to vote for my guy. [Network journalists know that] if everybody else is covering the jets flying overhead or the guy falling in a mud puddle then they'd better have that shot too. Because if they start talking to him about ethics and the Middle East problem, and the other networks show Ford falling down a flight of stairs, people are going to switch channels. [85]

Ailes resents the idea that the media's calling is more noble than his. Just as his commercials are designed to maximize votes for his candidate, their newscasts are designed to maximize ratings for their network:

> My only concern about them is their piousness in pretending that they're doing something else. They're trying to make their newscast the most exciting and visual and the least wordy and thoughtful. If they can do that they may get the highest ratings. There's nothing wrong with that, just admit it.
>
> Just say, "Folks, we're in show business and these candidates are in show business. You are the audience, and everybody is trying to get to you and entertain you. We'll give you whatever you want, because we're all in the business of selling." The thing that I object to is these journalists running around saying that Roger Ailes is doing something different from what they're doing. We're all in the same business."[86]

Perfecting and Puncturing the Picture

The shift from the traditional CBS news broadcast of the Cronkite era to the present was not simply a shift from a hard-news emphasis to an entertainment-oriented one. It was also a shift from one understanding of pictures to another. On the traditional "CBS Evening News," which aspired to be the "broadcast of record," pictures served a documentary function. "For the correspondent and producer, the principal challenge was to capture on film the quote that figured to be in the lead paragraph of the wire service story."[87] This meant that news film typically consisted of government officials or politicians speaking.

Today, pictures play a different role on the evening news. They function less as documents of news events than as a rapid succession of visually arresting images. Lesley Stahl aptly described this phenomenon in an interview with Bill Moyers.

> STAHL: As a reporter, I like to be able to wallpaper, as we say in television, my pieces.
>
> MOYERS: Wallpaper?
>
> STAHL: Wallpaper. Put pretty pictures up while I'm talking behind it. Pretty, interesting pictures, pictures with movement. Pictures that will capture the audience eye. I shouldn't want that, because I know that it's deceptive and the audience won't really hear what I'm saying. But I still like it. I like my pieces to have energy.[88]

The networks' use of pictures as "wallpaper," as images designed to capture and hold the viewer's attention, recalls the use of photos by picture magazines like *Life* a half-century ago. Like the networks today, *Life* in the thirties and forties used photography as both document and spectacle. Then as now, if the picture was compelling, it mattered little whether the subject was weighty or trivial, spontaneous or staged. Images of Hitler, Churchill, and Roosevelt coexisted with public-relations and novelty shots.

The difference is that *Life* celebrated pictures without embarrassment, without concern about their constructed character, whereas the image-conscious coverage that set the tone of political reporting in 1988 was born of the conflicting imperatives that network journalists confront. The "picture perfect" impulse prompts reporters and producers to seek the best pictures they can possibly get, even if this requires a certain complicity with the advance men and image makers who stage the media events. Meanwhile, the journalistic impulse prompts the same reporters and producers to expose as artifice the pictures they have helped produce. Since the picture no longer documents reality but distorts it, reality depends on the words that puncture the picture, that draw attention to the image as an image.

The first impulse, the need for the best possible picture, compels network producers to collaborate closely with the campaigns. Lesley Stahl explains that during the Reagan presidency, "The White House would get together with CBS producers to line up shots so the president would look good, and there would be balloons and flags. They sort of get together with our producers and say, 'What kind of an angle would you like to have?' "[89]

This collaboration continued during the 1988 presidential campaign. Thomas Rosenstiel of the *Los Angeles Times* reported that, toward the end of a Bush campaign speech, a campaign advance man would take network camera crews to an area specially arranged behind the podium. "On cue, Bush knows to turn around to the cameras so that he can be shot with balloons falling into the crowd behind him, a splendid shot."[90]

Susan Zirinsky, a senior producer at CBS News, gives vivid expression to the conflicting impulses with which television journalists struggle—to get the best picture, and yet to avoid being manipulated by it. She recalls the picture-poor days of the Carter administration, "when you couldn't even find out what time an event was being held." Reagan's media-conscious team made life easy by comparison. "During the [Reagan] campaign, pictures that I used to ask for all the time, such as a helicopter shot of the motorcade, suddenly became possible."[91]

In an interview with Martin Schram, Zirinsky reflected on the collaboration between network producers and the politicians' image makers.

> In a funny way, the [White House] advance men and I have the same thing at heart—we want the piece to look as good as [it] possibly can. . . . That's their job and that's my job. . . . I mean, I'm looking for the best pictures, but I can't help it if the audiences that show up, or that are grouped together by the Reagan campaign, look so good. I can't think of that. I can't factor that out of the piece. I show whatever is there. I show who shows up. I can't help it if they're great-looking people and it looks like a commercial."[92]

Zirinsky protests that this quote, taken alone, makes it seem as though she is in cahoots with the image makers, a suggestion she emphatically rejects. Although she shares their interest in producing the best possible picture for the evening news, she says she has the further job of "countering" the pictures. "The way you counter it is editorially—with script, with extra interviews, with extra sound bites," and above all by alerting viewers to the contrivance the pictures represent. Here Zirinsky voices the second impulse, the impulse to puncture the pictures she has worked so hard to get. "If you merely present the picture as the day, the event, you are playing into their hands. If you stop and say to the audience, 'This event was so orchestrated that they even cleared an entire field so that the press could take a picture,' you hope the public gains some understanding of the machinations involved. It's your own moral conscience as a journalist speaking."[93]

Those responsible for network coverage in the 1960s maintain that it was different in their day. When television pictures functioned more as documents than as visually compelling images, there was less need for complicity with the campaigns, and also less need to puncture the pictures. Shad Northshield, executive producer of the "Huntley-Brinkley Report" during the 1968 campaign, recalls, "Of course, we were always interested in pictures. Pictures were the stuff of what happened that day. As to pressuring reporters to come up with better pictures, no, I didn't do it." Northshield attributes the current demand for arresting visuals on the evening news to the "pervasive and destructive and pernicious and terrible" effect of the "bottom-line mentality" on network news.[94]

Frank Shakespeare, Nixon's media adviser, maintains that in 1968 the networks would have resented any attempt by the campaigns to collaborate on dramatic camera angles or backdrops. "They didn't want to be used. . . . If you tried to say 'This would be interesting to film rather than that,' or 'Get your camera over here rather than there,' . . . no, no, no. We didn't do that. There was a church-and-state line then. We were the politicians and they were the reporters. And we weren't in bed together."[95] Likewise, Sanford Socolow, senior producer of the "CBS Evening News" with Walter Cronkite in 1968, states bluntly that network complicity in campaign stagecraft was scorned in those days. "If someone caught you doing that in 1968, you would have been fired."[96]

Tom Bettag, who produced Dan Rather's newscast in 1988, argues that the traditionalists "remember those times as being better than they actually were." He maintains that the complicity Susan Zirinsky describes is nothing new. Reporters and camera crews have always tried for the best possible picture. "They want their pictures to look good, and the [campaign] people are trying to get their person to look good. There is an inherent complicity on both sides that has always been there." Bettag sees no alternative to seeking interesting and exciting visuals. "Either you pay attention to making it look good or you don't. If you don't, that's a conscious decision too. It will become a mess on the screen. Anything I shoot I try to make look as good and as visually interesting and exciting as I possibly can."[97]

Walter Cronkite, untempted by the image-conscious sensibility of modern television news, disagrees. "Our interest is not in getting the best possible picture of the candidate. Our interest is in covering the event as journalists. We hope to have a nice clean picture of the candidate. But if we're asked to shoot him so that you see his arms wave, or see him holding an American flag or something like that, to heck with that. That's not our problem. That's not our duty at all."[98]

In the film *The Wizard of Oz*, Dorothy's dog Toto pulls back the curtain to reveal that the "great and powerful Oz" is no wizard after all, but an illusion created by a man pulling levers. "Pay no attention to that man behind the curtain," the man thunders through his machine. But once the artifice is exposed, the wizard's authority is dissolved.

Television's image-conscious coverage has not worked that way. Through much of the eighties, network reporters tried to pull back the curtain on the elaborate image-making apparatus of the Reagan presidency and presidential campaigns, and yet no amount of attention to images seemed able to dissolve their hold. Why, then, did the reporters' words seem impotent to unravel the authority, the resonance, the evocative power of the images whose artifice they revealed?

One answer to this question, given by many television journalists themselves, is that on television, pictures swamp words. This is the often quoted lesson Lesley Stahl learned when the Reagan White House thanked her for what she thought was a hard-hitting report on Reagan's use of television. Despite her critical words, the public would remember the flattering visuals of Reagan that appeared on the screen as she spoke. Sam Donaldson also subscribes to what he calls "a simple truism about television: the eye always predominates over the ear when there is a fundamental clash between the two."[99]

On this theory, theater criticism fails to save the media from manipulation by the image makers because pictures speak louder than words. People liked watching the vivid images of Reagan saluting troops or riding a horse or posing with country-music stars. Indeed, that is the reason the networks were so tempted to show the pictures, newsworthy or not, in the first place. The problem for the reporter is that picture-perfect images are not easy to puncture. Enchanted by the pictures, people don't listen to the words. "You can do the hardest piece on a candidate," says Susan Zirinsky, "and if a person isn't paying attention, the message doesn't get through. Part of the problem in the Reagan campaign was that people weren't paying attention. They wanted the images."[100]

The notion that pictures swamp words, plausible though it is, misses a deeper difficulty with image-conscious coverage as a way of puncturing the images politicians construct. Part of the problem is that exposing an image as an image usually involves showing the image—whether a media event or a political advertisement—and so giving it further airtime. But more than this, the very unmasking of an image as an image can sometimes, paradoxically, heighten its appeal. What Daniel Boorstin wrote three decades ago has proven all too true of today's political reporting turned theater criticism. "We are frustrated by our very efforts publicly to unmask the pseudo-event. Whenever we describe the lighting, the make-up, the studio setting, the rehearsals, etc., we simply arouse more interest. . . . Information about the staging of a pseudo-event simply adds to its fascination."[101]

One example of an illusion that is enhanced rather than diminished by the revelation of its artifice is Disney World, and its newest attraction, Disney/MGM Studios, which takes visitors behind the scenes of the movies. The architecture critic Robert Campbell recently described the image-conscious aspect of Disney World in terms that could also be a commentary on television's image-conscious coverage of presidential campaigns.

I'd never understood why people seemed to be so fascinated by the things Disney World ostensibly presents—all those stagey rides in the Magic Kingdom, all those very obviously fake European villages at Epcot Center. . . . But now I think I understand. Disney World isn't really about the displays it seems to be about. Instead, it's about how those displays are created. . . .

"Frontstage Disney World is kind of a bore, but backstage Disney World is fascinating. And we're always being given tantalizing glimpses of that backstage. Those glimpses are what we love. . . . What's interesting is the machinery that makes the illusion work. On display at Disney World is the machinery of illusion—not illusion itself.[102]

At Disney/MGM, "[t]hey've made the backstage the frontstage." A whole city neighborhood appears to be made of streets and buildings. But "you can walk around behind these 'buildings' and see that they are nothing but painted plywood facades. . . . The fact of fakery—that's the essence of the Disney World experience."[103]

Similar assumptions inform today's television coverage of presidential campaigns. It, too, makes "the fact of fakery" a central theme. The frontstage—the speeches, the issues, the position papers—is a bore, but the backstage—the staging, the backdrops, the spin control—is fascinating. Network reporters and producers thought that covering the construction of images for television would alert viewers to the contrivance of those images, and so expose the artifice of the campaigns. They thought that revealing the media advisers and handlers and spin-control artists manipulating the levers of illusion would dissolve the illusion and replace it with reality. But it did not work that way. Unlike *The Wizard of Oz*, revealing the man behind the curtain did not diminish the hold of the image. The effect was instead like that of Disney/MGM studios. Revealing the painted plywood facade left the allure of the city intact.

Exposed Images:
Image Consciousness in Art
Photography and Popular Culture

CRITICS AND DEFENDERS OF TELEVISION NEWS GENERALLY AGREE that today's fast-paced, picture-driven, image-conscious style of campaign coverage is the product of technological, commercial, political, journalistic, and cultural factors which have all played a part in transforming the way television news covers presidential campaigns. But beyond the question of what caused the image-conscious turn of television news is the further question of what it means. What does the image-conscious sensibility of modern television news tell us about our society and ourselves?

In striking ways, television coverage of presidential campaigns displays motifs and sensibilities that find frequent expression in contemporary art, photography, and popular culture. The picture-perfect mentality, the self-conscious attention to the construction of images, and the focus on gaffes that reveal the artifice of the pose do not appear on television alone. They also figure with increasing prominence in contemporary culture and in our ordinary lives.

Image Consciousness in Everyday Life

The home video camera makes it far easier to record family events than the old eight-millimeter home movie camera. This technological change carries consequences for the role of images—and image making—in our lives. Not only birthdays and weddings and family vacations, but even such intimate moments as childbirth, are now captured on videotape. But as always with photography, the camera's eye is never innocent. The documentary ambition to record the moment lives in constant tension with the impulse to pose. As the *New York Times* recently reported, the growing use of home video cameras has meant that "lives become roles" in which people arrange their lives and occasions to accommodate the video camera. While many parents use the video camera, like the old home movie camera, to document the important moments of their lives, others fall into "talking like Hollywood types. [They] do not speak of taking the kids to the park and the zoo. They go 'on location.' "[1]

Our strenuous efforts to capture important moments on videotape often transform these moments by the self-consciousness the camera induces. Even children quickly learn that going to the park to be videotaped is a different experience from just going to the park. As writer Don Gifford notes, "The tapes made of family occasions would seem to promise spontaneity but . . . tend to be dominated by staged bits of action (just as still photographs of such occasions are so frequently dominated by the posed shot)."[2]

The popular television program "America's Funniest Home Videos," which receives over a thousand home videotape offerings each day, both reflects and promotes the video-conscious sensibility of modern American life. Gifford wonders how this new orientation is changing the way we see and live our lives. Much as image-conscious coverage of presidential campaigns leads to a focus on gaffes and gutter balls, he suggests that the growing image consciousness of ordinary life could have a similar effect. "The genuinely funny, unselfconscious family moments may be threatened with displacement by contrived, frenetic, half-comic scenes of pratfalls and other embarrassments."[3]

Television journalists find, to their surprise, that the people they cover are now fluent in the language of video production. Beth Pearlman is a producer for the CBS affiliate station WCCO in Minneapolis. She is struck by the way "media jargon has become public knowledge," and thinks this may be a consequence of television reporters' frequent emphasis on the apparatus of image making. "Now I'll go out on a story, and the person I'm going to talk to will ask me if I'm doing a feature or just a sound bite. Someone asked me the other day, 'Do you want to shoot B-roll before we have our interview?' B-roll is video that you run under the narration of the reporter. How do they know?"[4]

Television is not the only source of the image consciousness that informs everyday life. Giant video screens are now a familiar presence at rock concerts and large rallies, affording mass audiences a better view of the event that is unfolding "before their eyes." In the past, only those watching a baseball game on television could see an instant replay of a home run or a dazzling play in the field. Now the fans at the ballpark can also see the replay, thanks to the video screens that adorn most major-league stadiums. The image on the screen brings greater access to the game taking place on the field below.

Video consciousness and the play of images within images are familiar themes in popular entertainment and advertising. In the music video *Unforgettable*, Natalie Cole sings a duet with her deceased father Nat King Cole as she watches his image on a television set and video screen. Madonna's film *Truth or Dare* (1991) is a documentary that celebrates the pose and denies the distinction between the performer and the person, between the image and the self. Even as a doctor examines her ailing throat, Madonna wants the cameras to roll. Her friend Warren Beatty questions the "insanity of doing this all on a documentary." Madonna replies, "Why should I stop here?" Beatty chides her. "You don't want to talk off camera. You don't want to live off camera. There's nothing to say off camera. Why would you say something off camera?" Madonna's answer comes later in the song-and-dance number that sums her up. "Don't just stand there, let's get to it. Strike the pose, there's nothing to it. Vogue. Vogue."

Some recent television commercials have tried to draw on the authority of television images. An ad for American Express Traveler's Cheques shows a burglar breaking into a hotel room whose occupant is in the shower. As the burglar departs with the traveler's wallet, a television set in the room is shown airing the well-known American Express Traveler's Cheque commercial in which actor Karl Malden intones, "Don't leave home without them." According to the advertising agency that made the commercial, showing an image of an image makes the ad more realistic. "Putting the commercial frame within the television frame heightens the reality of being there."[5]

A recent newspaper ad for Radisson Hotels suggests that taking a vacation means taking pictures of ourselves vacationing. The ad does not show any of its hotels, but rather pictures of snapshots that people have taken while (presumably) vacationing at its hotels. "Picture Yourself at a Radisson Resort," the headline declares. To entice vacationers to stay at its resorts, the hotel chain offers a free camera. "We're so confident you'll have a picture-perfect vacation," the ad explains, "we'll give you a Konica Camera at check-in to capture all the memories."[6]

Given the focus on images of images in popular culture, it is perhaps unsurprising that politicians draw on similar themes to project their authority. Early in the 1992 primary season, Democratic presidential candidate Bill Clinton posed for a *Time* magazine photograph sitting on the floor in blue jeans, watching a videotape of one of his campaign commercials on a television screen. The remote-control device in his hands seemed to justify *Time*'s description of Clinton as "the custodian of his own image."[7]

During the 1988 campaign, Republican vice presidential candidate Dan Quayle sought belatedly to assert control over his own image. When Quayle was widely labeled in the press as a highly managed candidate, he replied in terms that accepted the notion that image making is the essence of political reality. Instead of rejecting the whole notion of "impression management," he proclaimed his independence from his handlers by resolving publicly to become his own handler and spin doctor. In the final weeks of the campaign, he proudly declared to reporters that henceforth, he would become his own image maker. "The so-called handlers story, part of it's true. But there will be no more handlers stories, because I'm the handler and I'll do the spinning. . . . I'm Doctor Spin, and I want you all to report that."[8]

It may seem a strange way for a politician to talk, but not so strange in a media-conscious environment in which authenticity means being master of your own artificiality. Towards the end of the 1988 presidential campaign, Michael Dukakis also tried to bolster his political fortunes by portraying himself as master of his own image. This attempt was best captured in a television commercial in which

Dukakis stood beside a television set and snapped off a Bush commercial showing (and ridiculing) his tank ride, and attacking his stand on
defense. "I'm fed up with it," Dukakis declared. "Never seen anything
like it in twenty-five years of public life. George Bush's negative
television ads, distorting my record, full of lies, and he knows it. . . ."

As it appeared in excerpts on the evening news, Dukakis's commercial displayed a quintessentially modern image of artifice upon artifice
upon artifice: television news covering a Dukakis commercial containing a Bush commercial containing a Dukakis media event. In a
political world governed by images of images, it seemed almost natural
that the authority of the candidate be depicted by his ability to turn
off the television set.

From television news to home videos, from advertising to entertainment, from Madonna to Michael Dukakis, a new image consciousness
pervades American popular culture. By the 1980s and 1990s, we had
come to see the world and to represent ourselves as a series of appearances and poses, without the old confidence that behind the appearance stood the real thing, behind the pose the true self.

This image-conscious outlook is not without precedent. The self-
conscious attention to the constructed character of images found
earlier expression in other parts of American culture, notably art
photography and film, in the 1950s and 1960s. As soon as television
began to have a significant impact as a means of mass communication, movie directors probed the new medium's vulnerability to artifice, fabrication, and deceit. Even as Walter Cronkite and Huntley
and Brinkley presided over the classic, image-innocent years of television news, art photographers such as Robert Frank, Lee Friedlander,
and Garry Winogrand, and pop artist Andy Warhol explored such
themes as the image as an image, the picture as a performance, and
the flaw that reveals the artifice of the pose.

Television in the Movies

Movies about television were among the early instances of pictures
about pictures. Since the inception of television, filmmakers have
explored the consequences of the new medium for politics and

selfhood. As early as 1948, Frank Capra's *State of the Union* dealt with television as a tool of political image making. Grant Matthews, an idealistic presidential candidate played by Spencer Tracy, begins his campaign as a crusader for social reform. Supported by his wife Mary (Katharine Hepburn), Matthews at first resists the manipulation of his advisers and remains true to his ideals. But soon the politicos and special-interest brokers prevail, and Matthews compromises his principles in hopes of victory.

Matthews agrees to deliver a ghost-written script that the politicians have written in a national broadcast to be televised from his home. His wife objects, imploring him to stand by his principles, to no avail. "That won't be Grant Matthews you'll hear in there tonight," she tells him. "It will be a shadow, a ghost, a stooge mouthing words that aren't your own."[9]

When the moment comes for Matthews to speak, he has a change of heart and throws away the script. As he begins to denounce the politicians and the image makers, the political operatives order the sound shut off. But Matthews, breaking through the artifice, asserts his mastery of the event. "Don't you shut me off," he demands. "I'm paying for this broadcast." He proceeds to lay bare the deceit of his campaign and to expose the contrivance of the broadcast itself. "This was no simple fireside broadcast, paid for by your dollars and dimes. This is an elaborately staged professional affair." At the last moment, Capra's hero struggles free of the image-making apparatus that surrounds him and asserts his integrity, his true self.

Subsequent heroes would not escape their entanglement with the television image so easily. In films of the fifties and sixties, television becomes a source of disempowerment and estrangement.

Elia Kazan's *A Face in the Crowd* (1957) is a parable of television's potential for power and duplicity. The public, which in Capra's film hungers for the genuine candidate, is present only as the crowd, the gullible audience yearning to believe but easily duped. The film chronicles the rise and fall of Lonesome Rhodes, an Arkansas drifter (played by Andy Griffith) who rises to national prominence as a folksy television personality, political kingmaker, and demagogue.[10]

Discovered by a woman from a local radio station, Marcia (Patricia Neal), who falls in love with him and promotes his career, Rhodes begins his radio career as a voice of the common man, genuine and unadorned, poking fun at the establishment. Before long he rises to stardom on national television, retaining his populist persona even as he becomes a Madison Avenue flack for his sponsor's product, "Vitajex pills."

Once authentic, Rhodes's folksy style becomes a wildly successful performance, magnified by his mastery of the medium. So adept does he become at television image making that he is enlisted to provide some "Madison Avenue coaching" for a senator with presidential ambitions. "Senator, I'm a professional and I have to look at the image on that screen the same as I would a performer on my show. And I have to say he'll never get over to my audience. Not the sixty-five million people who welcome me into their living rooms each week." After some resistance, the senator accedes to constructing a new television image so that he too can be sold to the public as successfully as Vitajex pills. One of the senator's powerful backers explains the need to change with the times. "Politics has entered a new stage—the television stage. Instead of longwinded public debates, the people want capsule slogans, . . . punch lines and glamor."

Unlike Capra's film, Kazan's offers its hero no redemption from television's politics of deceit, no moment when the authentic self vindicates itself and rises above the image. Unlike Grant Matthews, Lonesome Rhodes does not puncture his own pose. Infatuated with his own image and television fame, Rhodes becomes demagogic in his will to power, as manipulative and disdainful of those close to him as he is of his viewers.

In the climactic scene, Rhodes's performance is finally punctured by the disillusioned Marcia, who uses television to expose him. After a show, Rhodes, thinking he is off the air, ridicules the stupidity of his audience. Marcia switches on his microphone, allowing the viewers to hear their hero's disdain for them. The audience is outraged and disillusioned, and Rhodes's image is destroyed. So is Rhodes himself, who at the end of the film is left ranting and raving to the accompaniment of an applause machine.

Films of the 1960s and 1970s continue to explore how politics and selfhood are formed and deformed, constructed and deconstructed by the power of television. In *Medium Cool* (1969), by Haskell Wexler, the television image does more than empower or entangle an individual like Grant Matthews or Lonesome Rhodes; it comes to define social reality as a whole. The film deals with a television news cameraman (Robert Forster), who thinks of himself as neutral and detached, but finds himself implicated in the events he covers and, by his presence, transforms.

In the opening sequence, we see him callously filming an injured victim of a traffic wreck; only when his film is safely in the can does he call for an ambulance. In subsequent conversations, he and his colleagues reply to criticism of the media by insisting that they just "cover" reality, that the camera merely "records," that the soundman is but "an elongated tape recorder." But the events of the film, which unfold against the tumultuous backdrop of the violence and confrontation of 1968, erode the cameraman's claim to neutrality. Those he covers forcefully deny the innocence of the camera's eye.

Pursuing a human-interest story, the cameraman seeks out a black cab driver who found and returned a large sum of money. But the cab driver just wants to be left alone. His friends are hostile. They berate the cameraman for exploiting blacks, yet they crave the attention of his camera. They, too, want to be on television.

A friend of the cab driver, an angry young black man, rages against the artifice and power of television images. A "nobody" who shoots someone draws television coverage, the young man explains. "Then the cat lives, man. He really lives. A hundred million people see the cat on the tube, man, and they say, 'ooo, the former invisible man lives.' Everybody knows where he went to school. Everybody knows about his wife and kids and everything. . . . The tube is life. . . . You make him a TV star on the six, the ten and the twelve o'clock news."

The slogan "the tube is life" restates for the television age the old paradox of the camera. The pictures that look so real can be false and misleading, but people do not feel real unless they are in the television picture. Television is powerful because it confers a celebrity that has become a surrogate for identity and true recognition.

Medium Cool shows that neither the cameraman nor the public he films can escape their entanglement with television images. The cameraman finally overcomes his disengagement by falling in love with a woman from Appalachia (Verna Bloom), and befriending her son. But in the end, he, too, becomes an object before the television camera. As he drives with his woman friend to find her son, their car crashes. The film ends, as it began, with the crash being filmed—this time by a camera that turns toward the audience as the movie ends.

Like *State of the Union*, *The Candidate* (1972) tells the tale of a reform-minded candidate who is stripped of his ideals by professional image makers. When a young liberal lawyer, Bill McKay (Robert Redford), agrees to run for the U.S. Senate, the political advisers promise he can be his own man, since he has no chance of winning anyhow. But when victory appears within grasp, the handlers take over, reconstructing the candidate's identity along with his political beliefs. The cynical image making that *A Face in the Crowd* depicts with dark satire appears here as a routine aspect of the modern campaign.

In an early speech, McKay, still speaking in his own voice, declares, "Our lives are more and more determined by forces that overwhelm the individual." He soon finds himself a victim of the very forces he describes, as he loses control of his campaign and his identity as well. McKay, once critical of political image making, now watches images of himself on television.

Unlike Grant Matthews in *State of the Union*, the candidate of the seventies never breaks through the artifice to reassert his true self. When he wins the election, his disempowerment is complete. Surrounded by an enthusiastic crowd applauding the "people's candidate," McKay pulls his campaign manager aside and into a service elevator. His manager turns to him, "We've got sixty seconds of privacy. . . . What's on your mind, Senator?" McKay responds, "Marvin, what do we do now?"

Sidney Lumet's *Network* (1976), one of the most popular movies about the power and artifice of television images, depicts a television world driven by ratings pressures and entertainment values. The old news values of straight reporting are pushed aside in order to accommodate the glamor and glitz of entertainment shows. The tension between the camera as recorder of reality and instrument of artifice is gone. Artifice becomes the organizing principle for the reality television presents. People and events are constructed and contrived to be compelling television images.

The film begins with news anchorman Howard Beale being fired due to poor ratings. In despair, he becomes unhinged. Appearing on the air, he delivers a diatribe against the ills of the world and announces that he plans to blow his brains out the next week. In an absurd twist, ratings soar in response to Beale's mad ravings. His reward is his own show under the auspices of the entertainment division.

The new "Howard Beale Show," which features Beale's tirades, a soothsayer, and a TV gossip columnist, is an instant success. It rises on the wave of popular anger and exploits for entertainment purposes viewers' love-hate relationship with television (just as the movie itself plays to those same emotions in its audience). Beale builds his popularity by warning against television's power and artifice. "The only truth you know is what you get out of this tube. . . . We're in the boredom-killing business. . . . You're never going to get the truth from us. . . . You're beginning to think that the tube is reality and that your real lives are unreal. . . . You people are the real thing. We are the illusion. So turn off your television sets."

Paradoxically, the television audience applauds the message and ratings soar further. Beale's plea to "turn off your TV sets" is less a call to action than a form of entertainment. Television thus reduces words to media events, part of the seductive appeal that keeps people watching. As the hard-driving producer (Faye Dunaway) tells her boss, "He's articulating a popular rage. . . . I want that show."

The network gives Beale complete freedom of speech until he threatens the economic interests of the corporation that owns the network by urging his audience to send telegrams to the White House to protest an upcoming business deal. The head of the corporation decides that instead of taking Beale off the air, he will convert him by teaching him of the larger forces that render protest futile. In a dimly lit corporate boardroom he solemnly tells Beale, "You have meddled with the primal forces of nature. . . . You get on your little twenty-one-inch screen and howl about America and democracy. There is no America. There is no democracy. There is only IBM, ITT and AT&T. . . . The world is a collage of corporations inexorably determined by the immutable bylaws of business."

After Beale's encounter with the corporate executive, he preaches a prophecy of doom, telling his audience that "the individual is finished." His ratings fall and the network executives decide to have him assassinated on his own show. After a moment's silence, the audience applauds this too. The movie ends with the narrator observing, "It is the first time in history a man was killed for having lousy ratings."

In contrast to the high emotion and dark satire of *Network*, another satire on television, *Being There* (1979), achieves its effect through the absence of emotion. Directed by Hal Ashby (based on a screenplay by the author of the original novel, Jersy Kozinski), the movie is about the life of Chance (Peter Sellers), a gardener who has lived his life totally isolated from society, raised in effect by a television set. Television provides Chance with his only way of knowing the world.

The opening sequence shows Chance waking up in the morning to television images. Television sets are everywhere, even outside in the garden. When Chance learns from the housekeeper that his employer has died, he receives the news impassively as he continues to watch television at the kitchen table.

Chance's life after leaving his employer's home is a sequence of absurd incidents based on his attempts to deal with life as if it were television. Walking through a run-down neighborhood, he is confronted by a young tough who pulls a knife on him. Chance tries to turn aside the tough by pushing the button on the remote control device he still carries in his hand. Wandering the streets of Washington, he cannot tell the difference between real things and their television images. Surprised to see his own image on the video monitor in a store window, he backs up and is hit by a rich woman's car. Fearing a lawsuit, the woman (Shirley MacLaine) befriends Chance and invites him to her home. Amiable and disconnected from life, Chance's first request is: "May I watch television please?"

Dressed in the dated but expensive clothes of his former employer, Chance appears to be a man of independent means. When he identifies himself as "Chance the gardener," the woman mistakenly hears "Chauncy Gardner." Chance becomes the house guest of the woman and her husband (Melvyn Douglas), an aged business tycoon, and is swept into their lives of high finance and political influence. Without an identity of his own, Chance is the perfect receptacle for people's projections. They take his simpleminded homilies about gardening to be subtle metaphors of economic analysis.

They interpret his innocence and emptiness as a refreshing clarity and directness. The dying businessman tells Chance: "You have the gift of being natural."

Through no doing of his own, Chance moves into ever higher circles of power. His words are taken as economic insights by his patron and incorporated in a presidential address to the nation. Chance becomes a television authority in his own right, interviewed before a national audience.

The final scene of the movie is at the funeral for Chance's businessman friend, attended by the president and the pillars of government and high finance. The pallbearers are power brokers who discuss in hushed tones the need to find a new candidate for president. "What about Chauncy Gardner?" suggests one. "But what do we know of the man?" asks another.

"Absolutely nothing. We don't have an inkling of his past."

"Correct. That could be an asset."

"A man's past cripples him. His background turns into a swamp and invites scrutiny."

"Up until this time he hasn't said anything that could be held against him."

"The mail and telephone response from his appearance on that Burns show was the highest they've ever had, and it was 95 percent pro. . . ."

"I do believe, gentlemen, that if we want to hold on to the presidency our one and only chance is Chauncy Gardner."

Chance's weightlessness makes him the perfect candidate for a world governed by the ephemeral images emitted by the television screen. Unlike candidates whose identity must be remade by the image makers, Chance has no identity in need of reconstruction. A pure image, he is utterly selfless, without ambitions or interests of his own, and without an identity to resist the construction others place on his words and being.

Television as an object of satire, sometimes dark, sometimes surreal, gives way to lighter comic treatment in *Broadcast News* (1987). The long-standing worry about the authenticity versus the artificiality of the television image remains. It animates the work relations and even the personal relations of Jane Craig (Holly Hunter), a hard-driving young news producer, and Tom Grunick (William Hurt), the handsome but ill-informed news anchor.

Unlike earlier films about television, however, *Broadcast News* makes its peace with artifice. For the young producer, the line between authenticity and artifice is a matter of great conviction, but in practice the distinction proves elusive. Early in the film she delivers a harangue to her fellow broadcasters defending traditional news values: "We are being increasingly influenced by the star system. . . . Our profession is endangered. . . . We are being pressured to take a loyalty oath to profit and economy. . . . We are all secretly terrified by what is happening." Her bored audience files out one by one, until she finds herself speaking to an empty room. Only Tom Grunick, the handsome but empty young anchorman, lingers to praise her. Although romantically appealing to Jane, he represents everything she stands against.

But Craig herself is entangled in the artifice of television, even as she rails against it. While covering Central American insurgents preparing to engage in combat, she berates a network cameraman for asking them to lace up their boots for the camera. "We are not here to stage the news," she admonishes. As the camera crew stands poised for the shot, one of the soldiers momentarily stops lacing his boots. "You do whatever you want," Craig sternly instructs him. "You are free to choose for yourself." Perplexed, he shrugs and continues to lace his boots. The "authenticity" of the moment vindicated, the cameras roll.

For all her unwitting accommodation to the artifice of her profession, Craig still clings to the scarcely credible distinction between news and entertainment. The dramatic turning point in the movie is when Craig discovers that Grunick faked a tear in an emotional report that won high praise at the network. Outraged that her reporter friend was "acting," she breaks off her incipient romance with him. "I know you acted your reaction to the interview. It made me ill. . . . It's amazing. You commit this amazing breach of ethics and you act like it's nothing."

Jane's romance with Tom is over, but not their professional partnership. Some years later, she agrees to be his managing editor when he is named anchorman of the evening news. Unlike earlier films that rail against the pose, the deceit, and the emptiness of television imagery,

Broadcast News casts the poser (anchorman Grunick) as a winsome character, appealingly self-effacing. An anchorman for the age of Ronald Reagan, he is hollow but decent, comfortable with the artifice that surrounds him.

Taking Pictures of Pictures

In 1960, Garry Winogrand took a photograph that uncannily antici-pated the image-conscious style of coverage that television news would adopt a quarter-century later. The photo shows John Kennedy addressing the Democratic National Convention, and it portrays politics in the age of television as an array of images of images. Shot from behind the podium, it does not show Kennedy's face or the reaction of the delegates below. Instead, it shows Kennedy's back, and on the platform behind him, a portable television showing him delivering his speech.

From behind the scenes, Winogrand exposes the layers of images that constitute the political event. In the foreground of the photo-graph is the television; in the middle is the candidate gesturing to the crowd. In the background, out of focus, is the platform that holds the television cameras that are recording the image that appears on the screen.

Winogrand directs our attention from politics to the pose, from the political event to the irony of political form. Winogrand is not interested in the meaning of the event as experienced by its participants, but in the meaning of the scene as a picture about pictures.

Winogrand's picture of Kennedy signaled a departure from the traditional ambitions of both art and documentary photography. As art photography sought to interpret reality, documentary photography sought to record it, but both directed the viewer's attention to a reality beyond the photograph. The art photographers of the fifties and sixties undertook a different project.

Just as modernist drama denied the audience the suspension of disbelief and made us aware of the play as a play, the new photography made us aware of the frame as a frame. As modern playwrights had decades earlier made the scenery, scripting, and staging subjects of dramatic discourse, photographers of the postwar period took pictures that called attention to the conventions of photography—the camera angle, lens type, and depth of focus. They directed attention to the picture itself, to the image as an image.

This new photographic sensibility arose in conjunction with the rise of television. During the 1950s and 1960s, when television began to become a potent form for documentation and entertainment, it also became a powerful influence on the work of artists. Photographers began to photograph the television set as part of the social landscape. Artists began to explore and criticize the conventional ways in which the media invite us to see the world. The idealized visions of television, movies, advertising, and fashion themselves became the subjects of pictures.

The first stirrings of the new image-conscious photography had appeared in the work of the great documentary photographers of the Depression era. Even as they fulfilled their assignments for the Farm Security Administration, documenting conditions of poverty across the country, they subverted conventional images by taking pictures of pictures. Among the earliest ironic pictures of pictures were their photographs juxtaposing the promotional media of their day—movie posters, advertisements, and promotional billboards—and the impoverished American landscape.

In Atlanta, Walker Evans photographed a series of movie billboards, stretching like a large strip of film, in front of two bleak frame houses. The glamorous face of Carole Lombard in her new movie, *Love Before Breakfast*, is defaced by a blackened eye. In a photograph taken on Cape Cod, Evans shows an extreme close-up of a torn movie poster of a man protectively embracing a woman. By magnifying the tear and the wrinkles of paste underneath the poster, Evans exposes the very materials of its creation as they fall apart, and subverts its intended meaning. The paste marks extending from the corners of the man and woman's eyes look like fallen tears. A large rip forms a violent gash down the woman's forehead. The movie image has lost its power, and instead, Evans shows the drama within the drama of an image in decay.

Driving down the roadways of America, the photographers of the Depression captured the absurdity of American boosterism. A billboard that appears in several photographs shows a happy family driving their car with the slogan, "There is no way like the American way." Arthur Rothstein shows the billboard in a desolate part of Alabama. It reappears in a Russell Lee photograph of a barren stretch of American highway.

Unlike the disengaged stance of art photography in the sixties, the Depression-era "pictures of pictures" were made in the service of social criticism. The same was true of the work of another forerunner of modern image-conscious photography, the Swiss photographer Robert Frank. During the 1950s, Frank traveled through America taking photographs. His book *The Americans*, first published in 1958, revealed a truth that the idealized American images of the postwar era concealed. Watching a parade in Hoboken, New Jersey, Frank turned his camera away from the flags and festivities to photograph the onlookers. The camera looks up at a dingy brick building as two women watch the parade below, framed by the bleak, bare windows. A large American flag displayed between the windows obscures the face of one of the women. The other woman's face is barely visible in the darkened room. The American flag is a part of the mournful landscape.

Another picture in *The Americans* shows a television left on in an empty restaurant. A man in a suit, perhaps a politician, pontificates on the screen. But there is no life in the room, no response to the image. The artificial light of the television image coexists with the window light and the empty table. The face on Frank's television screen is not a compelling image, but an eerie electronic form.

Another photograph shows a smiling young woman sitting on a chair on a small stage in a television studio in Burbank, California. Frank's emphasis is on the artifice of the television image being created. The studio lights, the cables on the floor, the two-tiered stage where the woman sits are all visible.

Though the young woman is at ease posing for the television camera, Frank's photograph portrays the self as decentered and objectified. The young woman is in the background and off-center in the frame, her body half obscured by the elbow of a man standing in the foreground. Off at an angle we see her bright smiling face on a studio monitor. Frank highlights the split between the posing self and the televised self. In Frank's photo, the woman's smile seems less real than the studio equipment that transmits the image.

In Frank's photographs, the conventional meanings of images are transformed by their displacement. Not only the television but also various political, cultural, and religious icons—flags, movie stars, crosses—are dislocated. Instead of viewing the flag reverentially, Frank shows it obscuring a person's face. A beautiful star at a Hollywood movie premiere is shown out of focus. A statue of St. Francis seems to be blessing a gray and empty Los Angeles boulevard.

Brilliant in their dark documentation, Frank's photographs were a prelude to the image-conscious photography of the next decades. The art photographers of the 1960s, admiring though they were of Walker Evans and Robert Frank, rejected social criticism in favor of a distant, dispassionate stance toward the world they photographed. Their pictures about pictures directed attention away from the subject matter and toward the medium of photography itself. As Winogrand explained, "I photograph to find out what something will look like when photographed."[11]

A characteristic example of this distance is a photograph by Michael Ciavolino, dating from 1962, which shows a group of young people gathered around a table drinking beer. It looks like a typical snapshot except for the fact that the photographer printed the photograph encased within the contact sheet. We see the sprocket holes, the numbered frame, a portion of the image in the next frame, and the word designating the film type, "Panchromatic," all vividly on display.

The stress on the photograph as image comes out strongly in the work of Ken Josephson, who developed the theme of pictures of pictures by showing a hand jutting into the frame, holding a photograph or picture postcard of the scene being viewed, such as the Washington Monument or a Michigan beach.

Photographers began to use windows, mirrors, reflections, and the frame of the photograph itself to heighten the viewer's awareness of looking at images of images. In Lee Friedlander's book, *Self-Portrait*, the photographer appears in every frame as an intruding shadow or reflection. One photograph shows a public building with a photograph of John Kennedy in the window. Friedlander, his image reflected in the window as he takes the photograph, is standing outside looking in. Kennedy's face is obscured by a sign we cannot read, which obscures the face of the photographer himself.

In other photographs, Friedlander's shadow intrudes on familiar images in a way that undermines their conventional meaning. Our view of a hometown parade in Lafayette, Louisiana, is humorously disrupted by the shadow of Friedlander's head on a post in the foreground of the frame. The post itself disrupts the picture by dividing it in two. To the right of the post, the drum majorette, in shimmering body suit and white boots, casts her own shadow before her as she marches up the street, oblivious to the photographer's presence. In another photograph, the shadow seems to stalk its subject, appearing on the back of a blonde woman wearing a fur coat walking down a New York City street.

A photograph taken from a car in New York State shows a reflection of Friedlander taking the picture in the car's side mirror. The image of Friedlander itself occupies the side of the frame with the mirror and car window dividing the frame. Across the street, we see a roadside chapel with a cross and the words "God Bless America" on the roof.

Through the presence of his shadow or reflection, Friedlander refuses us the traditional documentary understanding of the photograph. Friedlander intentionally employs the "mistakes" of amateur photographers—shadows, reflections and distracting objects in the frame—to explore the photographer's role in making the picture.

Like Robert Frank in *The Americans*, Friedlander questions and disrupts images that are central to American cultural identity. But unlike Frank, who asked the viewer to enter the reality his photographs depicted, Friedlander, by his very presence, holds us back from entering another reality. He makes us aware of the picture as a picture, asking us to question the conventional way we see.

Photographers of the 1960s also explored the camera's potential for realism and fabrication by taking pictures of television sets. Like Robert Frank, they portrayed the television image in a way that heightened its artifice and subverted its power. A Diane Arbus photograph shows a Christmas tree and presents in an empty living room in Levittown, Long Island in 1963. Everything is orderly. Alongside of the tree is a lamp, the shade still covered with plastic. In the other corner is a television set. All the artifacts of suburban life are realistically portrayed, but drained of their usual meanings. The television, like the tree, is a testimonial to lifelessness.

In his book *Suburbia* (1972), photographer Bill Owens shows a similar Christmas living-room scene. The large television set, the top decorated with fake cotton snow and Christmas figures, is the focus of the picture. Ronald Reagan appears on the screen in an old movie, but no one is there to see him. He exists only as an amiable living-room fiction, an image within an image. In another Owens photograph, a family poses on their couch with the television tuned to a football game. The picture could have evoked the warm familiarity of a family snapshot, but Owen's wide-angle black-and-white image creates an ironic distance from his subjects' familiar engagement with the television set.

Lee Friedlander did a whole series of photographs of television sets turned on in empty rooms. Each photograph features a close-up of a televised face, a portrait oddly situated in the austere furnishings of what appear to be empty motel rooms. In one, the arch of the footboard of a bed crosses the lower center of the frame. Slightly off center, framed by two darkened doorways, the television shows a picture of a small child. The meaning of the image is ambiguous. We see it only as a form among forms.

Like the art photographers of the sixties, the pop artist Andy Warhol explored images of images, television images among them. Warhol is best known for his paintings of Campbell's soup cans, Coca-Cola bottles, Marilyn Monroe, and other icons of popular culture. By making copies of familiar images, Warhol changes the way we see them. While an ad for Campbell's soup directs our attention to the product, Warhol's serial reproduction, "200 Soup Cans," directs our attention to the packaging, to the soup can as an image. Similarly, while a glamorous photograph of Marilyn Monroe tempts the viewer to enter into the sexual fantasy she represents, Warhol's silk-screened reproduction of the photograph, entitled "Marilyn Six-Pack," focuses our attention on the merchandising of the image.

Sometimes Warhol begins with the most artificial of images, such as his "paint by numbers," series entitled "Do it Yourself." At other times, Warhol reproduces the most potent news images—race riots, a mourning Jacqueline Kennedy, car accidents—as if calling attention to the effects of the television replay.

The very act of reproducing, rearranging, and repeating images from the news, publicity photographs, and commercial products places the viewer in an ambiguous relation to the subject matter. On the one hand, Warhol's art of making pictures of pictures further distances us from the image, inviting our reflections on their meaning and effect. The serial images of celebrities and soup cans can be read as a critique of commercialism. The disaster series illustrates how the constant replays of the modern media—from sports highlights to national traumas—simultaneously transfix us and erode our emotional engagement.

On the other hand, Warhol's reproductions of celebrity portraits and commercial products play upon and enlarge our engagement with the image. Warhol himself aspired to celebrity status as he engaged in replicating celebrity images. "I love plastic idols," he proclaimed.[12] He became a media personality among media personalities. His reproductions of the celebrity images of Marilyn Monroe, Elvis Presley, and Elizabeth Taylor, far from puncturing the images, may depend for their effect on their enduring appeal. Similarly, in our consumer culture people have become accustomed to using advertisements as art—from stacking beer and Coke bottles to decorate dorm rooms to wearing T-shirts with advertising slogans. Warhol's serial images of Coca-Cola bottles and Campbell's soup cans seek a similar effect.

Warhol's pop art, like the photography of Winogrand and Friedlander, turns our attention away from the subject matter and toward the instruments of image making—the frame, the packaging, the pose. In this respect, it anticipates themes that television news would take up two decades later. In the same way, photography anticipated the increased presence of reporters in the stories they would cover. As photographers took pictures of pictures, they too assumed a more prominent role in the pictures they took—sometimes as a shadow lurking beyond the frame, sometimes as the subject of the picture itself.

Pictures as Performances

In Friedlander's self-portraits, the presence of his own image in the frame calls attention to the picture as a picture. In this respect it does for photography what Pirandello's modernist play, *Six Characters in Search of an Author*, does for drama. In Pirandello's play, the actors address the audience and speak of their roles, calling into question the tenuous line between appearance and reality, theater and life. The photographer's presence in the picture frame achieves a similar effect.

Even when Friedlander's image is not present in the photograph, his use of poles, mirrors, and other objects to disrupt the frame is "another reminder of the artifice and illusion at work in an otherwise very 'real-looking' two-dimensional picture," observes the critic Rod Slemmons. "Suddenly the proscenium arch appears."[13] The audience becomes aware of the play as a play.

Friedlander performed in the pictures he took, sometimes as shadow or reflection, sometimes as subject, but always as a kind of alien, dislocated presence. "Friedlander put himself in all these strange environments where he wasn't known, where he was a stranger, where he was wandering," observes the photographer Barbara Norfleet. This ironic mode of self-portraiture had the effect of heightening the pose, the self-distance of the subject. As Norfleet notes, Friedlander's photographs, which depict him as "this lonely wanderer, this homeless person, present in different environments that bear his reflection," show him "not as himself, but as a simulation of himself."[14] His self-portraits do not really portray the person of the photographer but rather an image of the person.

The theme of the photographer as performer is carried a bold step further in the work of Cindy Sherman. In the late 1970s, Sherman did a series of photographs called "Untitled Film Stills." Each photograph pictures a woman in a typical pose from a film. Sophisticated and naive, dominating and vulnerable, glamorous and plain, the women are caught by the camera in various dramatic poses. A young blonde woman looks at her reflection in the mirror. The cool vulnerability of her gaze reminds us of Grace Kelly or Marilyn Monroe. A dark-haired woman, simply dressed, stands defiantly in a doorway evoking the gritty sensuality of Sophia Loren in an Italian movie. A tough-looking brunette sitting in a chair smoking a cigarette resembles Joan Crawford. Still another, viewed from a low angle against a sharply etched background of city buildings, looks like a heroine from a Hitchcock film.

For all their various looks, settings, and genres, the photographs have one thing in common. Each is a self-portrait. It is Cindy Sherman who poses in every frame. The photographer is the sole subject of the photographs she takes, and yet no two photographs look alike. In each picture, she dons a different persona, a different disguise. The different looks and roles assure that, despite her presence in every frame, Cindy Sherman herself—the person as distinct from the pose—never actually appears.

As with Warhol, the repetition of images is essential to Sherman's art. Her photographs depend for their impact on being viewed as a series. And like Warhol's images, Sherman's pictures are copies of copies, illusions of illusions. But in Sherman, the self-referential aspect implicit in Warhol and explicit in Friedlander finds its ultimate expression, as she photographs herself posing as movie stars posing for photographs.

In a series of color photographs Sherman took in the 1980s, she poses as ordinary women fantasizing about the glamorous life, perhaps imagining themselves as movie stars. In each photograph, a young woman is seen staring, waiting, imagining. In one, a girl lies on a kitchen floor holding a crumpled piece of paper. In another, a young woman waits by the phone in her nightgown. In these pictures, Sherman seeks to document the reality of fantasy itself.

"There is a stereotype of a girl who dreams all her life of being a movie star," Sherman once explained in an interview. "She tries to make it to the stage in films and either succeeds or fails. I was more interested in the types of characters that fail. Maybe I related to that. Why should I try to do it myself? I'd rather look at the reality of these kinds of fantasies, the fantasy of going away and becoming a star."[15]

Sherman's work explores the many roles that women play, but leaves ambiguous her own stance toward those roles. Does she mean to celebrate or criticize the stereotypes she portrays? On the one hand, she never offers an alternative to the female stereotypes she depicts, never offers a vision of women unbound from the roles they occupy in her pictures. On the other hand, her self-conscious emphasis on the constructed status of women's roles may suggest an attempt to loosen their hold, to free women from their grip. As one commentator writes, "What raises Cindy Sherman's photos above the stereotype . . . is that she obviously knows quite well what's what with the women she is representing, and takes her distance from the self that she wraps herself in."[16]

Failed Images: Framing the Flaw

The focus on the failed image that reveals the artifice of the pose is yet another aspect of modern television news that the art photographers of the sixties and seventies had already explored. The most explicit treatment can be found in a series of photographs on media events by Garry Winogrand published under the title *Public Relations* (1977). With a background in both photojournalism and commercial photography, Winogrand had a keen eye for the artifice in media events. He focused on the show behind the show—the staging, the lighting and the role of the media in the drama of politics in the age of television.

Winogrand shows, with an ironic eye, the entanglement of the media and the politicians. A photograph of presidential aspirant Edmund Muskie shows him at an outdoor rally during the 1972 primary campaign. Neither the candidate nor the reporters and photographers who surround him are in control of the jumbled scene. Winogrand captures the chaotic choreography of the media jostling for position, pointing microphones and cameras, their faces displaying the odd off-guard expressions of people caught unawares.

Winogrand makes the candidate and the background setting look out of kilter; the statehouse behind Muskie appears to lean over and Muskie's podium tilts toward the crowd of reporters. By tilting his camera in a low-angle shot, Winogrand accentuates the way the candidate is "framed," undermined, foiled by the camera.

The double meaning of being "framed" suggests the tendency of image-conscious photography to puncture the pose by reframing the event to expose the flaws. Winogrand shows how the camera forms and deforms the events it covers in a photograph of an Eliot Richardson press conference in 1973. Sitting at a small table strewn with microphones, dressed in a suit with a handkerchief in his pocket, hands folded calmly before him, Richardson would look the picture of poise in a standard news photo shot from the chest up. But Winogrand's wide-angle shot makes Richardson look oddly isolated in a strangely empty room, a vast white wall looming behind him, with two incongruous house plants to either side.

The lifelessness of the scene is accentuated by the absence of anyone responding or listening to Richardson. The presence of the press is represented only by the microphones on the table, connected by wires to a clutter of small portable cassette recorders on the floor. The symmetry of this odd scene is upset only by a woman poking her head into the side of the frame to adjust her tape recorder.

Like Friedlander, Winogrand uses what would be considered mistakes in conventional photographs to artistic advantage. The misplacement of the central figure, heads and bodies poking into the frame, figures obscuring other figures, people caught in odd poses or with their eyes shut, are used to subvert the perfect picture. At a protest demonstration in Washington, D.C., following the Kent State shooting in 1971, the central drama is the odd juxtaposition of the press and protestors in the frame. A young woman is speaking in the center of the frame, but like Muskie, she is not the center of attention. A boom mike held by an unseen hand disrupts the frame. The television crews wearing gas masks look like alien beings in contrast to the students who are dressed in casual summer clothes.

Winogrand shows with irony and humor the way not only politicians but also ordinary people are image-conscious actors. The frontispiece of *Public Relations* is a wide-angle photograph of people taking photographs at an observation area at the Kennedy Space Center in 1969. They are all striking slightly different poses as they aim their hand-held cameras, oblivious to the photographer framing them in his picture.

In *Public Relations*, Winogrand emphasizes what the press tries so hard to deny, that they too are part of the performance. As artist and onlooker, Winogrand is not caught up in the contradiction of the press, who first seek the best possible picture of the politician, then try in their reporting to undermine it. When network reporters are criticized for collaborating with the advance teams of presidents or candidates, they insist that such collaboration is necessary to get a good picture. "What we're trying to do is make sure that we can see the President and what he does," explained Brit Hume in defense of network producers working with the Reagan White House to set up the shots. "All kinds of things can go wrong. You can have the president or the other candidate backlighted, for example, which means that he can barely be seen by the camera, or, because of the placement of people, the shot is blocked. We're trying to make sure our access to the story is not cut off."[17]

Unlike the television networks, Winogrand does not seek the

"perfect picture" in the first place. He is able to expose the artifice of media events without it. For Winogrand, the "technical" requirements of the shot are not reasons to collaborate with the image makers but conventions to be resisted and renounced. In Winogrand's photographs, not only the politicians but also the press are participants in the theater of contrivance.

The fact that picture after picture in *Public Relations* is about people taking pictures vividly illustrates how the line between authenticity and artifice, between document and fiction is crossed and recrossed. The focus on images that fail to meet conventional expectations is a way of jarring us into seeing in a different way.

This was precisely the effect of Walker Evans's photograph of the gashed and peeling movie poster in the 1930s, and of Robert Frank's photograph of the television set turned on in an empty highway restaurant. By placing billboards within a wider frame, photographers since the Depression have let the life outside the billboards provide ironic commentary on the idealized images they projected. Lee Friedlander provides a variation on this theme by using his shadow or reflection to create a flaw in an otherwise conventional scene or to deface a studio portrait or political poster. In each case, photographers transform an idealized image into an artifact that lacks the potency it might otherwise hold.

The Self Deformed

The eye for the flaw that deconstructs the pose is also an eye that deforms the self. The image-conscious sensibility, alive as it is to the constructed character of events and persons, suggests a view of the self that is at once liberating and disempowering. "You see someone on the street and essentially what you notice is the flaw," observed Diane Arbus. "It's just extraordinary that we should have been given these peculiarities. . . . If you scrutinize reality closely enough, if in some way you really, really get to it, it becomes fantastic. . . . Something is ironic in the world and it has to do with the fact that what you intend never comes out the way you intend it."[18]

Along with Winogrand and Friedlander, Diane Arbus was featured in a 1967 Museum of Modern Art exhibit entitled "New Documents." Her photographs in this and later exhibits drew large crowds and considerable critical attention. Trained as a fashion photographer, Arbus specialized in portraits that accentuated the deformities and abnormalities in the commonplace. One commentator has aptly described her work as "fashion portraiture gone horribly wrong."[19]

The sharp focus of Arbus's large-format camera transformed its subjects into strange caricatures of themselves. In a photograph labeled "Boy with a Straw Hat Waiting to March in a Pro-War Parade, N.Y.C. 1967," a young man stares at the camera with a deadpan expression dressed primly in a bow tie, jacket, and patriotic buttons. Arbus's use of the photographic flash does not so much illuminate and document the person as introduce an air of unreality. It makes the natural look unnatural, magnifying every physical imperfection and making symbols—like the American flag—look like props.

In Arbus's hands, the boy's pose is made to mock his ideals, and he becomes an unwitting participant in his own self-caricature. A photograph labeled simply "Patriotic Young Man with a Flag" goes a step further and makes the young demonstrator look like an escapee from a mental institution. Again, the use of the flash is a vehicle for bringing out the deformity in his expression. His eyes look upward, he smiles, he holds the flag, and it all seems like a dark form of madness.

The mundane subjects of family snapshots and photo albums—babies, children, and family groupings—fare no better under Arbus's scrutinizing gaze. In Arbus's sharp-focus close-ups, babies are not smiling but crying, their faces contorted and grotesque. A flower girl posed in front of a foggy landscape looks like an actor in a surreal drama. A little boy holding a toy hand grenade in Central Park is caught in a pose so contorted that it looks at once like the spasm of a nervous disorder and a gesture of barely contained violence.

Arbus's photographs are an assault on normalcy. In this assault, she, like Winogrand and Friedlander, makes high art out of the photographic mistakes and oddities that would end up in the reject pile of the amateur or fashion photographer. But Arbus also consciously sought out freaks, deviants, and the physically deformed. Freaks made her feel "a mixture of shame and awe. . . . Most people go through life dreading they'll have a traumatic experience. Freaks are born with the trauma. They've already passed their test in life. They're aristocrats."[20]

But the "aristocrats" of Arbus's photography, like her "normal" subjects, do not escape the indignity of exposure, the estrangement in the pose. In a photograph labeled "Mexican Dwarf in His Hotel Room," Arbus shows a man wearing only a hat and a towel covering his lower torso, staring with composure at the camera. Our eyes are directed to the deformities. The label of the photograph itself, "Mexican Dwarf," suggests that these two categories define his being. And so the inner life intimated in his smile is subsumed by his categorization as a "freak."

Another photograph—"A Jewish Giant at Home with His Parents in the Bronx"—shows how her labeling underscores the depersonalization of her subjects, her insistence on directing our attention to the odd violations of social categories and expectations. Beyond the labels, Arbus sets up an equivalence between the normal and the abnormal, between those like the "Tattooed Man" who choose their deformity and those like the "Woman with a Veil on Fifth Avenue," whose deformity is bestowed by Arbus through the distorting power of her camera lens. Twins in their party dresses posing for the camera look as surreal as another photograph of two mentally retarded women posing in party hats. In the end, we cannot determine to what extent the deformity we see is constructed by the distortion of Arbus's camera. If selfhood is constructed then so are its deformities. On what grounds can we distinguish, Arbus seems to ask darkly, between real deformities and artificially imposed ones?

Though less relentless in the pursuit of the grotesque than Arbus, Winogrand also features the self deformed. In contrast to Arbus, his subjects rarely pose for the camera. Instead, Winogrand shows the self deformed in the urban landscape. An oblique-angle photograph shows an outstretched arm protruding into the frame, giving money to a destitute man. The arm of the giver disassociated from his body is as alien an object as the boom microphones thrust into the frame in Winogrand's shots of media events. Other photographs show the self decentered by tilting the camera to make an otherwise normal-looking activity look out of kilter.

As the critic Jonathan Green notes, "There is no private world in

Winogrand's photographs. . . . Winogrand's tragicomic world emphasizes extreme human types and situations. He constantly juxtaposes the well-formed and the misshapen, the ordinary and the extraordinary. His viewpoint exaggerates the peculiarities of visual form and character, almost but not quite turning his subjects into caricatures."[21]

Sometimes Winogrand's pictures show people with physical disabilities, but unlike Arbus he does not make them the subject of fascination and awe. Winogrand widens the frame to show how the so-called normal people are implicated in a deeper deformity—the failure to relate to the life around them. Through the framing of the shot, he asks us to reflect on the formlessness of mass society, in which the problem is "not the number of people involved," as Hannah Arendt observed, "but the fact that the world between them has lost its power to gather them together, to relate and to separate them."[22]

A Winogrand photograph shot outside an American Legion convention shows how people pass by on the street ignoring a legless man near the center of the frame. In another wide-angle shot we see women walking down a Los Angeles boulevard, their figures defined by the sharp play of light and shadow cast by the sun. Other people wait for a bus. All are oblivious to a young man in a wheel chair who sits in the shadow of a building, his head drooped over his body.

Winogrand's view of life was deeply pessimistic. He did not believe, with the traditional documentary photographers, that exposure would lead to social reform. To expose was an end in itself, a logical and formalistic consequence of the camera's ability to expose images. "I look at the pictures I have done up to now," he wrote in an application for a Guggenheim grant, "and they make me feel that who we are and what we feel and what is to become of us just doesn't matter. Our aspirations and successes have become cheap and petty. I read the newspapers, the columnists, some books. I look at magazines (our press). They all deal in illusions and fantasies. I can only conclude we have lost ourselves."[23]

The loss of self is a theme, or at least an intimation, that has haunted the image-conscious turn of art, photography, film, and television in the last quarter-century. In their different ways, each of these media challenged the distinction between the event and the image, between the person and the pose. But what began as an impulse to unmask artifice, to expose the image makers, to deconstruct conventions that wrongly claimed the authority of nature, may have ended by denying the possibility of a self that is more than the poses it strikes or the roles it plays. As Andy Warhol ironically remarked, "If you want to know all about Andy Warhol, just look at the surface of my paintings and films . . . , and there I am. There's nothing behind it."[24]

For all its prominence in our image-conscious culture, however, the centerless self, disempowered and deformed, is not the only way we see ourselves. Tempted as we are to equate the person with the pose, we also retain contact with an older understanding of persons as bearers of characters or souls or essential selves that pictures sometimes succeed, and sometimes fail in capturing. This view goes back to photography's traditional aim of revealing the inner truth of its subject, the "spirit of fact" that transcends appearance. It recalls the insistence of Marcus Aurelius Root, the first photographic historian, that a portrait must "show the soul of the original—the individuality of selfhood which differentiates him from all beings, past, present or future."[25]

Closely related to the "spirit of fact" of the traditional daguerreotype is the notion of persons as embodiments of larger meanings and high ideals. The daguerreotypist Mathew Brady had this in mind when in the 1840s he undertook a "Gallery Of Illustrious Americans." The public figures in his portrait gallery would give expression to a distinctly American identity that celebrated both individuality and national purpose. This idealized, ennobling vision of the American self was carried into the twentieth century in the urban and industrial images of Jacob Riis and Lewis Hine, and in the portraits of dignity amidst depression by Dorothea Lange and Walker Evans.

In the decades since World War II, when art photography set about unraveling and deconstructing the American self, the traditional vision persisted in popular movies. Heroic figures, from Gary Cooper in *High Noon* to Sylvester Stallone in *Rocky* and *Rambo* to Harrison Ford in the Indiana Jones films, asserted their individuality even as they vindicated ideals larger than themselves. The maverick heroes of American movies from the forties to the nineties stand in sharp contrast to the disempowered, centerless selves represented elsewhere in the culture. Confronted with corrupt institutions, bumbling bureaucracies, or vast, impersonal structures of power, they launch out on their own, empowered despite their circumstances.

This cultural counterpoint provides the setting for contemporary political discourse. Ronald Reagan drew readily from the heroic images of the movies, as when he borrowed Spencer Tracy's line from *State of the Union* to great effect during a debate in the 1980 New Hampshire primary: "I paid for this microphone, Mr. Green!" Challenging Congress with the threat of a presidential veto, Reagan borrowed the line of Clint Eastwood's character, Dirty Harry, when he said, "Go ahead—make my day."

The persistence of the heroic image of the American self helps us understand the limits of image consciousness as a mode of political critique. Why did network reporters and producers find to their frustration that their repeated attempts to expose the image-making apparatus of Reagan and Bush did little to dissolve the hold of their images on the public? The answer is that certain pictures resist puncturing because they convey a truth or evoke an ideal that explains us to ourselves, that resonates with our deepest convictions.

In 1984, when Reagan stood on the bluff of a Normandy beach and recalled the heroic sacrifice of the "boys of Pointe du Hoe," it was artifice of the highest order, a carefully staged media event in which the president's practiced voice cracked with emotion at just the right moment. Yet no amount of attention to these facts could dissolve the power of the image. The reason is not simply that pictures overpower words. Reagan's words, after all, were a crucial part of the drama he created. The image resisted deconstruction because the pictures and the words taken together—for all their staging, for all their politically motivated design—spoke to something real, something genuine in America's understanding of itself. As television news, the ultimate document, becomes ever more entangled in artifice, the movies, home of fiction and fantasy, give expression to this rival vision of the American self.

Mythic Pictures:
The Maverick Hero in
American Movies

B Y MOST ACCOUNTS, 1968 WAS A YEAR OF UNRAVELING CERTITUDE and faith. Thousands of American soldiers had been killed or wounded in Vietnam. Thousands more returned home to a nation that did not recognize them as heroes. The Tet offensive gave the lie to the government's confident promise of victory against the Viet-cong. Eugene McCarthy scored a stunning victory against Lyndon Johnson in the New Hampshire primary, prompting the incumbent president to withdraw from the race. Not only liberal politicians but even Walter Cronkite came out against the war. Along with the assassinations of Robert Kennedy and Martin Luther King, Jr., and the riots in the inner cities, these tumultuous events called into question America's self-image as master of its destiny and force for good in the world. It was as if American life was finally playing out, in terms too obvious to deny, the dissonant, disempowered self-image that art photographers of the sixties had already glimpsed.

But even as events seemed to conspire against the traditional image of American mastery and virtue, Americans flocked to see *The Green Berets* (1968, directed by John Wayne and Ray Kellogg), with its patriotic theme song: "Fighting soldiers from the sky, fearless men who jump and die. Men who mean just what they say, the brave men of the Green Berets." In 1968, the movie was a top-ten box-office hit.

The popularity of the movie at a time of turmoil and doubt might be explained in a number of ways. Perhaps some, such as those Richard Nixon called "the silent majority," liked the movie because they supported the war and approved of the movie's message. Others may simply have enjoyed the movie as entertainment. But the appeal of popular movies is not limited to the ideologies they convey or the entertainment they provide.

Popular movies derive their appeal by engaging us in familiar narratives. For all the different stories they tell, they often reiterate certain myths and ideals that resonate with our collective self-understanding. What Erik Erikson observed about the enduring power of myth holds true for the myths that American popular movies convey: "It is useless to try to show that it has no basis in fact, or to claim it is fiction, and in fact nonsense. A myth blends historical fact and fiction in such a way that it 'rings true' to an era."[1]

As bearers of mythic pictures, American popular movies display a stance toward images that is different from that found in other realms of our culture. The image-conscious sensibility, so pronounced in the art photography of the sixties and the television news coverage of the eighties, takes a different form in popular film. While movies from *A Face in the Crowd* (1957) to *Network* (1976) to *Bob Roberts* (1992) have addressed issues of image creation and image manipulation in modern society, most popular movies do not seek to unravel or expose the myths that pictures convey. Unlike image-conscious art photography and television news coverage, which focus attention on the image as a way of puncturing the picture and dissolving its hold on us, most popular movies invite us to believe in the pictures we see. They ask us to enter the imaginary worlds they present, to be moved and engaged by them.

One of the most potent mythic images that the movies carried through recent decades of disillusion and doubt is the image of the maverick hero, a self-reliant American archetype who does things his own way, often outside established institutions, but who triumphs in the end, vindicating noble ideals.[2] The maverick hero has a long history in the American imagination, reaching back to Natty Bumppo, the frontier hero of James Fenimore Cooper's early-nineteenth-century novels, and finding classic expression in the cowboy heroes of Western novels and movies of the first half of the twentieth century. In popular movies from the sixties to the present, the maverick hero has assumed new forms. In contrast to the disempowered, centerless self represented in art photography and some movies, the maverick hero persists as a free and active agent, capable of exercising mastery even in the face of circumstances that seem to defy human control.

From frontiersmen to cowboys, soldiers to policemen, ordinary citizens to comic-book heroes of superhuman powers, American mavericks display several characteristic qualities. First, they typically prove their strength through one-on-one combat with their adversaries, most often in fistfights or shoot-outs. Drawing on his own strength and wits, the hero defeats the villain by himself, without depending on institutional support or technological advantages. Second, the maverick neither hungers for battle nor aspires to power. He is drawn into service reluctantly, and when his mission is done, he leaves the scene.[3] Finally, despite his fierce individualism, the maverick acts not for himself but on behalf of a community worthy of his efforts. He is at once an insider and an outsider—an insider in that he shares the highest ideals of the nation or community he serves, an outsider in that he is no organization man. He typically distrusts or disdains the officials with whom he must deal; more often than not, the institutions and organizations he encounters either corrupt the ideals he seeks to vindicate, or simply get in his way.

This insider-outsider quality enabled the American maverick to adapt to a period of deep disenchantment with American politics and institutions. Beginning in the 1970s, popular movies reflected the widespread disillusionment with large institutions of government and business. As Americans began increasingly to fear that vast structures of power defied individual control, the movies portrayed powerful corporations ruthlessly pursuing profits, security agencies abusing power in the name of questionable goals, law enforcement agencies engaging in corruption, foreign nations victimizing Americans, and supernatural forces exercising mysterious control over individuals.

This tendency is found across the whole spectrum of popular movies, whether they fall into the category of horror, science fiction, crime, or other leading genres. In *The Omen* (1976), characters hysterically utter the apocalyptic saying: "The Devil's child will rise from the world of politics." A scientist in the science-fiction thriller, *The Andromeda Strain* (1971) quips: "The establishment's going to fall down and go boom." In one of the later James Bond films, *The Spy Who Loved Me* (1977), a villain who heads a huge multinational corporation sends off nuclear missiles to destroy New York, remarking, "Observe, Mr. Bond, the instruments of Armageddon." In *Network* (1976) an aggressive program director argues that "apocalypse sells" to a public "clobbered on all sides by Vietnam and Watergate."

The maverick hero could survive this loss of faith in institutions because he was not identified with institutions in the first place. His identity depended instead on a mythic marginality. As an insider-outsider, he had always vindicated American ideals while rebelling against institutional constraints. The modern maverick hero was not vulnerable to the erosion of institutional authority; as a self-reliant individual, he always stood apart from the institutions he served.

John Wayne's Colonel Kirby, the hero of *The Green Berets*, is one in a long line of maverick heroes, a soldier with the soul of a cowboy. Over the Green Beret camp in the jungles of Vietnam hangs the sign, "Dodge City." When a skeptical newspaper reporter confronts Kirby about the brutal way Americans interrogate the enemy, he retorts cowboy-style: "Out there, due process is a bullet." Kirby is tough but kind, strong but sentimental. Like the classic cowboy, he defends a community too weak to defend itself. In the last scene of the movie, Kirby places a Green Beret's cap on the head of an orphaned Vietnamese boy, telling him, "You're what this is all about."

None of the Vietnam movies to follow played out the theme of the maverick hero with full confidence in the goodness of the fight. In *The Deer Hunter* (1978), *Apocalypse Now* (1979), and *Platoon* (1986), no hero would enjoy the moral certitude of Wayne's Colonel Kirby or emerge unscarred by the war.

At the same time, the image of the noble cowboy gave way to morally ambiguous variations. In the American westerns of the late sixties, the heroes were motivated more by money or adventure than by high ideals.[4] A year after *The Green Berets*, John Wayne played against type as the crude, drunken, one-eyed marshal Rooster Cogburn in the box office hit, *True Grit* (1969). In *Butch Cassidy and the Sundance Kid* (1969), Paul Newman and Robert Redford played engaging rakes with no higher purpose than to rob banks and have fun.

The dark side of the cowboy myth was painfully revealed in another big movie of 1969, *Midnight Cowboy* (directed by John Schlesinger).

Early in the movie, the hero, Joe Buck (Jon Voight), sings a cowboy song in the shower. He hopes to find his fortune by dressing up as a cowboy and becoming a hustler, catering to rich women in New York City. But his naive faith in the allure of the cowboy image brings him only poverty and failure. His seedy sidekick (Dustin Hoffman) tells him that even in the hustler's world, "no one wants that cowboy crap." As the failed hustler wanders the streets of Manhattan, he is surrounded by billboards displaying Madison Avenue's images of the good life, images that serve as ironic commentary on Joe's inability to live the myth.

The empty drive-in movie theater that opens the movie, and the bleak figure of the failed hero adrift in the urban landscape, evoke the photography of Robert Frank, Lee Friedlander, and Garry Winogrand. But even as the image consciousness of the art photography of the 1960s and 1970s reverberated in movies like *Midnight Cowboy*, the maverick hero did not die. Although westerns waned in popularity and Vietnam War movies became filled with painful ambiguities, the American maverick survived by adapting to changed social circumstances. In order to see how the maverick hero survived the coming of the image-conscious culture, it is important to establish the archetypes from which he is derived: the cowboy heroes of *Shane* (1953) and *High Noon* (1952), the citizen hero of Frank Capra's *Mr. Smith Goes to Washington* (1939), and the urban maverick represented by Humphrey Bogart in *Casablanca* (1942).

Classic Maverick Heroes

The movie western goes back to the days of silent films, but finds its fullest expression in two classics of the fifties, *Shane* (1953, directed by George Stevens), and *High Noon* (1952, directed by Fred Zinnemann).

Shane is a technicolor fable of fast action and moral certitudes. The hero, Shane (Alan Ladd), embodies the paradoxes and the triumphs of the maverick hero. He is a loner whose origins and full name are never revealed, yet his sense of selfhood and moral bearings are secure. He moves from place to place, the very embodiment of the rugged individualist of the frontier, yet assumes the identity of a homesteader in order to defend a community of farmers against a ruthless cattle baron. He is a gunfighter who can triumph in a lawless world, but who fights for a society of law and order.

Within the parable of the western, the hero is a man with sure moral bearings who plays the role of the enforcer only in the absence of law enforcement. Shane enters the lives of a homesteader family, Joe Starrett (Van Heflin), his wife Marion (Jean Arthur) and their son Joey (Brandon de Wilde) asking only for permission to cross their property and to stop for water. But he soon becomes involved in their conflict with the villains, a powerful cattle rancher named Riker (Emile Meyer) and his gang.

The selfish individualism of Riker, who exploits both the land and its people, is contrasted with the selfless individualism of Shane. "What are you looking for?" Riker asks Shane after failing to win him over to his side with a job offer. "Nothing," replies Shane. The laconic hero never articulates his principles, but acts to defend justice in a world without legal institutions. He takes up his gun only to defend those too weak to defend themselves. "A gun is a tool," he tells Marion Starrett. "No better, no worse than any other tool, an axe, a shovel, or anything. A gun is as good or bad as the man using it."

The later part of the movie illustrates just this point. Shane refuses to let the family man, Starrett, sacrifice himself against Wilson (Jack Palance), Riker's hired gun. He knocks out his friend and goes into town alone to confront and kill the gunfighter. Once this deed is done, the hero reinforces Marion Starrett's view that guns don't belong in the community. He tells young Joey Starrett that now that the gunfighter has been defeated, "I've got to be going on." "Why, Shane?" asks Joey. The reply is classic maverick, bringing to closure a moral parable which seamlessly reconciles self-reliance and community obligation. "A man has to be what he is. You can't break the law. I tried it and it didn't work for me. . . . There's no living with a killing. . . . Right or wrong, it's a brand. . . . Now you run home to your mother and tell her everything is all right. They're ain't any more guns in the valley."

In contrast to the bright tones of *Shane, High Noon* is a prelude to the morally ambiguous world that many modern heroes occupy. Though the movie celebrates self-reliance and individual agency, the film has the dissonant feel of a Robert Frank photograph. The world

that should look bright is murky; the central figure in the story—
Gary Cooper's sheriff, Will Kane—is not securely situated, but dis-
tanced from the community.

Unlike the outsider Shane, the hero of *High Noon* begins as the
insider who wants to move out, the sheriff who "cleaned up" the town
and now wants to retire, marry, and settle down in a new community.
Although Kane does not begin as a loner, circumstances soon force
him to become one. As he prepares to leave town with his bride, Amy
Fowler (Grace Kelly), he learns that Frank Miller, the feared gunfighter whom he sent to prison for murder, has been released and is
returning on the noon train to kill him. Three members of Miller's
old gang have already arrived in town to help their old boss get his
revenge.

Like Shane, Kane is a reluctant hero. He does not look for trouble,
but he stands firm in the face of it. Kane's friends urge him to leave
town with Amy as planned. At first Kane agrees, but out on the
prairie he stops and turns the buggy back to town. "It's no good. I've
got to go back," he tells his puzzled wife. "They're making me run. I
never run from anybody before." Back in town Amy urges her husband, "Don't be a hero. You don't have to be a hero—not for me." But
Kane loses his temper. "I'm not trying to be a hero. If you think I like
this, you're crazy. . . . This is my town. I've got friends here. I'll swear
in a bunch of special deputies. With a posse behind, maybe there
won't be any trouble."

Unlike the homesteaders in *Shane*, who are virtuous but weak
compared to the powerful rancher, the townspeople of *High Noon* lack
moral fortitude. As the clock ticks down dramatically to high noon,
the townspeople desert Kane one by one, offering one excuse after
another. Finally, as the noon train arrives, even Amy rides out of
town, because she is a Quaker and cannot condone violence. But
Kane does not leave. Like Shane, he is willing to stand alone and fight
for what he believes.

In *Shane* the mythic individualism of the hero is magnified by the
western landscape, but in *High Noon* the hero is isolated in the
enclosed world of the small town. Yet, he becomes a looming presence
in the stark landscape, the embodiment of individual agency in a
fallen world. In the dramatic climax of *High Noon*, Kane defeats the
villains in a protracted gunfight, aided at the last moment by his wife

Amy, who breaks with her Quaker teachings, and returns to take up a gun by her husband's side.

After Kane and Amy defeat the villains, the townspeople emerge from their hiding places and gather around the couple. In one of the most memorable scenes in American movies, Kane pulls off his badge, and throws it down in the dust. Without speaking to anyone, he gets in a buggy with his bride and rides out of town. He shows disdain for the cowardice of his community, but he has fulfilled his obligations to them and to himself. *High Noon* is a variant of the parable of *Shane*: self-reliance is distinguished from pure self-interest. It is enobled by a higher calling to defend the rights of the individual and the community, even when the community is weak and wayward.

In contrast to the classic cowboys, the citizen heroes of Frank Capra's movies of the 1930s and 1940s are typically rooted in their communities, but cast in conflict with the corrupt forces of the modern world. Though we often associate Capra with an idealistic vision of American institutions, his movies actually combine a deep cynicism about politics and big institutions with a redemptive vision of the citizen hero. In Capra's movies, the villains are greedy capitalists, corrupt politicians, and power-hungry newspaper moguls. In relation to the powers that be, the citizen hero is a virtuous outsider. He seeks neither fame nor glory, but is called by circumstance to assume civic responsibilities and reaffirm democratic ideals.

In *Mr. Smith Goes to Washington* (1939), Jefferson Smith (James Stewart), the popular head of a boys' club, is appointed by the governor to a vacant Senate seat. The party bosses figure that an idealistic "young patriot" who "recites Lincoln and Jefferson" will be the perfect cover for the special-interest land deal they hope to enact. They assume that young Smith is too naive to thwart their plans. At a banquet given to celebrate Smith's departure for Washington, the astonished hero exclaims, "I can't help feeling there's a mistake somehow."

Like the cowboy heroes, Smith is called to a mission he does not seek. At first, he is doubted by those who should be his supporters. Smith's savvy, world-weary secretary Saunders (Jean Arthur), mocks him behind his back, calling him "Daniel Boone," "Honest Abe," and "Don Quixote Smith." Yet, Smith proves that his patriotism is genuine, and that he has the strength and conviction to take on the

Washington establishment. When he is taunted by reporters that he is not a real senator but "an honorary stooge," he resolves to prove his mettle and proposes legislation to establish a national boys' camp, to be funded by small contributions from individuals.

By sheer coincidence, the site of the proposed camp is the exact location coveted by the party bosses for their real-estate scheme. When the bosses fail to dissuade Smith from pursuing his proposal, they try viciously to destroy his reputation. They enlist Joe Paine (Claude Rains), the senior senator from Smith's state, to accuse Smith falsely of trying to profit from the land the boys' camp would occupy. The party machine assembles a host of false witnesses and forged documents to incriminate him. Smith's fellow citizens, believing the charges, turn against him. Even the admiring boys from his club lose faith in their fallen leader. In despair, Smith packs his bags and decides to leave Washington.

This dark vision of Washington corruption is juxtaposed with Capra's mythic vision of the city, seen in his heroic shots of the monuments and buildings that both inspire Smith and provide the setting for his ultimate triumph. Saunders finds the defeated Smith sitting beneath the Lincoln Memorial. Once cynical, she has grown to love and respect Smith. She inspires him to stand up for his ideals and fight the political machine. "You didn't just have faith in Paine," she tells Smith. "You had faith in something bigger than that."

Once fortified, Smith returns to take on the establishment. Coached by Saunders, he uses Senate procedures to gain access to the floor. In plain and honest language, he exposes the corruption, graft, and deceit. Holding the Senate floor in an arduous but earnest filibuster, Smith reads from the Declaration of Independence and the Constitution. The national press that once ridiculed him now lauds him as a citizen hero. CBS Radio reports that the gallery is packed with people who have "come to see what they couldn't see at home, democracy in action." The people of Smith's state rally to him. The boys at the club print and distribute their own small newspaper to counter the lies the party bosses have printed in the newspapers they control throughout the state.

Smith's status as insider and outsider is now fully played out. He stands alone inside the Senate chambers and affirms American ideals, yet he speaks as the loyal outsider, the man who refuses politics as usual. Smith is vindicated in the end by the man who betrayed him, his mentor, Senator Paine. The consummate insider is finally moved by the moral suasion of the civic hero. Paine dramatically vindicates Smith before the assembled Senate. The movie ends to the strains of "My Country 'tis of Thee."

Capra's open-hearted idealists represent one side of the American archetype of the citizen hero. Humphrey Bogart's Rick Blaine in *Casablanca* (1942, directed by Michael Curtiz) represents another. Rick is a sophisticated urban hero without the innocence or naïveté of the classic western maverick or Capra's common man. He is the insider-outsider who makes a virtue of his marginality. Although he poses as a cynic, he is an idealist at heart. He feigns indifference to politics, yet fights for noble political causes. He appears selfish, but like Capra's heroes and the classic cowboys, acts selflessly to affirm social ideals.

Bogart's Rick has a hold on the popular imagination that goes beyond the film's engaging plot. He is the most stylized and modern of all the heroes, a consummate performer who never loses himself in his role. He cultivates his identity as a marginal man as a way of exerting his agency in an uncertain world. Unlike the cowboy, who scarcely speaks at all, and unlike Capra's plain-spoken idealists, Rick's agency is defined in good part by his memorable repartees: "And what in heaven's name brought you to Casablanca?" asks his friendly rival, the Vichy police Captain Renault (Claude Rains). "My health," Rick coolly replies. "I came to Casablanca for the waters." "What waters?" Renault replies. "We're in the desert." Rick responds with deadpan irony, "I was misinformed."

Part of the enduring appeal of *Casablanca* is its artful blending of sophistication and sentimentality, of self-distance and ardent passion, of modernism with classic American mythology. At his nightclub, "Rick's Café Américain," the hero creates a modern American identity in which style and panache are the defining qualities of selfhood. Yet from the beginning of the film, Rick's café is situated within a larger mythic landscape. Casablanca is the last stop on the refugees' path to "the new world," "the freedom of the Americas." Through the agency of the hero, Rick's café becomes the portal to a new life.

While Rick cultivates the stance of the neutral onlooker and political cynic, he is actually a highly principled man. "I suspect underneath that cynical shell, you're at heart a sentimentalist," Renault tells Rick. "Oh, laugh at it if you will, but I am familiar with your record." Renault then recites how Rick fought with the Spanish Loyalists and ran guns to Ethiopia. Though his credentials as a hero are impressive, Rick keeps them hidden. "The problems of the world are not my department," he tells the famous resistance fighter, Victor Laszlo (Paul Henreid), when Laszlo seeks his help in leaving Casablanca. Laszlo responds by evoking Rick's record, "Isn't it strange that you always happen to fight on the side of the underdog?"

Rick's nobility, hidden beneath a cynical exterior, is one of the defining characteristics of the urban maverick. He looks after his own staff, helps a young woman's husband win at gambling so that she will not have to compromise herself with Renault to get exit papers, and in the end makes the ultimate sacrifice by giving up the woman he loves in order to aid the cause of the resistance. "I'm no good at being noble," he tells Ilsa (Ingrid Bergman). "But it doesn't take much to see that the problems of three little people don't amount to a hill of beans in this crazy world. Someday you'll understand that." The last shot of the movie shows Rick walking off with Captain Renault into the fog of the small Casablanca airport, after the plane carrying Ilsa and Laszlo to freedom has departed.

The classic American heroes did not die out in the forties and fifties, but lived on in a world less innocent and credulous than the world of their origin. Even in a culture accustomed to deconstructing myths and unraveling rituals, we still are moved and engaged by the movies of the past. More than this, the maverick archetypes those movies defined have found their way, in new form, into our political imagination. Presidential candidates not only campaign with movie stars, but cast themselves within familiar movie archetypes—as mavericks against the establishment, as defenders of law and order, and as virtuous outsiders who will redeem American ideals.

Law and Order: The Maverick Cop

By the 1970s, the lawless frontier had not disappeared but moved to the crime-ridden city, calling forth such gritty cop heroes as Clint Eastwood's Dirty Harry. Eastwood's maverick police detective, Harry

Callahan, is at once an insider and an outsider. He fights for law and order, but also has to fight his own boss, the bungling police department, the downtown bureaucrats, and the lawyers who care more about the rights of criminals than of their victims. He gets the criminals in the end by breaking with the bureaucrats and drawing on his own resources.

Like other movies featuring cops and criminals, the camera work in Eastwood's Dirty Harry movies conveys a sense of both enclosure and exposure to danger in the urban environment: snipers shoot victims from tall buildings, gunmen hold passengers hostage on subways, individuals are lost in crowds or cornered in alleyways. The individual is exposed and abstracted in a pattern of buildings, streets and traffic, much as in the photography of Lee Friedlander, Garry Winogrand and other prominent art photographers of the 1960s and 1970s. Yet, even in an urban landscape that becomes alien and hostile, the hero of the movie exerts his mastery.

The underlying paradox of the Dirty Harry movies is that in order to enforce the law, the hero has to break the rules. In the first movie of the series, *Dirty Harry* (Warner Brothers, 1971, directed by Don Siegel) the district attorney is more concerned with protecting the rights of a psychopathic killer than those of his victims, smugly reminding Harry, "It's the law." Harry angrily retorts, "Then the law is crazy." In spite of the obstacles presented by his own department, Harry, through a series of daring feats, captures the killer. But he is so frustrated with the incompetence of the law enforcement bureaucracy that at the end of the movie he throws away his badge in disgust, just as Gary Cooper's righteous sheriff did in *High Noon*.

But in the next Dirty Harry movie, *Magnum Force* (1973, directed by Ted Post) the hero is wearing the badge again. The criminal justice system has not changed, but Harry has resigned himself to working within it, though he still insists on doing it on his own terms. This time he fights against a secret vigilante group of police officers within his own department, which kills criminals who might elude arrest and punishment. As the plot unfolds, Harry and his partner attempt to identify the sources of the conspiracy. In the climactic scene, Harry discovers that his own lieutenant is a member of the vigilante organization and exclaims in dismay, "When police become our executioners, when will it end?" Harry's boss cynically retorts, "You had your chance to join, but you preferred to stick with the system." In a line that defines the insider-outsider status of the maverick hero, Harry responds, "I hate the damn system, but until someone makes some good changes, I'll stick with it."

Still, Dirty Harry remains a maverick, disgusted by the failure of society to live by its ideals—ideals that he himself, though rough-hewn, hardened, and cynical, fights fiercely to defend. In *Sudden Impact* (1983, directed by Clint Eastwood), Harry is invited by a beautiful woman artist (Sondra Locke) to join her at an outdoor café. "What makes you think I'm a cop?" he asks. "I saw the commotion here the other day," she responds. "You're either a cop or public enemy number one." Harry answers, "Some people might say both."

ARTIST: Really, who?
HARRY: Oh, bozos with big brass nameplates on their desks and asses the shape of the seats of their chairs.
ARTIST: Why?
HARRY: Oh, it's a question of methods. Everybody wants results, but nobody wants to do what they have to do to get it done.
ARTIST: And you do?
HARRY: I do what I have to do.
ARTIST: I'm glad, Callahan. But you know you're an endangered species. This is the age of lapsed responsibilities and defeated justice.

Like Harry Callahan, the self-reliant hero of *Die Hard* (Twentieth Century Fox, 1988, directed by John McTiernan) thrives on being the man on the margin, resisting conventions yet redeeming society. The main elements of the plot are classic western. The hero is an outsider who comes into town and discovers that the bad guys have taken over. Overcoming great odds, he defeats them single-handedly. Once the job is done, he moves on. But the old story is overlaid with the most modern trappings. Far from being the classic loner, the hero of *Die Hard*, John McClane (Bruce Willis) is a man beset by marital problems. He is a New York City police detective who does not want to leave his job. His wife, Holly Gennaro (Bonnie Bedelia), has relocated to Los Angeles with their children to work as a high-powered executive at a Japanese-owned corporation. As the movie begins, McClane arrives in Los Angeles in hopes of saving their marriage.

But even on vacation he is ready for duty, his gun concealed in a shoulder holster underneath his casual clothes. It isn't long before he needs it. A heavily armed gang of international thieves breaks into the office party at his wife's corporation and takes everyone hostage. Alone and unseen, McClane reaches for his gun. The world has suddenly become uncivilized and brutal. Barefoot and in his undershirt, the maverick cop moves down the back stairs of the building.

The tension between the hero's role as insider and outsider becomes a central dramatic theme. McClane desperately tries to communicate with the outside world with a radio phone he has commandeered from the thieves, but he is foiled at every turn by the forces that are supposed to help him. Isolated inside the building he cries, "Come on, come on. Where's the fucking cavalry?" But when the modern cavalry arrives they fall flat on their faces. The police, SWAT team, and FBI forge their plans by the book and only succeed in playing into the thieves' hands, further endangering the hostages.

Caught in the crossfire between criminals and cops, the maverick cop is forced to wage his battle alone. The criminals try to kill him. The cops ignore him and refuse his advice. The thieves have superior technology, but they too play by the book, methodically proceeding with their plans. This is just the opening the maverick hero needs, because he is not playing by anyone's rules. Like Dirty Harry, he does what he has to do, even if it violates police procedures: "You won't hurt me, because you're a policeman," a cornered machine-gun-toting thief challenges McClane. "There are rules for policemen." McClane wryly responds, "Oh, yeah. That's what my captain keeps telling me."

In an exchange over the radio phone, the hero serves warning to Hans Gruber (Alan Rickman), the cold-blooded head of the international band of thieves, that he has "waxed" one of his men, and he will pursue the rest. But the arrogant foreigner has nothing but disdain for the hero and Americans in general:

> GRUBER: You know my name, but who are you? Just another American who saw too many movies as a child. Another orphan of a bankrupt culture who thinks he's John Wayne, Rambo, Marshal Dillon.

McClane: I was always partial to Roy Rogers. Actually, I really
    liked those sequined shirts.
Gruber: Do you really think you have a chance against us,
    cowboy?
McClane: Yippee Ki-Ay, motherfucker.

Unlike modern art photography or television news reporting, the
self-conscious references to American movies are not a means of
calling attention to the image as an image, but to the image as a myth
with real import. McClane, after all, is the genuine article. He lives
the myth, and embodies the culture the thieves disdain. Like other
cop movies, *Die Hard* contrasts the urbanity and sophistication of the
criminals with the unadorned and simple lifestyle of the hero.

Like Dirty Harry, who challenges a criminal holding a gun to a
hostage's head with the deadpan remark, "Make my day," McClane
asserts his control through a mastery of one-liners. Near the end of
the movie, when the evil Gruber is about to kill McClane, Gruber
again taunts him: "Well, this time John Wayne does not walk off into
the sunset with Grace Kelly." McClane coolly corrects him, "It's Gary
Cooper. Asshole." Before the beaten Gruber falls to his death, Mc-
Clane bids him farewell with Roy Rogers's classic sign-off, "Happy
trails."

In confronting the thieves, the maverick hero confronts the forces
in modern society that keep the ordinary citizen, the little guy, down:
privileged corporate types, criminals with their superior weapons,
arrogant rule-bound cops, and the media who treat the heroes' desper-
ate battle to save the hostages as just another dramatic event to be
exploited.

Gritty heroes like John McClane and Dirty Harry are just one variation of the maverick cop. In *Beverly Hills Cop* (1984) and *Beverly Hills
Cop 2* (1987), directed by Tony Scott, the same themes are played out
as comedy. Like the hero of *Die Hard*, police detective Axel Foley
(Eddie Murphy) is the outsider who comes to town and solves an
important crime before returning home. Like other mavericks, he
mocks authority and circumvents the rules at every turn.

In a comic variation on the insider-outsider theme, the hero dons
disguises, fabricates identities, plays with roles, moves between social

worlds. Axel Foley is a freewheeling black undercover cop from Detroit who solves cases that are beyond the police in posh Beverly Hills. In pursuit of the criminals, he effortlessly moves among various poses. First, he poses as an authoritative city building inspector, and dismisses a construction crew renovating a fancy home, claiming they have committed code violations. Later, he occupies the same home while the owners (and the construction crews) are away. In another scene, Axel gains access to a private club by posing as a flamboyant gay man who has had a liaison with one of the members. The discreet maître d' waves him in for fear he will make a scene. He then breaks out of his pose to confront the criminal maverick-style, one-on-one.

But far from eroding his identity, Axel's role playing proves how supremely secure he is. His mutable identities are a means of asserting his agency. This stands in contrast to the themes of modern art photography. When Cindy Sherman poses as different movie stars, her real self is hidden from view, submerged in the stereotype. The pose, she suggests in her cultural critique, is what selfhood has become. For the comic hero, the pose or disguise is a means of exercising his agency, of tricking fate, of overcoming social obstacles.

While many maverick heroes are police officers, others assume the role, without official sanction. In *Death Wish* (1974, directed by Michael Winner), the hero (Charles Bronson) changes from a mild-mannered middle-class professional to a cowboy-style vigilante after his wife is brutally murdered and his daughter raped by a group of urban thugs.

The hero of *Death Wish*, while stepping outside the law, enters a mythic role that validates his actions. As an urban cowboy, he reclaims his sense of agency and stands up for all the victims of crime. As he reminds his skeptical son-in-law, "What about the old American social custom of self-defense?" The police finally catch up with the hero, but rather than arrest him, they order him to leave town. The hero responds ironically, "By sundown, Inspector?" His last act in the movie is to break up the mugging of an older woman at the airport in his new home town. Smiling into the camera, he shares his triumph with the movie audience, shaping his fingers into a gun.

The popular movies *Billy Jack* (1971) and *The Trial of Billy Jack* (1974), directed by Tom Laughlin in collaboration with Dolores Taylor, feature a classic maverick in a counterculture setting. Billy

Jack dresses in western garb, is self-reliant, and skilled in one-on-one combat (karate), and lives by his own code of honor. A Vietnam veteran, he is against the war. A skilled fighter, he protects a "Freedom School" dedicated to nonviolent social change. A "half-breed," he finds his inspiration in Indian ways, but refuses their pacifism.

As in the Dirty Harry movies, there is a contrast between "good cops" who uphold the law and protect citizens, and "bad cops" who not only violate the law, but even threaten the life of the hero. Billy Jack becomes disillusioned with the law after witnessing police officers defending the interests of a corrupt businessman: "When policemen break the law, there isn't any law." Nonetheless, throughout the film he repeatedly comes to the aid of the weak but honest sheriff. In the most exciting sequences of the movie, Billy Jack, like Dirty Harry, takes on the role of the enforcer, single-handedly fighting town thugs or corrupt police officers who threaten the young people at the Freedom School.

In *The Trial of Billy Jack*, the themes of police corruption and state violence versus the purity of the maverick hero and the social causes he defends are replayed with even greater intensity. The corrupt police try to frame Billy Jack, and the violence escalates between the Freedom School and the townspeople, ending in a confrontation where many young people are wounded or killed. In the end the principle of nonviolence is redeemed as the students gather to honor their wounded teacher, Jean, the founder of the Freedom School, and to reaffirm her teachings. But this is only one layer of the movie's parable. Like the classic western hero, Billy Jack defends righteous principles while refusing to give up his maverick ways. Like Gary Cooper's sheriff in *High Noon*, he may respect pacifism, but he cannot practice it. A flawed world needs the maverick, whose status as insider and outsider gives him the independence to act, to exercise agency where others fail.

The Military Hero

The stars and stripes of the American flag fill the screen. General George Patton (George C. Scott) walks up and stands in the center of the screen backed by the massive flag. Strident, confident, sure of his country, he speaks:

> Men, all this stuff you've heard about America not wanting to fight, wanting to stay out of war is a lot of horse dung. Americans traditionally love to fight. . . . Americans love a winner and will not tolerate a loser. Americans play to win all the time. I wouldn't give a hoot in hell for a man who lost and laughed. That's why Americans have never lost, and will never lose a war, because the thought of losing is hateful to Americans.

The maverick's role as insider and outsider presupposes a secure place to stand. As a maverick hero fighting in the Second World War, Patton had such a place. The ideals he fought for were as unassailable as those of the maverick cops. The institutions these mavericks worked within were basically intact, though, in the case of the cops, usually flawed by bureaucratic incompetence and, sometimes, corruption. But the corruption was not all-pervasive. Most cops were good cops, just as most soldiers were good soldiers. Both cops and soldiers fought the good war. The enemy was clear and the cause just. If the maverick cop or soldier bent or broke the rules, it was in the context of principles that were being enforced. If he went too far, he was set straight. The institutional order remained secure.

In the case of the Vietnam War, the agency of the maverick was eroded because the hero entered a violent and chaotic world, bereft of a larger moral meaning that could vindicate the violence and provide the foundation for his actions. There was no firm place to stand, no clearcut enemy to fight. Without secure bearings, the struggle for agency was fought on other terms. The triumph of agency became survival itself, the ability to live with tragedies and moral ambiguities of the war, the ability to return home intact.

In 1970, the second year of the Nixon administration, three of the top ten movies—*Patton*, M*A*S*H, and *Catch-22*—were about war. Although none was about Vietnam, the making and reception of each was shaped by Vietnam experience.

Patton (Twentieth Century Fox, 1969, directed by Franklin J. Schaffner) takes place during the Second World War, but the movie plays to the ambivalent feelings of the American public during the

Vietnam era; was the war just or unjust, should the military stay or withdraw? By presenting Patton as a maverick, the filmmakers could make his character appealing to an American public deeply divided about war during the Vietnam era. Francis Ford Coppola, one of the screenwriters, tried to play upon the public's mixed feelings by portraying Patton as a quixotic figure, a "man out of his time." In this way, "people who wanted to see him as a bad guy could say, 'He was crazy, he loved war.' The people who wanted to see him as a hero could say, "We need a man like that now."[5] The movie lets the audience draw its own conclusions about Patton's character by romanticizing his self-reliance and spunk in taking on the military bureaucracy—the movie's subtitle is "Salute to a Rebel"—while simultaneously showing that he went too far, that he was an autocrat, not a democrat.

Like the maverick cops, Patton incorporates many elements of the classic cowboy and frontier hero. The hero is a self-reliant loner who has the daring to fight against great odds. Like other mavericks, Patton rejects the rationalized and technological methods used by big institutions in favor of fighting one-on-one. During a news conference, a reporter asks him what he thinks of "super weapons," and he responds, "There's no honor or glory in it." In an early sequence, the hero rushes into the street during an air raid and fires a pistol at the oncoming planes. In a later scene, Patton takes off in a jeep without informing the other generals on the staff, in an impulsive single-handed attempt to confront Hitler and the German command. When a foot soldier asks where he is going, Patton responds, "Berlin. I'm going to personally shoot that paperhanging son of a bitch."

For all the failings of its hero, Patton presents a positive and patriotic vision of America's mission in the Second World War. In M*A*S*H (directed by Robert Altman) the satire combines a sense of the absurdity of war with a celebration of the maverick hero. Korea is portrayed as a woebegone frontier, where the cause is not clear, and the cavalry has become a big military bureaucracy. The heroes, "Hawkeye" Pierce (Donald Sutherland) and "Trapper" John McIntyre (Elliott Gould) are surgeons in a Mobile Army Surgical Hospital. They are dedicated to their job, but refuse to accept the regimentation of army life.

Hawkeye and Trapper become pranksters, "court jesters" of the war.

They move in and out of their roles as professionals and renegades, purists and hedonists, idealists and cynics, asserting their mastery by healing the wounded, while circumventing the army bureaucracy at every opportunity. In the opening sequence, Hawkeye successfully steals an army jeep and drives himself to his unit. Later in the movie, Hawkeye and Trapper arrive at a military hospital, dressed in civilian clothes and carrying golf clubs, to operate on a general's son. In a confrontation at the hospital, they knock out a superior officer who tries to prevent them on procedural grounds from operating on an Asian baby. The heroes' foils are their sanctimonious coworkers, Major Houlihan (Sally Kellerman), the sexy head nurse, and Major Burns (Robert Duvall), a bumbling doctor, both of whom are ridiculous in their reverence for military protocol.

As a modern comedy, M*A*S*H, like other comedies of recent decades, partakes of the image consciousness prevalent in the culture, poking fun throughout at the way the camp gathers to watch World War II movies. But even as M*A*S*H calls attention to itself as a movie, it sustains the myth of the maverick hero. In the final scene, as Hawkeye prepares to leave, the chaplain blesses the jeep that will take him away as everyone gathers to say goodbye. Over the camp's loudspeaker, a voice announces, "Tonight's movie has been M*A*S*H." Despite this self-conscious gesture, the moral of the tale is more old-fashioned than postmodern. Although M*A*S*H mocks the myth that America only fights good and noble wars, it celebrates another—that the maverick hero, equipped with skill, irreverence and panache, can assert his individuality even in the face of the military bureaucracy, and ride off in triumph in the end.

In contrast to both *Patton* and M*A*S*H, *Catch-22* (directed by Mike Nichols) is a dark satire set during the Second World War without a redeeming vision of America's mission or the power of the maverick hero to triumph over his social circumstances. It portrays the military as a thoroughly oppressive and corrupt organization. The commanding officers order senseless bombing raids, have no regard for the safety of their men or the civilian population, and even collaborate with the enemy to have their own base bombed. The hero, Yossarian (Alan Arkin), a bomber pilot, copes with the military by becoming a maverick and a buffoon, engaging in outlandish acts of defiance. These acts range from refusing to carry out bombing missions to appearing naked at an awards ceremony. The military command tolerates Yossarian's bizarre behavior, for fear that he will expose their corruption if discharged.

Unlike the maverick cops or the heroes of M*A*S*H who cultivate their marginality to exert their mastery, Yossarian has little room to maneuver. His attempts to define himself as the outsider only entangle him further in the irrationality he seeks to escape. He is foiled by his commanding officer, the corrupt Colonel Cathcart (Martin Balsam), at every turn. When Yossarian feigns madness, he discovers the "Catch-22": the only way one can get out of combat duty is to be crazy, but the military insists that anyone who wants to get out of combat cannot be crazy.

The corruption of the military is so thorough, the situation so absurd, that Yossarian can assert his agency only by deserting the military. He tells a friend, "I'm going to call the deal off. . . . All I know is that I don't want to go to prison. I do not want to play Cathcart's game. . . . I've been fighting for my country. . . . I want to start fighting for myself." The last shot of the movie shows Yossarian, a small figure on a raft against a vast expanse of ocean, paddling his way to Sweden.

The isolation and estrangement conveyed by this image are also experienced by the heroes of many Vietnam movies. *Apocalypse Now* (Paramount, 1979, directed by Francis Ford Coppola) shows the military in a state of chaos, immersed in a war it cannot control. The film does not try to explore why America is in Vietnam. The war is simply presented as a hell one goes to in a distant and alien land. In such a world, we see the dark descent of the maverick hero. Agency is imperiled when no rules apply. Heroes once idealistic become renegades and fugitives. The two sides of the renegade maverick are represented by Colonel Kurtz (Marlon Brando) and Captain Willard (Martin Sheen). Kurtz, whose name is drawn from Joseph Conrad's protagonist in *Heart of Darkness*, is a war hero who descends into primitivism and madness after witnessing the effects of Vietnamese terrorism. He breaks with the United States military command and forms his own renegade army of Cambodian natives. The movie's climax involves the encounter between Kurtz and Captain Willard, the assassin commissioned by the American military command to find and "terminate" Kurtz.

After witnessing the senseless violence of the war, the murder of innocent Vietnamese children, and the indifference of American generals who order their men to risk their lives, while remaining safely distant from the fray, Willard has empathy for Kurtz's rebellion against his superiors. Before completing his mission and assassinating Kurtz, Willard, in an internal monologue, reveals his radical isolation from the institution he yet serves, "They were going to make me a major for this, and I wasn't in their fucking army anymore."

The themes of alienation and madness run through other movies about the Vietnam War, but their vision of the military as an institution is not as dark as that of *Apocalypse Now*. The heroes suffer; they bear witness to the senseless violence of the war, the victimization of the Vietnamese, the needless deaths of their comrades. But the theme that looms larger in these other movies is the victimization of the American soldier and his search for meaning and redemption upon his return home. The movies contrast the hero who survives and reclaims his sense of selfhood with his comrades who lose themselves in Vietnam, falling into madness and disillusion.

In *Coming Home* (1978, directed by Hal Ashby) most of the action takes place in America. The ongoing Vietnam War is discussed but never shown. The two central characters who served in the war express conflicting attitudes toward it. Bob (Bruce Dern), a marine captain, returns as a hero, but his war experience leaves him angry and conflicted. He still clings to his beliefs that the goals of the military in Vietnam were valid and that his own actions were honorable, but becomes increasingly unstable and disturbed. He begins to question his identity as a soldier. When his wife Sally (Jane Fonda) and her friend ask him how he received the leg wound that allowed him to return home, he responds with unexpected hostility: "There's nothing to tell. I'm a fucking hero and they're going to give me a medal." A later scene shows the presentation of Bob's medal by the base commander as a ritual without meaning. Bob has nowhere to turn, caught between his questioning of the legitimacy of the institution that has provided the framework for his life, while simultaneously feeling threatened by his doubts.

In contrast to Bob, Luke (Jon Voight) is able to channel his despair into personal protest. He is a disabled veteran who openly questions the legitimacy of the war. After the suicide of one of his friends in a veterans hospital, Luke chains himself to the fence of the military induction center to protest his friend's death and the war. At the movie's conclusion, Luke addresses a high-school assembly. In his wheelchair, dressed in jeans and the long hair of the counterculture, he is contrasted with the marine recruiter in formal military attire who has just addressed the students. Luke tells the students his own story, concluding, "I'm here to tell you it's a lousy thing." He begins to cry, but quickly recovers himself. "There's a lot of shit over there. I'm telling you there is a choice to be made." This sequence is intercut with shots of Bob at the beach, stripping off his marine corps uniform and swimming out to sea in an apparent suicide.

This contrasting response to the Vietnam War and the return home is also the dominant theme in *The Deer Hunter* (1978, directed by Michael Cimino). Unlike *Apocalypse Now* or *Coming Home*, *The Deer Hunter* does not criticize the war or the military. Nor does it show the Americans as perpetrators of violence. Instead, it presents in heightened form a tale of the victimization of the ordinary man who is stripped of his innocence by the war, yet is extraordinary by virtue of his ability to survive the experience without losing his sense of purpose. This theme is developed by comparing the different fates of three friends who go to Vietnam. Only one becomes the agent of his own destiny; the other two are victims of the furies of the war.

The first hour of the movie is infused with a quiet patriotism and commitment to the American way of life. It does so by presenting in rich evocative detail the texture of the lives of the three central characters, Mike (Robert De Niro), Nick (Christopher Walken), and Steve (John Savage), young men who have come of age in a Pennsylvania steel town, and are about to serve in Vietnam. The camera celebrates their hard work in the steel mill, their deer hunting, and the bonds they have with friends and community as they prepare for Steve's wedding.

The transition to the hellish battleground of Vietnam is abrupt and total. The friends experience the cruelty and senselessness of the war: the difficulty of distinguishing friend from foe, the atrocities committed by the enemy, capture and sadistic treatment by the Vietcong. Among the three, Mike emerges as the leader, but he cannot lead them out of the hell they are in. The men are soon separated and their fates are different. Steve is severely injured and returns home disabled for life. Nick is driven mad by the war, and finally kills himself. Mike, however, emerges as the true hero. He does not challenge institutions or break the rules, but he exhibits the self-reliance, diffidence, and cool rationality in the face of crisis that are characteristic of the maverick. "You are a maniac. A control freak," Nick goads him as they talk about deer hunting before leaving for Vietnam. But it is precisely his self-control and inner discipline that allow Mike to endure his brutal sojourn in Vietnam. Like the classic frontiersman, cowboy, and soldier, Mike is a quiet man, a natural leader, whether hunting deer with his friends in the forests of America or fighting in the jungles of Vietnam. His friends panic and fall apart, but Mike goes on. Like the frontier hero, he finds the path home because he is never truly lost. He is guided by an inner strength and conviction that even Vietnam cannot destroy.

Platoon (Hemdale Film Corporation, 1986, directed by Oliver Stone), also focuses on the theme of redemption in survival. The young hero Chris Taylor (Charlie Sheen), like Mike in *The Deer Hunter*, is a patriot who has chosen to go to Vietnam, but discovers there is no honor or glory there. But, unlike *The Deer Hunter*, in which the war is abstracted into an indefinable hell, *Platoon* examines the configurations of this hell with an unsparing eye. We see in much greater detail not only the brutality of the enemy, but the violence and lawlessness among the American troops, and their victimization of the Vietnamese people.

The young hero's gift and the measure of his heroism is that he bears witness to the dissolution of order, yet does not lose his faith or conviction. He affirms the democratic vision of America, even as he endures the hardships of Vietnam. He comes to Vietnam innocent of violence, and leaves knowing the darker side of his soul, yet like the heroes of the Bible and classical myth, he returns home strengthened by his trials.

The struggle within Chris's soul is represented by two authority figures, Sergeants Elias (Willem Dafoe) and Barnes (Tom Berenger). Both are seasoned veterans of Vietnam combat, but their characters are radically different. Sergeant Elias is a compassionate leader and protector of his men. Although skilled in jungle warfare, he is Christ-like in his compassion and fundamental pacifism. Off the battlefield, he is a child of the counterculture, listening to rock music and

smoking pot with his men. Sergeant Barnes is the polar opposite. He
is the incarnation of the violence and brutality of the war, a soldier
whose only goal is survival, a man who sees himself as beyond
common morality. Naturally the two men are adversaries, and finally
Elias reports Barnes for shooting a Vietnamese woman in cold blood
while she begged for her husband's life.

The dramatic turning point comes for Chris when he discovers that
Barnes has shot Elias while their platoon was scattered in the course
of the fighting. Since no one witnessed the crime, it appears that
Barnes will get away with it, and now Chris, pushed by the breakdown
of order, wants to step outside the law himself and kill Barnes. "Let
military justice do the job on him," a friend counters. "Fuck military
justice," responds Chris, now speaking the familiar language of the
cynical maverick cop. "Whose story are they going to believe?" But
unlike many modern maverick heroes, Chris has no position of authority, no freedom to move in and out of the institution he serves.
The army is now embodied in the cruel authority of one man. "I am
reality," Barnes taunts Chris and others he knows want to kill him.
But like the classic American hero, Chris refuses to submit. He
confronts his enemy one-on-one, but on his own terms, never descending to the brutality of his foe. Unable to bear Barnes's arrogant
disdain, Chris lunges at him, but Barnes wins the fight and threatens
to kill him.

Even after this encounter, Chris refuses to take revenge. As the
citizen hero, like the classic cowboy or the maverick cop, he is the
bearer of a common morality, which he breaks from only when
pushed to the extreme. It is only when Barnes tries to kill Chris (as he
did Elias) under cover of battle, that Chris is finally forced to mete out
his own justice. When he meets up with Barnes once again in the
chaos of battle, he kills Barnes in cold blood, even though Barnes is
wounded and defenseless.

This fateful act of violence, which is a radical departure from the
ethic of the classic cowboy and soldier, is the last test Chris endures.
As with the heroes of biblical and classical myth, the violence he
metes out and endures brings forth a deeper knowledge. Other Vietnam movies gesture toward hopes for redemption and renewal, but
Platoon ends with a homily on this theme. "I think now, looking back,
we did not fight the enemy," Chris reflects in a letter home. "We

fought ourselves. The enemy was us. The war is over for me now. But it will always be there for the rest of my days. . . . Those of us who did make it through have an obligation to build again, to teach others what we know, and to find goodness and meaning in this life."

Platoon reiterates a parable as old as the Puritans. For the Puritan, America represented a wilderness that tested the soul of man and of the community. The individual and the band of congregants often fell from the path. But they were exhorted and inspired to face their flaws and to redeem their virtue by a higher calling, a moral and civic purpose they were destined to fulfill. Vietnam is a similar wilderness through which the hero passes before returning home to reaffirm the true meaning of America.

In *Rambo: First Blood Part II* (1985, directed by George Pan Cosmatos) the maverick hero reemerges with a vengeance. John Rambo (Sylvester Stallone) is John Wayne's cowboy-soldier recast as primal man, the maverick as noble savage rising from the mud of Vietnam to redeem his honor and his agency. The archetypical maverick themes are boldly drawn—the individual against the institution, the vindication of patriotic ideals against political corruption and indifference, the affirmation of instinct and nature over civilization and technology, the celebration of self-reliance and one-on-one combat over modern warfare. In this post-Vietnam fable, the Vietnam veteran is no longer victim, but righteous avenger.

In the prologue of the film, the hero is introduced as the outcast who is the true idealist and patriot, the outsider who is asked to come back to tackle a task too difficult and dangerous for others. In the first scene we see Rambo on a prison work crew. We first hear his name when a guard calls out to him. Rambo's former commanding officer, Colonel Trautman, (Richard Crenna) of the Green Berets has come to the prison to ask Rambo to help rescue prisoners of war still in Vietnam. Rambo has the perfect credentials for the mission. He is a decorated Vietnam veteran and himself an escapee from a POW camp. "Sir, do we get to win this time?" asks Rambo. "This time it's up to you," responds Trautman.

Fired by his commitment to the cause, Rambo finds that he is foiled by the institution he serves. He soon learns that his trusted Green Beret commander, Colonel Trautman, will not lead the mission. Instead, an arrogant congressman, Murdock (Charles Napier), is running the show. Much to his surprise, Rambo is ordered only to find the POWs and take pictures. Others will perform the rescue. The movie contrasts the modern military technology the organization commands with the superior natural instincts of the hero. "Don't try the blood and guts routine," Rambo is admonished. "Let technology do the work." Rambo responds maverick-style, "I've always believed the mind is the best weapon."

Like other mavericks, Rambo has a single symbolic weapon, in this case a large knife, which he carefully sharpens in preparation for the mission. In a series of quick cuts the movie contrasts close-ups of Rambo's knife and his bare muscles with medium shots of the high-tech equipment being readied. Once Rambo is airborne, the fancy equipment fails immediately. As he attempts to parachute out of a plane, he becomes entangled in the ropes and is left dangling from the plane. About to die before he has even begun, Rambo cuts himself free with his knife.

Liberated from the encumbrances of modern technology, Rambo moves through the jungle with the ease of an American frontiersman in virgin forests. In contrast to the heroes of Vietnam War movies, he is undaunted by the dangers the jungle presents. The hero of *Platoon* cringes at the sight of snakes; Rambo picks one up and confidently tosses it aside. Armed with only his knife and a bow and arrow, Rambo is in complete command. He knows that men like Murdock consider him expendable, but in the jungle he is a free man, free to carry out the mission on his own terms.

Rambo attains this freedom, paradoxically, when Murdock orders a helicopter support mission aborted and abandons him in the jungle. Deserted, Rambo becomes empowered. On his own, he successfully takes on the forces of both superpowers, relying on instinct and artful sabotage. In a series of daring exploits he outwits Vietnamese soldiers and their heavily armed Russian counterparts. In each encounter he works with his primitive weapons or skillfully uses the superior technology of his enemy against them. The hero's final coup is commandeering a Russian helicopter to transport all the POWs back to the American camp in the jungle.

The drama of the individual against the institution is most vividly portrayed in Rambo's confrontation with Murdock. After Rambo returns to base with the freed American prisoners, he goes into the high-tech control room and machine-guns all the equipment. He then confronts Murdock, who still hides behind his institutional role: "Rambo, I don't make the orders. I take them like you." Rambo pulls out his large knife, threatening Murdock. "You know there are more men out there. You know who they are. Find them or I'll find you."

Like the cowboy and the maverick cop, Rambo walks off alone in the end. Having righted the wrongs, he is ready to leave. Like John Wayne's Davy Crockett in *The Alamo* (1960), Rambo does not want medals or accolades. He brushes off Trautman's remark that he should get a second Medal of Honor for his service on the mission, "You should give it to them [the POWs]. They deserve it more." Like Wayne's Green Beret hero, Colonel Kirby, Rambo is a homespun patriot, a man of few words but deep convictions. His rage is directed at the betrayal of ideals, but he honors the ideals themselves. "Hate [my country]? I'd die for it. . . . I want what every other guy who came over here and spilled his guts wants. For our country to love us as much as we love it."

Love of country and patriotic ideals also infuse movies about the military that are set in the post-Vietnam era. *Top Gun* (1986, directed by Tony Scott), for example, is a modern replay of a John Wayne movie, free of the doubts and ambiguities characteristic of so many movies of the Vietnam era. The hero is a gifted young Navy pilot, Pete Mitchell (Tom Cruise), who goes by the name Maverick. The movie takes place at the elite Navy training school for fighter pilots, nicknamed "Top Gun," where men learn the "lost art of aerial combat" and become "the top fighter pilots in the world." The movie unselfconsciously praises what Vietnam era movies so often scorned: selfless obedience to orders. "We don't make policy. . . . We are the instruments of that policy," instructs their commanding officer. The "best of the best" carry out their duty with pride, and the movie celebrates them in sequence after sequence of breath-taking aerial photography.

True to his nickname, Maverick is a misfit. He is praised as "a hell of an instinctive pilot," but his superiors worry that he is a "wild card" who may be unreliable in combat. His playful antics give them further cause for concern. He buzzes the control tower, making a superior officer spill his coffee. He flies upside down and takes a photograph at the same time. His prowess defies the books, and he is not afraid to challenge his teachers. Off duty, Maverick is freewheeling and fun-loving. As one instructor tells him, "Son, your ego is writing checks your body can't cash."

But, unlike many maverick heroes of the 1970s, the hero's conflict is not with a corrupt or ineffective institution. The military is exemplary in every respect. The elite fighter training school represents a chance to be the best he can be. The conflict lies, rather, in Maverick himself. In the quiet interludes between the flying sequences we learn that his wildness and rule breaking are associated with the death of his father, also a star Navy pilot, whose plane was shot down under ambiguous circumstances during the Vietnam War.

Maverick has an older instructor who provides him with guidance, in the father-figure role so often and skillfully played by John Wayne. He tells Maverick his father was a great hero, but that the circumstances of his death were kept classified because he had crossed over "the wrong line" in aerial combat. Maverick's faith in his father is restored, but he is still haunted by the loss of his flying partner, and still unsure whether he can fly under the pressure of combat. The hero's final test and triumph comes after he graduates from Top Gun and his squadron is in battle over the Indian Ocean. He overcomes a moment of panic and engages the enemy, outwitting and destroying their planes against great odds. After his successful mission, he returns to his ship to buzz the control room in a flyby, once again making a controller spill his coffee. But Maverick is fundamentally a hero who is integrated with his organization. He is the outsider who has come all the way in, a John Wayne-style hero for the 1980s, wholly at ease with the institution he serves.

As *Top Gun* shows, the maverick can be a loyal insider or, as *Rambo* illustrates, a loyal outsider who walks away from the institution once the job is done. The maverick hero enables the movies to absorb the critique of institutions while retaining the mythic resources that empower the hero. Through the maverick hero, rugged individualism can be reconciled with institutional affiliation, self-reliance with social obligation. Most important of all, individual agency and power can be affirmed in a modern world where (outside the movies) the individual feels powerless and diminished. What is intriguing about popular movies is that many present the same social landscape as the art photographers. The difference is the figure in the landscape.

Instead of being fragmented, the individual is empowered. No longer caught within the frame, the figure is animated, mobile, breaking free of social constraints.

Super-Heroes: Ordinary-Extraordinary Men

A variation on the insider-outsider role of the maverick is the hero with a double identity—now the common man, now the super-hero. Unlike the maverick, the super-hero does not rebel against the methods and practices of the institutions he serves. He is usually a conventional person who works cooperatively with organizations, defending their goals and respecting their practices. In *Superman* (1978, directed by Richard Donner), the hero's mission is to fight for "truth, justice, and the American way." Superman (Christopher Reeve) upholds these ideals both in the role of Clark Kent, the shy, bumbling, bespectacled newspaper reporter, and when he dons his costume and becomes a super-hero. Superman represents the fantasy of immense individual power, always exercised on behalf of the community.

The Superman movies replay the law-and-order theme, without the social and moral ambiguities that beset the maverick cop. Superman never has to do dirty work, fire a gun, or endure the disdain of his superiors. He is the all-American cosmic enforcer who flies above the fray. His identity as a common man is both a contrast and a complement to his identity as super hero. In the persona of Clark Kent he is a laughable if well-intentioned wimp, whose idea of confronting a gun-toting mugger is to sermonize, "You can't solve society's problems with a gun." As Superman, no criminal is a match for him. He can catch bullets in his bare hand, prop up the president's plane when an engine fails, divert a nuclear warhead from its target, and even bring the dead back to life. But Clark Kent represents an essential aspect of Superman's character. He is a nonviolent hero, a modest man who never seeks fame or glory.

Superman's dual identity as ordinary citizen and extraordinary being is distinctively American. In marked contrast to the Nietzchean conception of a superman characterized by a will to power and a disdain for common morality, Superman is a self-effacing team player. When he brings the crooks back to prison at the conclusion of the first movie, the grateful warden says, "This country is safe thanks to you." "Don't thank me, warden," replies Superman. "We're all part of the same team." Like James Stewart's citizen hero in *Mr. Smith Goes to Washington*, Superman is an unabashed patriot, a believer in the American ideals of family, community, and individual service. He embodies the distinctly American paradox of being the uncommon common man.

This paradox has been part of the Superman myth ever since he made his comic-strip debut in 1938. But unlike the earlier comic strips, the Superman movies (1978, 1980, 1983, 1987) incorporate a double message. On the one hand, they play the story straight, reveling in the hero's feats, celebrating his homey virtues, and elaborating on the cosmic nature of his calling. The first movie, for example, is interspersed with mythic sequences in which Superman goes into outer space where his dead father from Krypton (Marlon Brando) instructs and guides him in the use of his powers. But even as the movie moves within the myth, it also steps outside it, self-consciously calling attention to the story's form, and winking to the audience in a series of inside jokes. On the way to rescue Lois Lane (Margot Kidder), for example, Superman looks longingly at a phone booth (the classic place for quick changes in the comic-book versions of the story); but it is a modern booth, open to the elements rather than enclosed, so he must change in a hotel. In romantic and rescue scenes, the tone shifts from sentimental to satirical, always drawing on the audience's awareness of how the new version of the story departs from the old.

However, this self-conscious attention to the story's plot and form does not unravel the mythic elements of the movie. By vacillating from the fanciful to the satirical, the movie widens its appeal to include both sophisticates and believers, parents and children. Underlying the satire, the simple plot, the stereotypic characters, and the extraordinary special effects is a parable of individual agency rooted in commitment to the community.

Batman (Warner Brothers, 1989, directed by Tim Burton) is also based on a comic-strip character, and is another variation on the Superman theme. The tone of the movie, however, is darker. Batman's (Michael Keaton) double identity has a different cast, too. Unlike the mild-mannered Clark Kent, who comes from the middle

American heartland, Batman's other self, Bruce Wayne, is a rich, self-assured millionaire, who lives in a grand house with a butler. Like Superman, he has lost his parents at an early age, but the cause of their death strikes much closer to home, evoking a deeply shared anxiety in the audience: his parents were murdered by muggers in a city alleyway as young Bruce watched in helpless horror. The plot is further tied together by the revelation, toward the end of the movie, that Batman's evil adversary, the Joker (Jack Nicholson), was the mugger who killed his parents years before.

Although the setting of Batman is fantastic, the themes of urban lawlessness and disorder, crime and retribution closely parallel movies like *Dirty Harry*, *Die Hard* and *Death Wish*. The hero is a lone fighter against crime who bails out a well-intentioned but weak police department. "The police have got it wrong," Batman tells Vicki Vale (Kim Basinger), the ace photographer who is covering his exploits. Through a masterly analysis of the clues, Batman has determined that the Joker has poisoned hundreds of chemicals that go into cosmetic products, and urges Vale to take the information to the press. But she hesitates:

VALE: A lot of people think you're as dangerous as the Joker.
BATMAN: He's psychotic.
VALE: Some people say the same thing about you.
BATMAN: What people?
VALE: Well, let's face it. You're not exactly normal, are you?
BATMAN: It's not exactly a normal world.

In contrast to Superman, Batman is a super-hero who still must prove himself. Like Dirty Harry, Batman is scorned and doubted by the people he serves. Undaunted by the doubts of others, Batman proves himself in feat after daring feat. Yet with all his powers, he is decent and self-effacing. He only becomes Batman as a last resort. He would much rather lead a normal life.

Yet another version of the hero with a double identity is Indiana Jones of Steven Spielberg's mythic adventure films, *Raiders of the Lost Ark* (1981), *Indiana Jones and the Temple of Doom* (1984) and *Indiana Jones and the Last Crusade* (1989). In one part of his life, he is Dr. Jones, dedicated academic and archaeologist, the picture of convention in his staid suit and glasses, a man whose passion is facts and footnotes. But in the other, more expansive part of his life, he is Indiana Jones, archaeologist-adventurer, world traveler, and maverick hero, who thinks nothing of climbing out the window to escape his clamoring students.

Like the classic maverick hero, Indiana (Harrison Ford) does not initiate his missions, but is called upon by others who need his special skills, yet often end up disparaging or betraying him. The rich American businessman who hires Indiana to search for the Holy Grail in *Indiana Jones and the Last Crusade* turns out to be a Nazi. Though good guys (American army intelligence officers) hire Indiana in *Raiders of the Lost Ark*, they too foil him in the end. After Indiana locates the Ark, they thank him and pay him handsomely, but they will not let him have access to it. "We have top men working on it," they claim. "Who?" asks Jones, who is himself, together with his partner, Marcus (Denholm Elliott) among the top men in the field. "Top men," the intelligence officer stonewalls. "Fools, bureaucratic fools," Jones grumbles to his partner and lover Marion (Karen Allen). The last scene of the movie shows that the officer has lied; the sacred Ark is filed away and forgotten in a cavernous government warehouse in a box marked "top secret."

But aside from this dramatic example of bureaucratic betrayal, Indiana's adventures are set comfortably in the past, free of the moral and political ambiguities that plague contemporary maverick cops and soldiers. The good and bad guys are defined with comic-book clarity, and Indiana pursues them with the earnest dedication of a boy-hero from an adventure book. "Nazis, I hate these guys," he says to himself looking up at an Austrian castle with the self-assured innocence of Tom Sawyer or the Hardy Boys. Like other mavericks from the movies, Indiana thwarts his technologically superior foes using simple old-fashioned methods. Instead of carrying a gun, Indiana has a special whip, which he uses like a cowboy's lasso to disarm his enemies. In *Raiders of the Lost Ark* he chases a Nazi truck riding a white horse. In *Indiana Jones and the Last Crusade*, he rides on horseback against a rocket-shooting Nazi tank, leaps from his horse to the tank, picks off the Nazis one by one, and frees his father (Sean Connery), also an archaeologist, held captive inside. He pursues his enemies across the world, dons disguises, and masters modern technology with ease.

Despite his special gifts, Indiana is never portrayed as a grand figure. Like many American heroes, he is "revered" with irreverence. He is at once larger than life and continually cut down to size. Indiana's father orders him around and calls him "Junior" when they work together to find the Holy Grail in *Indiana Jones and the Last Crusade*. Indiana's partner and lover, Marion, in *Raiders of the Lost Ark*, is a feisty maverick in her own right. When he first visits her in Nepal she punches him for neglecting her for so long and forces him to take her along on his mission because he owes her money. The irreverent attitude toward the hero is also conveyed through self-conscious parody of the genre itself. In one episode, Indiana confronts a huge Egyptian brandishing an enormous sword. Instead of going one-on-one in heroic combat, whip against sword, Indiana nonchalantly pulls out a gun and shoots his enemy instead.

Through the character of Indiana Jones, Spielberg's movies are able to both mock and sustain their mythic elements. Like many maverick heroes, Indiana is a skeptic when it comes to grand ideals and myths. "We cannot take mythology at face value," he lectures his students near the beginning of *Indiana Jones and the Last Crusade*. "Archaeology is the search for facts, not the truth." When others, including his father and his older colleague Marcus, speak of the extraordinary spiritual powers of the Holy Grail, Indiana pooh-poohs this as a "bedtime story."

Once his father is captured by the Nazis, however, Indiana temporarily sheds his modern skepticism and becomes a believer. After his father is shot by the Nazis near the place where the Holy Grail is hidden, Indiana learns that only the healing power of the Grail can save him. Following his father's instructions and using his own inner resources, Indiana recovers the Grail and heals his father. Once his mission is accomplished, the tone of the movie quickly shifts from spiritual to earthy, from classic myth to the homegrown American kind, in which irreverence is mixed with reverence, humor is mixed with homage. "What did you find, Dad?" Indiana asks his father. "Illumination," his father responds. "And what did you find, Junior?" This paternal condescension breaks the mood at once. But as they ride off, father goodnaturedly defers to son. "After you Junior," he says teasingly. As the camera lingers affectionately on the departing figures, we are suddenly back to the landscape of American

mythology, with father and son riding off into the sunset like cowboys in a western epic.

Like the Indiana Jones movies, George Lucas's mythic space adventures, *Star Wars* (1977), *The Empire Strikes Back* (1980), and *Return of
the Jedi* (1983), fuse classical and contemporary myths through the
pairing of two contrasting heroes. Luke Skywalker (Mark Hamill) is a
virtuous, idealistic, young Jedi knight who learns to use the power of
good, "the Force" to overcome the imperial foes. His partner and
friend, Han Solo (Harrison Ford), is a crude but endearing maverick
who lives the myth in irreverent opposition to it; who does not
espouse ideals, yet redeems the ideals in the end; who appears at first
as a mercenary, but ends by nobly sacrificing his own interests for the
sake of the virtuous band of rebels.

Early in the saga, Han Solo dismisses the spiritual teachings of the
Jedi knights: "I've been from one side of the galaxy to another. I don't
believe in a mystical force." He is not even willing to help rescue the
captured Princess Leia until Luke Skywalker suggests there will be a
reward. In contrast, Luke Skywalker believes in the cause of the
rebels, and aspires to be a virtuous knight. Through his character, the
Lucas movies can give full expression to their classical mythic elements. In the climactic scene of *Star Wars*, as the rebels begin their
attack on the space station of Darth Vader, the leader of the imperial
forces, Luke hears the voice of his mentor telling him "the Force will
be with you always." Luke turns off the fancy computer in his space
craft and flies into the enemy stronghold, trusting his deeper instincts. Along with Han Solo and the other rebels, he destroys the
space station in this mythic version of a classic war movie.

This type of scene also replays, with more explicit mythic import,
the confrontations of maverick cops with their technologically superior foes. In *Die Hard* the cop hero has nothing but instinct and
intuition to rely on as he faces the heavily armed terrorist-thieves.
"Think, think," he tells himself when he realizes he must go it alone.
In *Sudden Impact*, Harry Callahan makes constant, though self-
deprecating, references to being "psychic" and "intuitive" when it
comes to outwitting criminals. This reliance on intuition is shared by
Luke Skywalker's maverick partner, Han Solo, as well.

Most American heroes are self-effacing, more likely to believe in intuition and instinct than grand ideals, more likely to be called to the cause than to be initiators of the struggle. They fight on the right side, but not always with the right attitude. Sometimes they are idealists like John Wayne's Davy Crockett and Colonel Kirby, but often they are skeptics and cynics like Humphrey Bogart's Rick Blaine or Clint Eastwood's Harry Callahan. Their cynicism, however, masks a deeper idealism. They are willing to sacrifice for the good of others, even as they insist on remaining autonomous from institutions and unfettered by their constraints.

The typical mythic structure sets the hero apart from the institution he serves. John Wayne movies make this point by showing that the hero can be a self-reliant maverick who calls his own shots while working within institutions. Clint Eastwood movies make the point by setting the hero against the law enforcement bureaucrats. *Star Wars* makes the point by drawing the lines between the institution and the individual in bold mythic lines—good versus evil, the individual against the empire. Since part of the American way is to resist institutional conformity, to rebel against authority, the maverick as insider-outsider or as the bearer of a double identity is well-suited to sustaining the myth. Social criticism and the celebration of institutions easily coexist.

The distinctive character of American heroes can be seen by contrast with the popular British hero, James Bond. From the first James Bond movie, *Dr. No*, in 1962, to the present, these spy-adventure films have ranked among the top-ten box-office draws for Americans. Like the modern American mavericks, Bond is a professional whose work demands a high degree of self-reliance and the ability to engage in one-on-one combat. But unlike the typical American maverick, Bond's relationship with his superiors is unproblematic and the secret organization he serves is presented in a glowing light.

In American movies the hero is rarely an agent or spy. The FBI and CIA are more likely to be portrayed as arrogant bureaucracies that foil the hero, or worse, as rogue organizations, immoral and conspiratorial, that threaten the hero's life. In *Three Days of the Condor* (1975), the CIA is depicted as a violent organization that kills its own members in interdepartmental power struggles. In *Marathon Man* (1976), the hero is hunted by "the Division," a secret government organization that "fills in the gap between the FBI and CIA," that rationalizes collaboration with Nazi war criminals by telling the hero, "We cut both ways." In *The Eiger Sanction* (1975), Clint Eastwood plays a cynical hired assassin who joins the CIA to do some good for his country, but quickly learns that there is little difference between the CIA and the enemies they fight.

In contrast, the officials of the British Secret Service are not cold and brutal bureaucrats, but witty, charming, and highly competent. They support the hero on his dangerous missions with an impressive array of state-of-the-art technology. If Bond falls off a cliff, a parachute suddenly pops out to bring him safely to the ground. If an enemy corners him, a concealed weapon pops out to foil his foe.

Unlike the American hero, who is plain-spoken, self-effacing, and ill at ease among sophisticates, James Bond represents the fantasy of ultimate mastery in every sphere. He is the "Renaissance man" of the modern age, a master at moving in and out of roles and poses, a man at ease in many cultures. There is no tension between nature and civilization, self and society. He is not the New-World hero who has to define himself against society, but the Old-World hero, already comfortably civilized, the ultimate insider.

In other respects, though, Bond resembles the American maverick. He is backed up by technology, but he is not a technocrat. He works cooperatively within a highly rationalized organization, but he is not an organization man. He is supremely independent, versatile, and innovative. The fancy gadgets of the Secret Service get Bond into the enemies' strongholds, but once inside, he is on his own to face the vast technology of his foes.

Like the American maverick, James Bond expresses his agency and command through the laconic remark, the pun that shows that he can say the right thing when words would fail the ordinary person. Bond, however, is a much more self-conscious and self-satisfied hero. He does not have to fight abuse and disdain like Dirty Harry and his fellow maverick cops. Nor does Bond display any of the homespun idealism of Superman. In Bond's stylized realm, questions of ideology are beside the point. There is no tension between his roles as insider and as outsider; he is the consummate insider with an outward gaze, a performer with a self-conscious appreciation of his own act. "I hope you enjoyed the show," he remarks to his Russian partner, the beautiful Triple X in *The Spy Who Loved Me* (1977), after he has fought off several villains in front of some Egyptian tombs.

Though James Bond is from the outset an image-conscious hero, with every plot combining fast action and tongue-in-cheek humor, by the 1970s another element is added to the image consciousness— winking references to American movies. In *The Spy Who Loved Me* (1977), for example, the villain's henchman is a hulk of a man with metal teeth and braces, named "Jaws," who at one point, kills a shark by gripping it in his powerful mouth. In *Moonraker* (1979), Bond smashes a bad guy against a piano and says, "Play it again, Sam." When Bond rides with others across a plain dressed as gauchos, the theme from the popular television western "Bonanza" plays. When Bond cracks a secret scientific code, the background music mimics that of another Steven Spielberg hit movie, *Close Encounters of the Third Kind* (1977).

The image consciousness and winking allusions parallel the style of the hero himself and enhance the stylish, tongue-in-cheek quality of the films. Just as Bond's puns and one-liners prove his mastery over every situation, so the references to movies and other icons of American popular culture prove once again the ability of blockbuster movies both to mock and magnify their own myths.

Citizen Heroes: Triumphs of the Common Man

In vivid contrast to the glamorous, urbane, and stylishly self-conscious Bond, most American heroes are cut from rougher cloth. Rarely moving in the spheres of the elite, they are more likely to be men of the people. Nowhere is the American fable of the triumph of the ordinary man more directly told than in *Rocky* (1976) and its many successful sequels (1979, 1982, 1985, 1990). *Rocky* is the story of an Italian boxer, Rocky Balboa (Sylvester Stallone), a nobody who becomes somebody, an underdog who becomes a champion. Like the heroes of Frank Capra's movies, Rocky is a common man of uncommon character.

The first movie in the series, *Rocky*, is a simple story of a boxer who makes good on his own terms. This modern Horatio Alger story chronicles the hero's rise from loser to national hero. But the deeper story of *Rocky* reiterates a core theme running through Capra's movies—the virtue and incorruptibility of the ordinary citizen.

Like so many American heroes, Rocky finds his life changed by a stroke of fate. Apollo Creed, America's champion boxer, is looking for a new challenger for a fight on the Fourth of July. Apollo comes up with a scheme that will boost attendance and hype the fight. "Give a local boy a shot on this country's birthday," he tells his inner circle. "I like it," responds his manager. "It's very American." "No," says Apollo smiling, "It's very smart." After looking at film footage of various boxers, he decides on Rocky. Apollo, who is black, wants a "snow-white contender," and Rocky fits the part. "Apollo Creed meets the Italian Stallion," Apollo laughs, ever the self-conscious performer. "It sounds like a monster movie."

Like Capra's Jefferson Smith or John Doe, Rocky is cast in a role by the established powers, who want to use him for their scheme. Like Capra's heroes, Rocky remains true to himself amidst the phoniness and the hype. He is the self-reliant hero without pride or overreaching ambition. For Rocky the fight represents his opportunity to prove himself. Without fancy equipment or staff, he trains in his neighborhood gym, and runs every morning at dawn down the streets and back alleys of the city. For Rocky, the fight is not a show but a personal quest. He sets his own goal, not to win but to go the distance and to be standing after fifteen rounds.

Apollo, in contrast, is the consummate performer, a prideful champion who sees patriotism as merely something to exploit in a media event in which he will star. He enters the fight dressed as Uncle Sam and throws silver dollars to the crowd. By contrast, Rocky quietly prays in preparation for the fight and appears without fanfare. Rocky succeeds in lasting the fifteen rounds and proves his heart and skill as a fighter.

In the sequels to *Rocky*, the hero returns to the ring, and continues to display the virtues of self-reliance, patriotism, and faith. The simplicity and authenticity of the hero are continually contrasted with the false and fabricated images the media creates. In *Rocky II*, for example, the hero is cajoled into making television commercials, at which he miserably fails. He must constantly resist attempts to refashion and glamorize his image.

Rocky IV casts the Rocky story within a broader mythic framework.

This late Cold War parable pits Rocky against the monstrous Russian fighter Drago. Drago is presented as an automaton, the powerful embodiment of Russian technology and totalitarianism. Rocky's erstwhile opponent Apollo, now a friend, takes on Drago against Rocky's advice, and in a bloody battle is killed.

Rocky then decides to fight Drago to redeem the death of his friend. As he prepares for the fight Rocky assumes the mantle of the classic citizen hero. He is the natural man, while Drago is a creature of technology and steroids. When he goes to Russia to fight Drago, Rocky recreates the American frontier on Russian soil, and finds his strength there. He lives in a simple cabin, "no sparring, no TV." He trains alone in the snow—loading rocks, pulling sleds, carrying huge logs, scaling the lonely mountains, with only his trainer and brother-in-law providing moral support. When his wife joins him in his lonely outpost his rejuvenation is complete. He is ready to take on the seemingly invincible Russian.

Fighting on foreign territory in front of a hostile crowd, Rocky once again wins the hearts of his detractors. The hero is pummeled by his Russian foe, but refuses to give in. Somehow he finds the strength to fight his way to victory, and the Russians who once booed him now chant his name. The movie ends with the victorious Rocky draped in an American flag, being carried aloft by ordinary Russians in defiance of the party officials.

The Rocky stories are pure American fable with no dark vision to complicate the dream. In Oliver Stone's *JFK* (1991), by contrast, the citizen hero finds corruption at the center of the dream. In *JFK*, Stone addresses the event that came to symbolize the violence that threatened the American dream—the assassination of John F. Kennedy. Stone argues through his movie that Kennedy's murder was not the doing of a lone gunman, as the Warren Commission concluded, but the result of a conspiracy conducted and concealed at the highest levels of government. He suggests that beyond the tragedy of Kennedy's death is the deceit and corruption of American democracy itself.

It is difficult to imagine a darker portrayal of American institutions. Capra's cigar-chomping party bosses and conniving capitalists seem benign by comparison. Despite the severity of Stone's indictment, however, the point of his movie is not to reveal a hollowness at the core of the American dream. On the contrary, the story his movie tells is the classic myth-affirming tale of a maverick hero who pursues the truth against all odds and seeks to validate America's noblest ideals. The hero in this case is Jim Garrison (Kevin Costner), the New Orleans district attorney who sought to prove that Kennedy's assassination was the result of a conspiracy. Garrison is portrayed as the citizen hero, the true patriot whose unwavering idealism and perseverance give us faith in a democracy that is threatened by institutional decay.

Like Capra's heroes, Garrison embodies the best of American virtues. He is a dedicated family man, a hard worker, and a concerned citizen. But like Gary Cooper's sheriff in *High Noon*, he finds that taking a stand leads to isolation. Even his wife Liz (Sissy Spacek), like Amy Fowler in *High Noon*, at first fails to understand the importance of his mission. "You care more about John Kennedy than you do about your own family," she complains when he fails to show up for an Easter dinner. "All day the kids were saying, 'Where's Daddy?' What am I supposed to tell your kids, Jim?" Garrison replies, "I don't know what to tell them. How about the truth? I'm doing my job to make sure they grow up in a country where justice will not be an arcane, vanished idea they read about in a history book, like dinosaurs or the lost continent of Atlantis."

Some of *JFK*'s dramatic techniques are strikingly reminiscent of *Mr. Smith Goes to Washington*. When Garrison goes to Washington to meet with an important informant (Donald Sutherland), the scene takes place in front of the Lincoln Memorial, where Jefferson Smith's secretary-friend urged him to confront the party machine. Garrison's informant, a retired intelligence operative, describes how members of the CIA conspired with military officials and other government figures to assassinate Kennedy. "I never realized Kennedy was so dangerous to the establishment," Garrison earnestly replies. As they move to another location, the Washington Monument now looming in the background, the informant urges Garrison to continue his investigation.

Just as Jefferson Smith took his case to the Senate floor, Jim Garrison offers his argument before a jury in the trial of Clay Shaw, a businessman who once worked for the CIA. Garrison accuses Shaw of participating in the assassination conspiracy, but his speech to the jury is about the fate of American democracy. "The ghost of JFK confronts us with a secret murder at the heart of the American dream. He forces on us the appalling question of 'What is our Constitution made of?' What is the future of a democracy where a president can be assassinated under suspicious circumstances while the machinery of legal action scarcely trembles? I submit that what took place on November 22, 1963 was a coup d'état."

But even the dark secret at the heart of the American dream does not turn the citizen hero to cynicism. Instead, he urges redemption in the regenerative vision of the mythic American frontier. "We had better find the truth," Garrison asserts, "or we might just as well build ourselves another government like the *Declaration of Independence* says to when the old one ain't working, just a little farther out west. An American naturalist wrote, 'A patriot must always be ready to defend his country against its government.'"

Garrison loses the case, but not his ideals or his determination to fight. After the verdict, reporters surround him, asking if he plans to resign. "Hell no," he replies, and vows to continue his investigation. The film closes with Garrison walking away from the crowd, walking arm-in-arm with his wife and young son, bathed in a mythic golden light.

JFK plays out in vivid terms two tendencies present in contemporary American political culture. On one level, it expresses the fear that American institutions are in the grip of powerful forces that defy our understanding and control, while at the same time it displays the persistence of the classic maverick hero. His insider-outsider status and his self-reliant idealism equip him to survive, and even flourish, in a world that frustrates conventional action.

On another level, Stone's movie powerfully displays a tendency, some would say a danger, implicit in the image-conscious culture we inhabit. This is the tendency to blur the distinction between the event and the image, between document and art. Stone's movie is a skillful melange of actual documentary footage, simulated documentary footage, and dramatic reenactments. Often, the images appear and disappear so quickly that it is difficult to distinguish the real images from the fabricated ones. Clips of Eisenhower, Kennedy, and the famous Zapruder home movie of the assassination in Dallas are interspersed with documentary-like reenactments and traditional

Hollywood acting. Perhaps Stone intended by this technique to enhance the veracity of his movie, to lend documentary weight to the claims the movie made; perhaps, on the other hand, he sought to confer mythic dimensions on an actual event, to ennoble a controversial prosecutor with the mantle of art. Whatever Stone had in mind, his movie reminds us that, in contemporary culture, the boundary between the event and the image may be more precarious than we sometimes suppose.

Epilogue

TAKEN TOGETHER, THE IMAGE-CONSCIOUS SENSIBILITY AND THE aspiration to the mythic contend in our culture and provide the setting for much of contemporary political discourse. As sophisticates of the video age, we are alive as never before to the artifice that constitutes the pose. We are as fascinated by how images are made as we are by what they mean. In art photography, movies, and political discourse, we have elevated the image-making process to a subject in its own right. In some moods we are connoisseurs of the slickly produced image, whether in political ads, pop art, or popular movies. In other moods we are outraged by the distortions and deceits that images purvey.

Fascinated though we are with the process of image making, another side of us believes in the images we see. This belief stems from the fact that images are bearers of meanings, enduring carriers of ideals and myths. It also stems from our continuing confidence in the camera's ability to record reality and document facts.

These two cultural tendencies, our self-consciousness about image making and the persistence of mythic ideals, have played themselves out in intriguing ways in American politics, and in television coverage of politics, since the 1968 campaign. While the network evening newscasts increasingly focused attention on how the campaigns constructed images for television, the candidates, for all their mastery of television techniques, still conducted their campaigns by invoking traditional ideals. In 1980 and 1984, Ronald Reagan masterfully tapped into American myths, often using the movies as the sources for his political metaphors. In 1988, George Bush drew on these same themes, casting himself as the patriot who would defend the country against its foes and defend the values of family, community, and self-reliant individualism against big government.

For all its attention to the stagecraft of the Bush and Dukakis campaigns in 1988, the image-conscious reporting of the networks failed in two respects. It inflated the importance of the process of image making without adequately assessing the meaning of the images themselves. As I have argued, calling attention to the image as an image may not be enough to dissolve its hold. The reason is not that images are more powerful than words, but that certain images resonate with meanings and ideals that run deep in American culture.

To be successful, criticism of politicians who claim to uphold American ideals cannot rest with simply revealing that they pose for pictures against flattering backdrops. Who in this modern age of television does not stage events for the camera? The networks, after all, stage their evening newscasts every night with backdrops, carefully written scripts, and makeup for their anchors and reporters. The stagecraft of the newscasts may be more polished now, but it has always been part of broadcasting the news. A veteran reporter of the 1968 campaign recollects, "we were all sitting around talking and someone said, 'Nixon is wearing makeup.' I said, 'Look around, guys. Everybody at this table is wearing makeup. Where do we get off criticizing the politicians?' We were in theater, but we didn't like the idea."[1]

To plan or stage an event for the press does not in itself falsify its content, as the history of press coverage of political events amply demonstrates. Before a Vietnamese Buddhist monk burned himself to death in 1963 in protest against his government's policies, his supporters notified the Associated Press, which recorded the event in a famous photograph. Similarly, leaders of the civil-rights movement learned to time their demonstrations so that television could carry their message to the nation. Communicating through television images is part of modern discourse. The distinction between real and pseudo-events must be judged not on the method of presentation but on the content of the event itself.

To fulfill its documentary purpose, political reporting must engage the content of political candidates' ideals and assess the substance of their claims. For example, when Bush rode a boat on Boston Harbor in 1988, coverage should not have rested with the revelation that he contrived a media event to undermine Dukakis's reputation as an environmentalist; instead, it should have assessed each candidate's record and program on the environment. Similarly, when Ross Perot campaigned in 1992 as an outsider to politics, as an entrepreneur in the spirit of American individualism, the coverage should have focused, as some of it did, on how well the image fit with the facts of his career, not simply on his standings in the polls or his skills at impression management.

Some failures of image-conscious coverage were corrected in the 1992 campaign coverage. The networks, inspired by the "ad watches" developed by print journalists and local television in their coverage of the 1990 campaigns, began systematically checking the veracity of candidates' commercials, instead of using them as illustrations of campaign image making. ABC's "World News Tonight" announced that it would "avoid sound bites that are designed exclusively for TV news consumption." The "CBS Evening News" declared that it would run no sound bite of a presidential candidate less than thirty seconds in length. NBC sought to break with the syndrome of short sound bites by airing three-and-a-half-minute excerpts of the candidates' stump speeches.[2] Newsweek magazine, in full-page newspaper ads touting its convention coverage, promised, "No sound bites. No stories driven by photo ops. No 'in depth' reporting in 90 seconds."[3]

Meanwhile, image-conscious coverage as a style of political reporting had spread from television news to print journalism. Reporting on an Illinois rally for Bill Clinton and Al Gore, the New York Times described the campaign's efforts to gather a good crowd and then observed, "It looks so much better on the evening news when the heartland is crowded."[4] Another Times story reported on the Democratic ticket's appearance at a town meeting in West Virginia, where a statue of John Kennedy "loomed behind the men as they spoke, an irresistible television shot."[5] Under the headline "Playing Diplomat on Television," a New York Times story on the Bush campaign noted,

"The President's media consultants could hardly have scripted a better picture than the sight over the weekend of George Bush as Commander in Chief, an American flag draped behind him and the Presidential seal in front of him."[6]

For their part, political candidates, sensing the disenchantment of the public with politicians and media alike, explicitly renounced the politics of sound bites and image consciousness. Independent candidate Ross Perot found that to an electorate wary of artifice, campaigning as the earnest citizen and political outsider was a promising political strategy. He publicly resolved that he would be a candidate without handlers, and in a much-reported sound bite, deflected questions about details of his economic policy by saying, "I am not going to sound-bite it."

Despite the networks' promises, the shrinking sound bite continued to shrink. The average sound bite was only 8.8 seconds in the primaries and 8.4 seconds in the general election.[7] But the 1992 campaign did signal an end to television campaigns waged primarily on the network evening newscasts. Seeking more sustained television exposure than the nightly newscasts afforded, President George Bush and challengers Bill Clinton and Ross Perot made frequent use of other television venues, including talk shows and quasi-news programs such as "Larry King Live" (CNN), "Donahue" (syndicated), "Arsenio Hall," (syndicated), "Today" (NBC), "Good Morning America" (ABC), "This Morning" (CBS), and even MTV. On some of these programs, the candidates were able to answer questions for one or two hours of unedited airtime, making possible a return to a more extended form of political discourse.

Critics of this development, including some from the networks and some print journalists, complained that the candidates' new emphasis on talk shows and "infotainment" programs was a way of circumventing professional journalists; answering questions from viewers or talk-show hosts offered the benefits of favorable television exposure without the challenge of probing, critical questions from hard-news reporters.

But this objection, while valid in principle, overlooked the extent to which the network evening newscasts had already abandoned sustained attention to hard news in favor of entertainment-driven stories and production techniques. The fast pacing and quick cutting, the slick graphics and short sound bites, the shift in emphasis from political coverage to soft-news, life-style, and human-interest stories, had hardly left the network evening newscasts a bastion of sobriety and substance. It is not clear that the public learned less watching Bush, Clinton or Perot on a talk show than watching the slickly produced packages of images and words that the evening news presented.

The politicians' 1992 campaign against image-conscious politics attempted to draw its power by connecting with the mythic dimensions of the American popular imagination. As disillusion with politics has grown in recent years, Americans have come to doubt the ability of any power or person to exercise meaningful control over events, or to make a fundamental difference in the course of the nation's collective life. Vast structures of power and intractable domestic problems seem to defy the mastery of presidents, let alone ordinary citizens.

In response to the growing sense of disempowerment, a number of presidential candidates, groping for an idiom of agency, have intuitively portrayed themselves in the mode of the maverick hero depicted in American movies—as outsiders to Washington and the political establishment, as redeemers of the ideals betrayed by unresponsive political institutions. In 1968 and 1972, the conservative Southern populist, George Wallace, ran as the angry outsider, the critic of the "pointy-headed bureaucrats" who disempowered ordinary Americans by such policies as "forced busing" to desegregate schools. In 1972, the liberal Midwestern populist, George McGovern, sought to cleanse the American soul from its corruption by the Vietnam War, bidding the country, "Come home, America," in a refrain of redemption. In 1976, Jimmy Carter, combining the Southern and progressive strands of populist protest, ran against Washington and won the presidency. In 1992, Paul Tsongas, Jerry Brown, and Ross Perot tried, with varying degrees of success, to tap the mood of discontent by presenting themselves as outsiders to the Washington establishment who nonetheless stood as embodiments of American ideals.

But the most successful practitioner of the insider-outsider politics of the mythic American maverick hero was Ronald Reagan. Not only did he run against government while seeking the presidency in 1968, 1976, and 1980, but even as a sitting president, Reagan managed, to the frustration of his political opponents, to present himself as the righteous outsider to the government he led. More than just an outsider, Reagan stood, like the citizen heroes of Frank Capra and the cowboy heroes of American myth, as the redeemer of American individualism and idealism.

It was during the 1980s, in the wake of Reagan's successful evocation of mythic American imagery, that the television networks most decisively turned to an image-conscious style of political reporting. Instead of focusing on how Reagan's and Bush's ideals fit with their policies and programs, the networks became fixated on the image-making process itself, a fixation that, ironically, only served to highlight the successes of Reagan and Bush in manipulating the media.

It was not that the networks favored the Republicans in their political coverage. They focused equally on the gaffes and "failed images" of both sides. But because the networks shifted their emphasis from the content of political speech to techniques of image manipulation, they unwittingly gave an advantage to the side that ran the most effective media events, sound bites and political ads.

As the newscasts came to focus on the process of image making rather than on the content of the images themselves, they unintentionally adopted a stance quite similar to that of the art photographers of the 1960s. Like the art photographers, television reporters became iconoclasts, trying to expose images and thereby to break their hold. But like the art photographers and pop artists, they found themselves bound to the very images they attempted to deflate. Like Andy Warhol's pop art or Cindy Sherman's movie-star poses, television news began to generate copies of copies, as it repeatedly aired the ads and media events of the campaigns.

The same questions that cultural critics asked of Warhol's or Sherman's art can also be asked of television news. Does the repetition of fabricated images amount to critical commentary or does it reinforce the power of illusion, by never moving beyond the artifice of image making? Are Warhol's serial images of Coca Cola bottles or Marilyn Monroe an ironic commentary on our consumer society or a celebration of it? When Cindy Sherman photographs herself posing as various movie stars, does she liberate us from the stereotypes she depicts, or does she reiterate and entrench those stereotypes?

The paradox of the television reporting of the 1988 campaign is that the reporters made an idol of the image. But, unlike the art photographers, television reporters were obliged as journalists to document reality, to break through the illusions to the facts. Some of the news reports did just that. But as exemplary as these reports were, they were overshadowed by the pervasive emphasis on image-conscious coverage.

Like the reporters, politicians too found themselves unwittingly entangled in the image-making process, even as they tried to call attention to the artifice of their opponents. In 1988, Dukakis could not escape from image-conscious politics even though he disdained it. Though George Bush successfully campaigned for president in the wake of Reagan's successes, he, too, found himself speaking openly— if sometimes unwittingly—about the images he sought to create on television. At a heated point in the 1988 television debate with Dukakis, Bush, before delivering a crack about Dukakis's tank ride, inadvertently revealed that the joke was not spontaneous, but scripted in advance by his media advisers: "Is now the time to bring out our one-liners?" Bush wondered aloud.

As president, Bush became notorious for his inarticulate, yet self-conscious, tendency to expose his own attempts at image construction. Instead of simply stating where he stood on the issues, Bush would speak of the way he wanted to be "perceived" or "positioned." Asked about one-time Klansman David Duke's candidacy for governor of Louisiana, Bush responded, "We have—I have—want to be positioned in that I could not possibly support David Duke, because of the racism and because of the bigotry and all of this." Another version of Bush's self-conscious exposure of his own attempts at image construction came when Bush "read his stage directions aloud," as the columnist Michael Kinsley put it. In a visit calculated to convey his concern for the economic plight of New Hampshire voters shortly before the 1992 New Hampshire primary, Bush toured the state declaring, "Message: I care."[8]

The drawbacks of modern image consciousness should not obscure its liberating aspects. In reasonable proportion, there is nothing wrong with reporters showing when and how politicians stage events. More important, the underlying skepticism behind image consciousness, the desire to expose and unmask the false pose, is an essential ingredient of political reporting, as long as reporters do not simply balance perceptions but ultimately pursue the facts.

More generally, the skepticism that underlies the image-conscious strand of our culture is an important corrective to the way myths are used to whitewash reality and to exempt established conventions from critical examination. Robert Frank's powerful photographs in *The Americans* peeled back the self-satisfied and complacent view of the 1950s purveyed in public boosterism and television comedies like "Ozzie and Harriet" and "Father Knows Best." Frank documented another and more troubled side of American life, which burst forth in the social turmoil and social reform programs of the 1960s. Frank's work was a central influence on the art photographers of the 1960s who challenged the conventional ways we view society.

The critical exploration of image making can also be a corrective to the false impressions created by the maverick heroes of the movies. The maverick hero, after all, has promulgated illusions as well as ideals. One example is the way John Wayne movies shaped the image of war for soldiers who went to Vietnam. In his book *Born on the Fourth of July*, Vietnam veteran Ron Kovic observes:

> Like Mickey Mantle and the fabulous New York Yankees, John Wayne in *The Sands of Iwo Jima* became one of my heroes. We'd go home and make up movies like the ones we'd just seen or the ones that were on TV night after night. . . . On Saturdays after the movies all the guys would go down to Sally's Woods . . . with plastic battery-operated machine guns, cap pistols, and sticks. We set ambushes, then led gallant attacks, storming over the top, bayoneting and shooting anyone who got in our way. Then we'd walk out of the woods like the heroes we knew we would become when we were men.[9]

Kovic's book, like many other documentary and fictional accounts of the Vietnam experience, illustrates the shock and disillusion of discovering that the war did not play like a John Wayne film.

The ability to stand back from the ideals and myths that shape our lives is a positive achievement of the image-conscious sensibility that has come to infuse our culture since the Second World War. The limitations of this stance, whether expressed in art photography or in television news, lie in its tendency to distract us from the meanings that images convey, and in its tendency to assume that merely calling attention to images as images will dissolve their power.

The nineteenth century saw in photography the promise of a picture more perfect than art could produce, yet understood nonetheless the importance of the pose. What separates our time from Daguerre's is a shift in sensibility, in emphasis and outlook. Daguerre and his generation were intrigued with the realism of photography; they attended to the pose as a way of capturing the truth about the subject.

We image-conscious sophisticates of the late twentieth century are alive above all to the artifice of the image. From Andy Warhol's hyper-realistic pop art to the interchangeable use of political advertisement footage and actual news footage on the evening news to the rise of the television docudrama, our culture blurs the distinction between realism and artifice almost to the vanishing point.

For Daguerre, the distinction was clear. Photography was one thing, his theater of illusions another. He admonished the young artist not to paint the fabricated scenes of the theater of illusions, but to "go out of doors," lest the artist produce a copy of a copy. We, on the other hand, are fascinated with copies of copies, images of images. If Daguerre's generation, in its naïveté, failed to glimpse the potential of the camera to distort reality rather than record it, we, in our sophistication, may risk losing the capacity to behold the "spirit of fact" to which the perfect picture can still aspire.

Notes

Introduction

1. I reported this and other findings in early form in "TV Tidbits Starve Democracy," *New York Times*, December 10, 1989; "The Incredible Shrinking Sound Bite," *New Republic*, May 28, 1990; and "Sound Bite Democracy: Network Evening News Presidential Campaign Coverage, 1968 and 1988," June 1990, a research paper published by Harvard University's Kennedy School of Government. For a subsequent study on sound bites, see Daniel C. Hallin, "Sound Bite News: Television Coverage of Elections, 1968–1988," *Journal of Communications* 42 g 2 (Spring, 1992): 5–24.

2. Cartoon by Doug Marlette of *New York Newsday*; *New York Times*, March 8, 1992, p. E4.

3. Norman B. Judd to Abraham Lincoln, June 6, 1860, quoted in Harold Holzer, Gabor S. Boritt, and Mark E. Neely, Jr., *The Lincoln Image: Abraham Lincoln and the Popular Print* (New York: Scribner, 1984), 67.

4. The sample of movies from 1968 through 1991 is drawn from *Variety's* list of top-grossing movies, based on rentals to distributors. I also watched a sample of fifty of the top movies from the period 1930–1968, to provide a context for the analysis of the contemporary movies.

Chapter 1. Picture Perfect

1. Beaumont Newhall, *The Daguerreotype in America* (New York: Dover, 1976), 16. I am indebted to Newhall for the material about Daguerre from which I drew my account.

2. William Henry Fox Talbot, an Englishman, independently invented the photograph using a different process in the 1830s. For accounts of others involved in the invention of the photograph see Beaumont Newhall, *The History of Photography* (Boston: Little, Brown, 1986) and Jean-Claude Lemagny and Andre Rouille, *The History of Photography* (Cambridge: Cambridge University Press, 1987).

3. Richard Rudisill, *Mirror Image* (Albuquerque: University of New Mexico Press, 1971), 57.

4. Oliver Wendell Holmes, "The Stereoscope and the Stereograph," in *Photography: Essays and Images*, ed. Beaumont Newhall (Boston: New York Graphic Society, 1980), 54.

5. Rudisill, *Mirror Image*, 54.

6. Harold Francis Pfister, *Facing the Light* (Washington, D.C.: Smithsonian Institute Press, 1978), 140.

7. Ibid., 142.

8. Robert A. Sobieszek and Odette M. Appel, *The Daguerreotypes of Southworth and Hawes* (New York: Dover, 1976), ix.

9. Marcus Aurelius Root, *The Camera and the Pencil* (Pawlet: Helios, 1971 [1864]), 143.

10. Newhall, *The Daguerreotype in America*, 44.

11. Pfister, *Facing the Light*, 140; Newhall, *The Daguerreotype in America*, 78.

12. Mark Twain, *Life on the Mississippi* (New York: Penguin Books, 1986, [1883]), 278.

13. Max Kozloff, *Photography and Fascination* (Danbury: Addison House, 1979), 79.

14. Stephen Hess and Milton Kaplan, *The Ungentlemanly Art: A History of American Political Cartoons* (New York: Macmillan, 1968), 3. Thomas C. Leonard notes that this famous remark by Tweed may be apocryphal, but provides an astute analysis of the power of pictures in *The Power of the Press* (Oxford: Oxford University Press, 1986), 108.

15. Robert Sklar, *Movie-Made America* (New York: Vintage, 1975), 3, 22.

16. Niccolò Machiavelli, *The Prince*, ed. Quentin Skinner and Russell Price (Cambridge: Cambridge University Press, 1988), 63.

17. *Boston Globe*, May 1, 1991.

18. The account of Spielberg's visit was provided by Congressman Mike Synar of Oklahoma. Interview with author, May 10, 1991.

19. This quotation and the information about the Democrats' attention to camera placement during the Bork hearings was provided by a Democratic adviser who wished to remain anonymous. Interview with author, October 24, 1991.

20. This statistic comparing the 1968 and 1988 general election campaign coverage is based on an analysis of the campaign newscasts mentioned on pp. 1–2.

21. Rod Slemmons, *Like a One-Eyed Cat: Photographs of Lee Friedlander* (New York: Abrams, 1989), 12.

22. Patrick S. Smith, *Andy Warhol's Art and Films* (Ann Arbor: UMI Research Press, 1986), 117.

23. Erving Goffman, *The Presentation of Self in Everyday Life* (Edinburgh: University of Edinburgh, 1958), 10.

24. Marcia Tucker, "Mechanisms of Exclusion and Relation: Identity" in *Discourses: Conversations in Postmodern Art and Culture*, ed. Russell Ferguson et al. (Cambridge: MIT Press, 1990), 92.

25. Holmes, "The Stereoscope and the Stereograph" (1859) in Newhall, *Photography*, 60.

26. Thomas L. Johnson and Philip C. Dunn, *A True Likeness: The Black South of Richard Samuel Roberts, 1920–1936* (Columbia: Algonquin Books of Chapel Hill, 1986), 6.

27. Transcribed from a videotape of NBC's 1984 Republican Convention coverage.

Chapter 2. The Rise of Image-Conscious Television Coverage

1. Figures are for Democratic and Republican candidates appearing on ABC, CBS and NBC weekday evening newscasts from Labor Day to election day, 1968 and 1988 (over 280 newscasts in all). Since the networks did not offer Saturday and Sunday evening newscasts during the periods studied, weekend newscasts are omitted to insure comparability.

   All quotations from the newscasts, unless otherwise attributed, come from this sample.

2. For an excellent account of the growing role of political consultants and media advisers in American politics, see Larry Sabato, *The Rise of Political Consultants* (New York: Basic Books, 1981).

3. Michael Deaver, a public-relations expert in charge of Reagan's media, offered an account of his work in his book, *Behind the Scenes*

(New York: William Morrow, 1987). Accounts of Deaver's role can also be found in Martin Schram, *The Great American Video Game* (New York: William Morrow, 1987), and Mark Hertsgaard, *On Bended Knee: The Press and the Reagan Presidency* (New York: Farrar, Straus and Giroux, 1988).

4. Don Oliver, interview with author, May 9, 1991.

5. David Schoumacher, interview with author, January 27, 1991.

6. Frank Shakespeare, interview with author, January 14, 1991.

7. The quotations from Roger Mudd and the political consultant are from Lee Dembart, "A Mudd Report on Candidates Rejected by Cronkite Program," *New York Times*, June 8, 1976, p. 67.

8. Roger Mudd, interview with author, December 2, 1991.

9. John Hart, interview with author, March 12, 1990.

10. Jill Rosenbaum, interview with author, January 9, 1991.

11. Tom Bettag, interview with author, April 17, 1991.

12. Susan Zirinsky, interview with author, May 13, 1991.

13. Leonard Garment, interview with author, February 5, 1991.

14. Joseph Napolitan, interview with author, January 28, 1991.

15. Bob Schieffer, interview with author, January 9, 1991.

16. Jeff Greenfield, interview with author, March 9, 1991.

17. On the role of political ads in the 1968 and earlier campaigns see Edwin Diamond and Stephen Bates, *The Spot* (Cambridge: MIT Press, 1988), and Kathleen Hall Jamieson, *Packaging the Presidency* (New York: Oxford University Press, 1984).

18. Joseph Napolitan, interview with author, January 28, 1991.

19. Frank Shakespeare, interview with author, January 14, 1991.

20. Roger Ailes, interview with author, July 15, 1991.

21. Jill Rosenbaum, interview with author, January 9, 1991.

22. Andy Franklin, interview with author, January 8, 1991.

23. Brian Healy, interview with author, January 9, 1991.

24. Sanford Socolow, interview with author, December 1989.

25. Ted Koppel, interview with author, February 20, 1991.

26. Reuven Frank, interview with author, May 15, 1991.

27. Quoted in Randall Rothenberg, "Controversy in Commercials Used to Gain Extra Publicity," *New York Times*, January 8, 1990, p. D8.

28. Quoted in "Rift Over Campaign Films," *New York Times*, August 11, 1988, p. D19.

29. Bill Crawford, interview with author, April 17, 1991.

30. Quoted in Rothenberg, "Controversy in Commercials."

31. Ted Koppel, interview with author, February 20, 1991.

32. *Time*, October 3, 1988, 18.

33. John Sasso, interview with author, March 9, 1991.

34. Roger Ailes, discussion, The Joan Shorenstein Barone Center, Harvard University, November 28, 1990.

35. Walter Cronkite, interview with author, May 28, 1991.

36. David Broder, interview with author, February 20, 1991.

37. The source wished to remain anonymous. Interview with author, 1991.

38. Roger Ailes in *Campaign for President: The Managers Look at '88*, ed. David R. Runkel (Dover, Mass.: Auburn House, 1989), 136.

39. Andrew Savitz, interview with author, February 23, 1991.

40. John Sasso, interview with author, March 9, 1991.

41. Tim Russert and Bill Wheatley, interview with author, January 8, 1991.

42. Richard Salant, interview with author, April 6, 1991.

43. Kathryn Murphy, interview with author, May 1989.

44. Dayton Duncan, interview with author, May 1989.

45. The Stahl incident is related in Schram, *The Great American Video Game*, 26.

Chapter 3. Contesting Control of the Picture

1. Bill Wheatley, interview with author, April 19, 1991.

2. Bill Wheatley, interview with author, January 8, 1991.

3. Ibid.

4. Bob Schieffer, interview with author, January 9, 1991.

5. Ted Koppel, interview with author, February 20, 1991.

6. Sanford Socolow, interview with author, June 4, 1991.

7. Walter Cronkite, interview with author, May 28, 1991.

8. Shad Northshield, interview with author, April 22, 1991.

9. Tom Bettag, interview with author, April 17, 1991.

10. Susan Zirinksy, interview with author, May 13, 1991.

11. Dan Rather, interview with author, September 23, 1991.

12. Walter Cronkite, interview with author, May 28, 1991.

13. Don Hewitt, interview with author, April 22, 1991.

14. *New York Times*, April 22, 1990.

15. Thomas Dwight to Theodore Sedgwick, February 7, 1789, quoted in David Hacket Fischer, *The Revolution of American Conservatism* (New York: Harper Torchbooks, 1965), 91.

16. Fisher Ames to Theodore Dwight, March 19, 1801, quoted ibid., 135.

17. Samuel Henshaw to Theodore Sedgwick, April 15, 1789, quoted ibid., 133–34.

18. Ibid., 146.

19. Gil Troy, *See How They Run: The Changing Role of the Presidential Candidate* (New York: The Free Press, 1991), 14, and generally, 7–19.

20. Ibid., 16.

21. Ibid., 22.

22. Ibid., 23–24.

23. Ibid., 30–36.

24. Ibid., 39.

25. Harold Holzer, Gabor S. Boritt, and Mark E. Neely, Jr., *The Lincoln Image: Abraham Lincoln and the Popular Print* (New York: Scribner's, 1984), 11–14.

26. Ibid., 70.

27. Ibid., 71–78.

28. Troy, *See How They Run*, 142–43.

29. Ibid., 149.

30. Ibid., 164.

31. See Becky M. Nicolaides, "Radio Electioneering in the American Presidential Campaigns of 1932 and 1936," *Historical Journal of Film, Radio and Television*, 8 (1988): 115–38.

32. Ibid., 126; see also Erik Barnouw, *A History of Broadcasting in the United States* (3 vols. 1966–70) *The Golden Web*, vol. 2 (New York: Oxford University Press, 1968), 51.

33. *New York Times*, June 28, 1936, quoted in Nicolaides, "Radio Electioneering," 130.

34. Sevareid, *CBS Evening News*, October 11, 1968.

35. *New York Times*, June 28, 1936, quoted in Nicolaides, "Radio Electioneering," 131.

36. Quoted ibid., 124.

37. Quoted in Troy, *See How They Run*, 170.

38. Ibid., 170, 171.

39. Thomas C. Leonard, *The Power of the Press: The Birth of American Political Reporting* (New York: Oxford University Press, 1986), 102.

40. Michael Schudson, *Discovering the News: A Social History of American Newspapers* (New York: Basic Books, 1978), 93.

41. Ibid.

42. See Neil Harris, "Iconography and Intellectual History: The Half-Tone Effect," in *New Directions in American Intellectual History*, ed. John Higham and Paul K. Conkin (Baltimore: Johns Hopkins University Press, 1979), 196–211.

43. Leonard, *The Power of the Press*, 100.

44. Harris, "Iconography and Intellectual History," 203.

45. Ibid., 203–4.

46. Ibid., 204.

47. Ibid., 204–5.

48. Walter Cronkite, *Theodore H. White Lecture, November 15, 1990* (Cambridge: The Joan Shorenstein Barone Center, Harvard University, 1990), 23–24.

49. Daniel Boorstin, *The Image* (New York: Atheneum, [1961] 1987), 133. Wallace quoted in John Bainbridge, *Little Wonder, or The Reader's Digest and How It Grew* (New York: Reynal and Hitchcock, 1945), 36.

50. Boorstin, *The Image*, 133–34.

51. Ibid.; Bainbridge, *Little Wonder*, 53.

52. Quoted in Irving Howe, *The Idea of the Modern in Literature and Art* (New York: Horizon Press, 1967), 20.

53. Quoted in Roland Marchand, *Advertising the American Dream* (Berkeley: University of California Press, 1985), 3–4.

54. Quoted in Troy, *See How They Run*, 130.

55. Quoted in Nicolaides, "Radio Electioneering," 121.

56. Walter Lippmann, *Drift and Mastery* (Englewood Cliffs, N.J.: Prentice-Hall, [1914] 1961), 53.

57. *Life*, November 23, 1936, 3.

58. Advertisement in *Life*, December 28, 1936, 73.

59. Reuven Frank, *Out of Thin Air: An Insider's History of Network News* (New York: Simon and Schuster, 1991), 183–84.

60. Dick Salant, *CBS News Standards* (New York: CBS, internal document, April 14, 1976), 38.

61. Charles Quinn, interview with author, January 10, 1991.

62. Don Hewitt, interview with author, April 22, 1991.

63. Ibid.

64. Ibid.

65. Walter Cronkite, interview with author, May 28, 1991.

66. Theodore White, *The Making of the President, 1960* (New York: Atheneum House, 1961), 329.

67. Daniel Boorstin, *The Image: A Guide to Pseudo-Events in America* (New York: Atheneum, 1961), 41.

68. Ibid., 36.

69. Richard Nixon, *Six Crises* (Garden City, N.Y.: Doubleday, 1962) 422.

70. Frank Shakespeare, interview with author, January 14, 1991.

71. Ibid.
72. Russ Bensley, interview with author, January 25, 1991.
73. John Hart, interview with author, March 12, 1990.
74. Timothy Crouse, *The Boys on the Bus* (New York: Ballantine Books, 1973), 149–50.
75. Michael Deaver, interviewed by Bill Moyers, *The Public Mind*, "Illusions of News," PBS (New York: Journal Graphic Inc., November 22, 1989), 5.
76. Quoted in Martin Schram, *The Great American Video Game* (New York: Morrow, 1987), 33.
77. Quoted in Peter J. Boyer, *Who Killed CBS?* (New York: Random House, 1988), 15.
78. Edwin Diamond, "Stay Tuned for Television News," *New York Magazine*, March 16, 1987, 30–33. On the changes in the economics of network news, see Peter J. Boyer, *Who Killed CBS?*, Ken Auletta, *Three Blind Mice* (New York: Random House, 1991), and Ben Bagdikian, *The Media Monopoly* (Boston: Beacon Press, 1983).
79. Murrow is quoted in Robert MacNeil, *The People Machine* (New York: Harper and Row, 1968), 18.
80. Shad Northshield, interview with author, April 22, 1991.
81. John Ellis, interview with author, March 6, 1991.
82. Boyer, *Who Killed CBS?*, 141.
83. Bob Schieffer, "The New Politics: Some Basic Questions," Society of Professional Journalists Fellowship Lecture, Minneapolis, Minnesota, June 5, 1990, 14.
84. Michael Deaver, interviewed by Bill Moyers, "Illusions of News," 2.
85. Roger Ailes, interview with author, July 15, 1991.
86. Ibid.
87. Boyer, *Who Killed CBS?*, 134.
88. Moyers, "Illusions of News," 4.
89. Lesley Stahl, interview with Bill Moyers, "Illusions of News," 2.
90. Thomas B. Rosenstiel, "TV Political Coverage—Timing, Image, Doughnuts," *Los Angeles Times*, October 23, 1988, p. 15.
91. Susan Zirinsky, interview with author, May 13, 1991.
92. Schram, *The Great American Video Game*, 55.
93. Susan Zirinsky, interview with author, May 13, 1991.
94. Shad Northshield, interview with author, April 22, 1991.
95. Frank Shakespeare, interview with author, January 14, 1991.
96. Sanford Socolow, interview with author, December 1989.
97. Tom Bettag, interview with author, April 17, 1991.
98. Walter Cronkite, interview with author, May 18, 1991.

99. Quoted in Mark Hertsgaard, *On Bended Knee: The Press and the Reagan Presidency* (New York: Farrar, Straus, and Giroux, 1988), 25.
100. Susan Zirinsky, interview with author, May 13, 1991.
101. Boorstin, *The Image*, 44, 38.
102. Robert Campbell, "Fabulous Fakery," *Boston Globe*, February 27, 1990, pp. 57, 59.
103. Ibid.

Chapter 4. Exposed Images

1. Georgia Dullea, "Camcorder! Action! Lives Become Roles," *New York Times*, August 15, 1991, pp. 1, C10.
2. Don Gifford, "What We See When We Cut to the Videotape," *New York Times*, May 20, 1990, p. H31.
3. Ibid.
4. Beth Pearlman, interview with author, May 27, 1991.
5. See Randall Rothenberg, "Commercials Get a New Star: Television," *New York Times*, August 13, 1990, p. D6.
6. Radisson advertisement, *New York Times*, January 19, 1992, p. 22.
7. *Time*, January 27, 1992, 21.
8. Reported by Jackie Judd on ABC (October 11, 1988), and Ken Bode on NBC (October 11, 1988).
9. All of the movie quotations in this book are from viewing the films, not from reading the scripts.
10. An article by Todd Gitlin also discusses *A Face in the Crowd* and other movies about television, exploring the question of how movies gradually came to terms with the powerful presence of television. See Gitlin, "Down the Tubes," in *Seeing Through Movies*, ed. Mark Crispin Miller (New York: Pantheon Books, 1990), 14–48.
11. Quoted in Jonathan Green, *American Photography* (New York: Harry N. Abrams, 1984), 99.
12. Ibid.
13. Rod Slemmons, *Like a One-Eyed Cat: Photographs by Lee Friedlander, 1956–1987* (New York: Harry N. Abrams, 1989), 117.
14. Barbara Norfleet, interview with author, May 6, 1991.
15. Quoted in Elis Barents, ed., "Introduction," *Cindy Sherman* (Amsterdam: Stedelijk Museum Amsterdam, 1982), 8.
16. Ibid., 9.
17. John D. Callaway, Judith A. Mayotte, and Elizabeth Altick-McCarthy, *Campaigning on Cue* (Chicago: University of Chicago,

William Benton Fellowships Program in Broadcast Journalism, 1988), 85.

18. Diane Arbus, *Diane Arbus* (New York: Aperture, 1972), 1–2.

19. Lewis Baltz, "American Photography in the 1970s" in *American Images: Photography 1945–1980* (New York: Penguin Books, 1985), 161.

20. Ibid., 3.

21. Jonathan Green, *American Photography* (New York: Harry N. Abrams, 1984), 112, 113.

22. Hannah Arendt, *The Human Condition* (Chicago: University of Chicago Press, 1958), 52–53.

23. Quoted in John Szarkowski, *Winogrand* (New York: The Museum of Modern Art, 1988), 34.

24. Patrick S. Smith, *Andy Warhol's Art and Films* (Ann Arbor: UMI Research Press, 1986), 114.

25. Marcus Aurelius Root, *The Camera and the Pencil* (Pawlet: Helios, 1971 [1864]), 143.

Chapter 5. Mythic Pictures

1. Erik H. Erikson, *Childhood and Society* (New York: W. W. Norton, 1963), 327–28.

2. My analysis of the maverick hero is based in part on my study, *American Fantasy: Social Conflicts and Social Myths in Films of the 1970s*, Ph.D. diss., State University of New York at Stony Brook, May, 1982. I further developed the theme of the maverick hero as insider and outsider in "How the White House Was Won," *The New Republic*, November 12, 1984.

3. I am indebted to Robert B. Bly's excellent study, *A Certain Tendency of the Hollywood Cinema, 1930–1980* (Princeton: Princeton University Press, 1985) for the term "reluctant hero."

4. For an intriguing study of the changes in American western movies see Will Wright, *Six Guns and Society* (Berkeley: University of California Press, 1975).

5. Stephen Farber, "Coppola and the Godfather," *Sight and Sound* 41 (1972): 220.

Epilogue

1. David Shoumacher, interview with author, 1991.

2. See Renee Loth, "ABC Says It Will Drop 'Sound-Bite' Coverage," *Boston Globe*, September 11, 1992, p. 13, and "CBS Vows to Serve Up Chewier Sound Bites," *TV Guide*, July 18, 1992, 25.

3. *New York Times*, July 13, 1992, p. D14.

4. Don Terry, "Candidates and Issues Stir Small-Town Frenzy," *New York Times*, July 22, 1992, p. A14.

5. Gwen Ifill, "Clinton Finds Time to Take on GOP," *New York Times*, July 20, 1992, p. A10.

6. Richard L. Berke, "Playing Diplomat on Television," *New York Times*, July 29, 1992, p. A12.

7. Average length of candidate sound bites on the network evening newscasts of ABC, NBC, and CBS. The primary election statistic is from Ann N. Crigler, Marion R. Just, and Timothy E. Cook, "Local News, Network News, and the 1992 Presidential Campaign," unpublished manuscript (1992), 9. The general election statistic is from S. Robert Lichter, "Campaign '92 Project," Center for Media and Public Affairs, Washington, D.C., 1992.

8. *New Republic*, April 27, 1992, 6.

9. Ron Kovic, *Born on the Fourth of July* (New York: Pocket Books, 1976), 54, 55.

Index

ABC, 14, 170; balancing of political pictures and perceptions by, 52, 53; blurring of commentary and political reporting by, 55, 56; campaign gaffes and mishaps as subjects on, 48, 49; media advisers and, 43, 44, 45; political commercials on, 35–36, 37, 39–40, 41; political image making on, 33, 34; presidential debates in 1988 on, 30; profits and ratings and, 85

Adams, John, 71

Advertising: photography's use of images from, 108–9; television images used as part of, 96–97; use of political figures in, 42. *See also* Political commercials

Advisers: Lincoln's use of photography and, 4. *See also* Handlers; Media advisers; Political consultants

Agnew, Spiro, 48–49

Ailes, Roger, 38, 40, 42, 44, 46, 49, 72, 84, 87

Alamo, The (movie), 23, 151

Allen, Karen, 156

Altman, Robert, 142

American Express, 96

American Legion, 47

Americans, The (Frank), 109, 111, 174

"America's Funniest Home Videos" (television program), 16–17, 95

Ames, Fisher, 70

Anchormen. *See* Television journalists

Andromeda Strain, The (movie), 126–27

Apocalypse Now (movie), 127, 144–45, 146

Arbus, Diane, 19, 111, 118–20, 121

Arendt, Hannah, 121

Arkin, Alan, 143

"Arsenio Hall" (television program), 170

Arthur, Jean, 129, 131

Ashby, Hal, 104–5, 145

Associated Press, 168

Astaire, Fred, 11, 22

Auletta, Ken, 85

Bagdikian, Ben, 85

Baker, James, 45, 72

Balsam, Martin, 144

Basinger, Kim, 155

Batman (movie), 154–55

Bazell, Robert, 52, 60

Beatty, Warren, 96
Beckel, Bob, 44
Bedelia, Bonnie, 136
Being There (movie), 104–5
Bennett, James Gordon, 75
Bensley, Russ, 84
Berenger, Tom, 147
Bergman, Ingrid, 134
Bernard, Stan, 45
Bettag, Tom, 32, 64–65, 66, 90–91
"Beverly Hillbillies, The" (television
     program), 85
Beverly Hills Cop (movie), 138
Beverly Hills Cop 2 (movie), 138
Billy Jack (movie), 139
Bloom, Verna, 101
Bob Roberts (movie), 125
Bogart, Humphrey, 128, 133, 159
Bond films, 127, 159–61
Boorstin, Daniel, 16, 18, 77, 82–83,
     92
Bork, Robert, 13, 179n19
Born on the Fourth of July (Kovic), 174
Boyer, Peter, 85, 86
Brady, Mathew, 4, 10, 122
Brando, Marlon, 144, 154
Brinkley, David, 98
Broadcasters. *See* Television journalists
Broadcast News (movie), 105–7
Broder, David, 47
Brody, Rick, 24, 25, 57
Brokaw, Tom, 22, 41–42, 48, 53–54
Bronson, Charles, 139
Brooker, C. F. Tucker, 76
Brown, Edmund G., Jr. (Jerry), 29, 171
Burton, Tim, 154
Bush, George: campaign gaffes and
     mishaps by, 47–48; image making
     on television by, 32–33, 34, 173;
     Persian Gulf war and, 13; tradi-
     tional themes used by, 168. *See
     also* Presidential campaign—1988
Butch Cassidy and the Sundance Kid
     (movie), 127

Cable television, 12
Cameras. *See* Photography; Video cam-
     eras

Campaigns. *See* Presidential campaign
     headings
Campbell, Robert, 92–93
Candidate, The (movie), 102
Candidates. *See* Politicians; Presidential
     campaign *headings*
"Candid Camera" (television program),
     17
Capra, Frank, 99, 128, 131, 162, 164,
     172
Carter, Jimmy, 89, 171
Cartoons, political, 10, 13, 72, 178n14
Casablanca (movie), 128, 133–34
Catch-22 (movie), 141, 143–44
CBS, 17, 57, 74, 81, 85, 170; blurring
     of commentary and political re-
     porting by, 55; campaign gaffes
     and mishaps as subjects on, 48,
     49, 50, 51; criticism of Reagan's
     1984 campaign on, 58–59; enter-
     tainment values and, 86, 87;
     media advisers and, 44; political
     commercials on, 34, 36, 37, 38,
     39, 41; political image making on,
     27, 30, 31, 32, 33; profits and rat-
     ings and, 85; sound bites on, 62,
     65; television news documentaries
     and, 80–81
"CBS Evening News" (television pro-
     gram), 39, 63, 64, 84, 87, 90, 169
"CBS Morning News" (television pro-
     gram), 29
CBS News Standards (handbook), 85
Chancellor, John, 25, 55
Childs, Marquis, 75
Church, Frank, 29
Churchill, Winston, 88
CIA, movie portrayals of, 159, 160
Ciavolino, Michael, 110
Cimino, Michael, 146
Citizen heroes in movies, 131–33, 148,
     161–66, 172
Civil-rights movement, and television,
     81, 168
Clay, Henry, 72
Clement, Frank, 81
Clinton, Bill, 97, 169, 170, 171
Close Encounters of the Third Kind
     (movie), 161

CNN, 12, 170
Cochran, John, 41
Cohen, Richard, 85
Colbert, Claudette, 11
Cole, Natalie, 96
Cole, Nat King, 96
Coming Home (movie), 145
Commercials. *See* Advertising; Political commercials
Congress, 13, 123; citizen hero in movies and, 131–33
Connery, Sean, 156
Conrad, Joseph, 144
Consultants. *See* Handlers; Media advisers; Political consultants
Coolidge, Calvin, 73
Cooper, Gary, 13, 122, 130, 138, 140, 164
Cooper, James Fenimore, 125
Cop heroes, 134–40, 158
Coppola, Francis Ford, 142, 144
Cosmatos, George Pan, 149
Costner, Kevin, 164
Cowboy heroes, 127–28, 128–29, 130–31, 139, 142
Crawford, Bill, 41, 65–66
Crenna, Richard, 149
Criticism: conflict between photographs and words and, 76–77. *See also* Theater criticism
Cronkite, Walter, 29, 34, 39, 46, 63–64, 67, 77, 82, 87, 90, 91, 98, 124
Cruise, Tom, 151
C-SPAN, 12
Culture. *See* Popular culture

Dafoe, Willem, 147
Daguerre, Louis, 7–8, 10, 175
Daguerreotype, 8, 9, 11, 178n1, 178n2, 178n3, 178n6, 178n8, 178n9
Daley, Richard, 25
Death Wish (movie), 139, 155
Deaver, Michael, 26, 75, 84, 85, 179n3
Deer Hunter, The (movie), 127, 146–47
Democratic party, 13, 71–72, 107
De Niro, Robert, 146
Depression, 11, 79, 80, 108, 118

Dern, Bruce, 145
de Wilde, Brandon, 129
Diamond, Edwin, 85
Die Hard (movie), 136–38, 155, 158
Diorama (theater of illusion), 7–8, 10, 175
Dirty Harry films, 134–36, 138, 140, 155
Disney/MGM Studios, 92–93
Disney World, 92–93
Documentary aspect of the camera: in everyday life, 20–21; image consciousness and, 2, 5–6, 14–18, 22; movies and, 11, 165–66; photography and, 2, 8–9, 11, 20–23, 79–80, 107, 167, 175; picture magazines and, 79, 88; television journalism and, 3, 12, 17–18, 69–70, 80–81, 87–88, 108; video camera and, 21–22
Dr. No (movie), 159
"Donahue" (television program), 170
Donaldson, Sam, 31, 49, 53, 56, 92
Donner, Richard, 153
Doonesbury cartoon, 13
Douglas, Melvyn, 104
Dukakis, Michael, 173; campaign gaffes and mishaps by, 49, 50–51; control of image of, 97–98; on image making, 70; media advisers and, 45. *See also* Presidential campaign—1988
Dunaway, Faye, 103
Duncan, Dayton, 51
Duvall, Robert, 143
Dwight, Thomas, 70

Eastwood, Clint, 123, 134–35, 136, 159, 160
Edison, Thomas, 11, 73
Editing techniques, television, 65–66, 67
Eiger Sanction, The (movie), 160
Elections. *See* Presidential campaign *headings*
Elliott, Denholm, 156
Ellis, John, 86
Emerson, Ralph Waldo, 9, 10

Empire Strikes Back, The (movie), 158

Entertainment: campaign coverage influenced by value of, 63, 86, 170–71; campaign gaffes and mishaps seen as, 50; image consciousness and, 16–17; picture magazines and, 78–79; video camera technology and, 96

Erikson, Erik, 125

Evans, Walker, 79–80, 108, 110, 118, 122

Face in the Crowd, A (movie), 99–100, 102, 125

Fairness: balancing of equal time and perceptions and, 26, 51–54; meaning of, 52

Farm Security Administration, 108

"Father Knows Best" (television program), 174

FBI, movie portrayals of, 159, 160

Federalists, 70–71

File footage, and political commercials, 41–42

Films. *See* Movies

Fonda, Jane, 145

Ford, Gerald, 50

Ford, Harrison, 122, 156, 158

Forster, Robert, 101

Frank, Reuven, 40, 80, 86

Frank, Robert, 19, 98, 109–10, 111, 118, 128, 174

Franklin, Andy, 39

Friedlander, Lee, 15, 18, 98, 110–19, 128, 135

Gable, Clark, 11

Garment, Leonard, 33

Gifford, Don, 95

Goffman, Erving, 18

Goldwater, Barry, 40

"Good Morning America" (television program), 170

Gould, Elliott, 142

Grant, Ulysses S., 76

Green Berets, The (movie), 23, 124–25, 127

Green, Jonathan, 120–21

Greenfield, Jeff, 33

Griffith, Andy, 99

Hamill, Mark, 158

Handlers: image making and, 43–47, 72; political commercials critical of, 38, 170. *See also* Media advisers; Political consultants

Harding, Warren, 73

Harper's Weekly (magazine), 10, 76–77

Harris, Neil, 75

Harrison, William Henry, 71–72

Hart, John, 31, 83, 84

Healy, Brian, 29, 39

Hearst, William Randolph, 74

Heart of Darkness (Conrad), 144

Heflin, Van, 129

Henreid, Paul, 134

Hepburn, Katharine, 99

Heroes: alienation and madness themes and, 144–45; citizen hero theme and, 131–33, 148, 161–66, 172; cop hero theme and, 134–40, 158; cowboy myth and westerns and, 127–28, 139, 142; as individual against the institution, 149–51; individualism and, 126–27, 129, 130, 152; insider-outsider quality of, 126, 132–34, 138–39, 153; maverick hero theme and, 125–27, 128–34, 141, 171, 174; military hero theme and, 140–53; morally ambiguous world and, 129–30; movie themes with, 23, 100, 124–66; North in Iran-Contra hearings as, 13; politicians' use of themes with, 123, 168, 171–72; return home theme and, 145–47; super-hero theme and, 153–61

Hewitt, Don, 67–68, 81–82

High Noon (movie), 13, 122, 128, 129–31, 140, 164

Hine, Lewis, 122

Hoffman, Dustin, 128

Holmes, Oliver Wendell, 8, 20

Home videos, 17, 94–95
Hoover, Herbert, 73
Horton, Willie, 36–38, 41, 53
Hume, Brit, 14, 30, 34, 37, 56, 117
Humphrey, Hubert, 27–28, 34. *See also* Presidential campaign—1968
Hunter, Holly, 106
Huntley, Chet, 34, 98
"Huntley-Brinkley Report" (television program), 40, 64, 80, 86, 90
Hurt, William, 106

Image consciousness: blurring distinction between event and image in, 165–66; dilemma for television journalists over, 3–4; documentaries and, 17–18, 22; everyday life and, 94–98; photography and, 15–16, 94–123; political debates and, 82; presidential campaign coverage and, 14–15, 24–60, 87–93; rise of, 2, 5–6; self and, 22
Image making: control of, 69–70; as focus of political campaigns, 14; historical overview of use of, 70–75; media advisers and, 46–47, 86, 89–90; popular culture and roles in, 15–16; presidential campaign in 1968 and, 31, 90; presidential campaign in 1988 and, 30, 31–32, 90–91; Reagan and, 22–23; social criticism and, 16; television focus on use of, 14, 17–18, 83–84
Indiana Jones and the Last Crusade (movie), 122, 155, 156, 157
Indiana Jones and the Temple of Doom (movie), 122, 155
Indiana Jones films, 122, 156–58
Individualism: movie heroes and, 126–27, 129, 130, 152; presidential campaigns and, 169. *See also* Self
Iran-Contra hearings, 13
It Happened One Night (movie), 11

Jackson, Andrew, 71
James Bond films, 127, 159–61

Jefferson, Thomas, 70, 71
Jennings, Peter, 30–31, 41, 48, 53, 54
JFK (movie), 163–66
Johnson, Lyndon, 40, 124
Josephson, Ken, 110
Journalists. *See* Print journalists; Television journalists
Judd, Jackie, 37

Kazan, Elia, 99–100
Keaton, Michael, 154
Kefauver, Estes, 82
Kellerman, Sally, 143
Kellogg, Ray, 124
Kennedy, Jacqueline, 112
Kennedy, John, 169; movies on, 163, 165–66; Nixon's debate with, 14, 26, 82; photography and, 107, 110. *See also* Presidential campaign—1960
Kennedy, Robert, 124
Kidder, Margot, 154
King, Martin Luther, Jr., 124
King, Rodney, 21
Kinsley, Michael, 173
Klauber, Edward, 74
Kodak camera, 11
Koppel, Ted, 39–40, 42–43, 62–63, 83
Kovic, Ron, 174
Kozinski, Jersy, 104

Ladd, Alan, 128
Landon, Alfred E., 74
Lange, Dorothea, 80, 122
"Larry King Live" (television program), 170
Laughlin, Tom, 139
Lee, Russell, 109
Life (magazine), 12, 78–79, 88
Lincoln, Abraham, 4, 72–73, 76
Lippmann, Walter, 78
Locke, Sondra, 136
Lombard, Carole, 108
Look (magazine), 78
Love Before Breakfast (movie), 108
Lucas, George, 23, 158
Lumet, Sidney, 102–3

McCarthy, Larry, 38, 41
McGinniss, Joseph, 16, 42–43, 44, 64
McGovern, George, 84, 171
Machiavelli, Niccollò, 12
Mackin, Cassie, 84
MacLaine, Shirley, 104
McLuhan, Marshall, 16
McTiernan, John, 136
Madonna, 96, 98
Magazines, picture, 12, 78–79
Magnum Force (movie), 135
Making of the President, 1960, The
    (White), 42
Malden, Karl, 96
Marathon Man (movie), 159
M*A*S*H (movie), 141, 142–43, 144
Mass communication, photography as
    form of, 11. *See also* Newspapers;
    Print journalists
Maverick heroes: movies and, 125–66;
    politicians and, 171, 174
Media. *See* Newspapers; Print journal-
    ists; Television
Media advisers, 14, 42–47; books on,
    42–43; as celebrities, 45–46; im-
    age making and, 68–69, 83; media
    advisers on work of, 43–44, 169;
    number of television reports on,
    43; techniques of, 46–47; televi-
    sion producers and, 86, 89–90;
    television ratings and, 85–86; tele-
    vision reporters and, 43–44, 47;
    voice coach for radio as, 74. *See
    also* Handlers; Political consultants
Media events, and political campaigns,
    3, 27–34, 123, 168–69. *See also*
    Photo opportunity; Staging events
    for television
Medium Cool (movie), 100–102
Meyer, Emile, 129
Michelson, Sig, 81
Midnight Cowboy (movie), 127–28
Military heroes in movies, 140–53
Mr. Smith Goes to Washington (movie),
    23, 128, 131–33, 154, 164
Monroe, Marilyn, 15, 19, 112, 113,
    114, 172
Moonraker (movie), 161
Morse, Samuel, 7–8

Morton, Bruce, 30, 36, 37, 49, 50, 51,
    57–58
Movies: as common frame of reference,
    6; cultural dominance of, 11;
    heroes in, 23, 122–23, 124–66;
    image making and, 4–5, 125; loss
    of self as theme in, 121–22; pho-
    tography's use of images from, 108,
    114–15; Reagan's use of images
    from, 22–23; references to movies
    within, 137–38; rise of popularity
    of, 11; television portrayed in, 98–
    107
Moyers, Bill, 88
MTV, 170
Mudd, Roger, 29
Murphy, Eddie, 138
Murphy, Kathryn, 51
Murrow, Edward R., 17, 85–86
Music videos, 96
Muskie, Edmund, 24, 57, 116, 117
Myers, Lisa, 32–33, 44

Nadar, 10
Napier, Charles, 149
Napolitan, Joe, 33, 38
Nast, Thomas, 10
Natural sound, 66–67
NBC, 22, 57, 80, 81, 84, 169, 170;
    balancing of political pictures and
    perceptions by, 52, 54; campaign
    gaffes and mishaps as subjects on,
    48, 49, 50; media advisers and,
    44, 45; political commercials on,
    34, 39, 40, 41; political image
    making on, 27, 32; profits and rat-
    ings and, 85, 86; sound bites on,
    25
"NBC Nightly News" (television pro-
    gram), 61
Neal, Patricia, 99
Network (movie), 102–4, 125, 127
Networks: campaign gaffes and mishaps
    used by, 48–49, 51; tension be-
    tween reality and artifice of image
    in, 2–3. *See also* ABC; CBS;
    NBC; Television
Newman, Paul, 127

New Republic (magazine), 73
Newspapers: advertising images in, 97.
    See also Print journalists
News programs. *See* Television
News reporters. *See* Television journalists
Newsweek (magazine), 74, 169
New York Herald (newspaper), 75
New York Sun (newspaper), 74
New York Times (newspaper), 78, 83, 95, 169–70
Nichols, Mike, 143
Nicholson, Jack, 155
"Nightline" (television program), 62–63
Nixon, Richard, 125; 1960 campaign of, 14, 26. *See also* Presidential campaign—1968
Norfleet, Barbara, 114
North, Oliver, 13
Northshield, Shad, 64, 86, 90

Oliver, Don, 27, 28
Omen, The (movie), 126
Owens, Bill, 111–12

Palance, Jack, 129
Patton (movie), 140–42, 143
Pearlman, Beth, 95–96
Perkins, Jack, 28
Perot, Ross, 169, 170, 171
Persian Gulf war, 13, 23
Photography: as art, 9–10; collaboration between photographer and subject in, 9; consciousness of image making in, 15–16, 94–123; control of picture in, 11–15; deformed self in, 118–21; distinction between appearance and reality in, 10, 175; documentation of world by, 8–9, 11, 20–22, 79–80, 107; fabricated self in, 18–19; failed images in, 116–18; focus on image in, 107–8, 110–11, 113–14; invention of, 8; mass communication and, 11–12; movies and entertainment as subjects for, 108, 114–15;

picture magazines and, 12, 78–79, 88; political campaign use of, 4, 72–73, 76; pop art's use of, 112–13; popular culture and, 11; portraiture with, 4, 9, 21, 113, 114, 122; presidential campaigns as images for, 116–17; promotional media used in, 108–9; realism and, 2, 4, 7, 9, 10–11; social criticism and, 16, 76, 108–9, 110; television and, 108, 110–12; visual reorientation of public toward, 75–76; words overwhelmed by, 76–77
Photojournalism. *See* Photography; Print journalists
Photo opportunity, 3; number of, 14; television reporting of, 14; use of term in 1968 news coverage, 14, 31. *See also* Media events; Staging events for television
Picture magazines, 12, 78–79, 88
Pirandello, Luigi, 113–14
Platoon (movie), 127, 147–49
Poe, Edgar Allan, 8
Political campaigns. *See* Presidential campaign *headings*
Political cartoons, 10, 13, 72, 178n14
Political commercials, 3, 34–42; balancing of equal time and fairness concerning, 26, 51–54; Bush's Horton ad in 1988 campaign and, 36–38, 41, 53; Bush's "revolving door" prison commercial as, 26; comparisons among, 53–54; criticism of use of, 39–40; explanations for increased attention to, 38–39; fact correction by reporters covering, 35–36, 44; file footage using, 40–42; Johnson's "Daisy ad" in 1964 campaign and, 40; media experts used for evaluation of, 45; network news coverage and use of, 35, 61–64; 1968 campaign and, 34–35; results of attacks on, 36–38; television's appetite for visual images with, 40
Political consultants, 4, 12–14, 26, 42–

Political consultants (*Cont.*)
    47, 179n2. *See also* Handlers; Media advisers
Political reporters. *See* Print journalists; Television journalists
Politicians: campaign gaffes and mishaps by, 47–51; compression of speeches by, 78; control of television images and, 12–14; image-making process and, 173; mastery of television imagery by, 26; political cartoons and images of, 10, 13, 72
Polk, James, 72
Pop art, 15–16, 19–20, 112–13, 172
Popular culture: fabricated self in, 18–19; image consciousness in, 5–6, 15–16; movies as common frame of reference in, 6, 11; photography and, 11, 19, 111; Reagan's image making and use of, 22–23; television and, 12, 16–17
Portraiture: photography and, 4, 9, 21, 113, 114, 122; political use of, 4; pop art and, 19, 113
Post, Ted, 135
Presidential campaigns: appreciation of production values in, 2; control of television images in, 14–15; entertainment values and, 170–71; gaffes and mishaps as television subjects during, 47–51; ideal of disinterested politics in, 71–72; image making as focus of, 4, 14, 24–70, 167–73; maverick hero theme in, 171–72; movies on, 99–102; photographs of candidates used in, 4, 72–73, 76; photography's use of images from, 116–17; radio broadcasts used in, 73, 74–75, 78, 82; talk shows and "infotainment" programs used in, 170; television's pivotal role in, 25–26; tension between reality and artifice of image in, 2–3; traditional ideals invoked in, 168
Presidential campaign—1796, 71
Presidential campaign—1800, 71
Presidential campaign—1840, 71–72

Presidential campaign—1844, 72
Presidential campaign—1852, 72
Presidential campaign—1860, 4, 72–73
Presidential campaign—1920, 73
Presidential campaign—1932, 73–74, 78
Presidential campaign—1936, 74
Presidential campaign—1948, 81
Presidential campaign—1956, 81, 82
Presidential campaign—1960, 14, 26, 82–83, 107
Presidential campaign—1964, "Daisy ad" in, 40
Presidential campaign—1968, 1–2, 56, 74; blurring of television commentary and political reporting during, 55–56; campaign stops as media events during, 28–29; conflict between political words and images on, 57–58; criticism of coverage of, 64–65; gaffes and mishaps as television subjects during, 47–49; image making during, 31, 72, 83, 90; little usage of photo opportunities during, 14; maverick hero theme in, 171–72; network balancing of pictures and perceptions during, 54; political commercials during, 34–35, 38–39; size of anchorman's televised image during, 18; sound bite length during, 2, 24–25, 58, 65–66, 67, 170, 187n7; television time devoted to visuals of candidates without their words during, 25
Presidential campaign—1972, 84
Presidential campaign—1976, 29–30, 171
Presidential campaign—1980, 168, 171
Presidential campaign—1984: criticism of imagery used in, 58–59; image making during, 72, 123, 168; media advisers and, 43; Reagan's use of popular images in, 22–23
Presidential campaign—1988, 1–2, 56; blurring of commentary and political reporting during, 55–56;

conflict between political words
and images in, 57, 58, 60; control
over images in, 97–98; criticism of
imagery used during, 60; gaffes and
mishaps as television subjects during, 47–48, 49–51; Horton ad in,
36–38, 41, 53; image making during, 30–31, 31–33, 70, 90–91,
173; media advisers and, 43, 44,
46; network balancing of pictures
and perceptions during, 52–54;
"revolving door" prison commercial in, 26; size of anchorman's
televised image during, 18; sound
bite length during, 2, 25, 58, 65–
66, 67, 170; staged events in, 169;
television coverage of political
commercials during, 35–38, 39,
40–42, 61–62; television time devoted to visuals of candidates
without their words during, 25
Presidential campaign—1992, 61, 97,
169, 170–71, 187n7
Presidential debates: in 1960, 82–83; in
1988, 30–31
Presley, Elvis, 19, 113
Press conferences: gaffes and mishaps
during, 48–49; political commercials as, 39
Print journalists: compression of information for, 77–78; image
consciousness of, 169–70; image
making during campaigns and, 70–
71; media advisers and, 42; picture
magazines and, 12, 78–79; television journalists influenced by, 16;
visual reorientation to photographs
and, 75–76; words overwhelmed by
pictures and, 76–77
Producers, and media advisers, 86, 89–
90
Production techniques: political campaigns and, 2, 63, 67–68; public
knowledge of, 95–96
Profits, and television ratings, 85–86
Public opinion: movies on Vietnam War
and, 141–42; political campaign
coverage and, 69, 75–76, 82–83,
170

Public relations, and political campaigns, 73–74
Public Relations (Winogrand), 116, 117,
118

Quayle, Dan, 38, 97
Quinn, Charles, 57, 81

Radio: movies with campaigns involv-
ing, 99–100; political campaigns
with, 73, 74–75, 78; political debate of 1960 on, 82
Radisson Hotels, 97
Raiders of the Lost Ark, The (movie),
155, 156–57
Rains, Claude, 132, 133
Rambo (movie), 122, 137
Rambo: First Blood Part I (movie), 149–
51
Rather, Dan, 45, 46–47, 48, 64, 66–67
Ratings, television, 63, 64, 67–68, 85–
86, 102–3
Reader's Digest (magazine), 77
Reagan, Nancy, 72
Reagan, Ronald, 1, 111; criticism of imagery manipulation by, 58–59;
entertainment value of news and,
85, 86, 89; heroic images used by,
123, 168, 171–72; media advisers
and, 44; photography and, 117. *See
also* Presidential campaign—1984
Realism: movies and, 11; photography
and, 2, 4, 7, 9, 10–11; television
and, 12, 16, 102, 104; tension be-
tween artifice of image and, 2–3
Redford, Robert, 102, 127
Reeve, Christopher, 153
Reporters. *See* Print journalists; Televi-
sion journalists
Reston, James (Scottie), 83
Return of the Jedi (movie), 158
Reynolds, Frank, 55, 56
Richardson, Eliot, 116
Rickman, Alan, 137
Riis, Jacob, 122
Roberts, Richard Samuel, 21
Rocky films, 122, 161–63

Rogers, Ginger, 11
Rollins, Ed, 44
Roosevelt, Franklin, 73–74, 79, 88
Root, Marcus Aurelius, 122
Rosenbaum, Jill, 38–39
Rosenthal, Thomas, 89
Rothstein, Arthur, 109

Salant, Richard, 50, 85
Sands of Iwo Jima, The (movie), 174
Sasso, John, 45–46, 50
Satire, television as object of,
    102–5
Savage, John, 146
Savitz, Andrew, 49–50
Schaffner, Franklin J., 141
Schieffer, Bob, 30, 33, 62, 86
Schlesinger, John, 127
Schoumacher, David, 27–28, 48, 83
Schram, Martin, 89
Schudson, Michael, 75
Scott, George C., 140
Scott, Tony, 138, 151
Scott, Winfield, 72
"See It Now" (television program),
    17
Self: fabrication of, 15–20, 22, 98–102;
    deformed, 19, 188–222; heroes
    and, 122–23; image consciousness
    and, 22, 121–22; movie heroes
    and, 23, 96, 98–107, 122–66;
    photography and, 8–10, 18–20,
    107–22. *See also* Individualism
Self-Portrait (Friedlander), 15, 110
Sellers, Peter, 104
Selling of the President, The (McGin-
    niss), 16, 42–43, 44, 64
Serafin, Barry, 43
Sevareid, Eric, 55, 74
Seward, William Henry, 72
Shakespeare, Frank, 28–29, 38, 44, 83,
    90
Shane (movie), 128–29, 130
Sheen, Martin, 144, 147
Sherman, Cindy, 114–15, 139, 172
Siegel, Don, 135
Six Characters in Search of an Author
    (Pirandello), 113–14

"60 Minutes" (television program), 67,
    68, 81
Slemmons, Rod, 114
Smith, Lou, 25
Social criticism, and photography, 16,
    76, 108–9, 110
Socolow, Sanford, 39, 63, 90
Sound bites, 62; average length of, 2,
    25, 58, 170, 187n7; compression
    of information for, 65, 77; conflicts
    between images and, 57; editing
    techniques and length of, 65–66,
    67; emphasis of pictures over words
    on, 63–64; 1968 presidential cam-
    paign with, 29; natural sound in,
    66–67; pacing of, 63; political
    commercials and, 41–42
Southworth, Albert, 9–10
Spacek, Sissy, 164
Spielberg, Steven, 13, 23, 155, 161
Spin control, 14. *See also* Handlers;
    Media advisers; Political consul-
    tants
Spy Who Loved Me, The (movie), 127,
    161
Staging events for television, 26–34,
    80–87, 123, 168–69. *See also* Me-
    dia events; Photo opportunity
Stahl, Lesley, 36, 44, 46–47, 58–59,
    60, 88, 89, 91–92
Stallone, Sylvester, 122, 149
Star Wars (movie), 158
State of the Union (movie), 23, 99, 102,
    123
Stevens, George, 128
Stewart, James, 22, 131, 154
Stone, Oliver, 147, 163, 165–66
Suburbia (Owens), 111–12
Sudden Impact (movie), 136, 158
Sutherland, Donald, 142, 164
Sununu, John, 38
Super-heroes in movies, 153–61
Superman movies, 153–54
Supreme Court, 13, 71
Synar, Mike, 179n18

Talk shows, 170
Taylor, Delores, 139

Taylor, Elizabeth, 19, 113

Taylor, Paul, 80

Teeter, Bob, 47

Television, 24–60; advertising images on, 96–97; appreciation of production values in, 2; balancing of pictures and perceptions on, 26, 51–54, 93; blurring of commentary and political reporting on, 54–56; campaign stops seen as media events for, 28–30; compression of information for, 65; conflict between words and images on, 56–60, 92–93; Congressional hearings on, 13; consciousness of image making for, 31–32, 168–70; constructing images for, 27–34; control of political images on, 69–70; criticism of images on, 27, 32; documentary aspect of, 3, 17–18, 69–70, 80–81, 87–88, 108; emphasis of pictures over words on, 62–64; entertainment programming on, 16–17; entertainment values influencing news on, 50, 63, 86, 170–71; gaffes and mishaps as subjects on, 47–51; image making as focus of, 14, 17–18, 83–84; Iran-Contra hearings on, 13; meaning of fairness in, 52; media advisers and, 42–47, 86, 89–90, 169; movies on, 98–107; photography's use of images from, 110–12; pictures as "wallpaper" on, 88–89; pivotal role of, 25–26; politics and control of images in, 12–14; presidential debates and image making for, 30–31; pressure for ratings in, 63, 64, 85–86; reality and, 12, 16, 102, 104; sound bite average length of on, 2, 25, 58; sound bite construction for, 29, 57–60, 170, 187n7; staging event for, 168–69; talk shows and "infotainment" programs in, 170; tension between reality and artifice of image in, 2–3, 92–93, 105–6; time devoted to visuals of candidates without their words on, 25.

See also ABC; CBS; NBC; Networks; Political commercials

Television journalists: audience reaction to criticism of political image making by, 33–34; blurring of commentary and political reporting by, 54–56; criticism of political reporting by, 32–33; dilemma of image consciousness for, 3–4, 26–27, 91–93; fact correction for political commercials from, 35–36, 44; image making process and, 32, 172–73; images overriding criticism by, 59, 91–92; media advisers and, 43–44, 47; production techniques and, 95–96; size of televised image of, 18; sound bites used by, 29–30

Theater criticism, as a style of political coverage, 14, 33–34, 92–93. See also Image consciousness

Theater of illusion (Diorama), 7–8, 10, 175

"This Morning" (television program), 170

Three Days of the Condor (movie), 159

Threlkeld, Richard, 35–36

Time (magazine), 12, 45, 72, 79, 97

"Today" (television program), 170

Top Gun (movie), 151–52

Top Hat (movie), 11

Tracy, Spencer, 23, 99, 123

Trial of Billy Jack (movie), 139, 140

Troy, Gil, 71

True Grit (movie), 127

Truth or Dare (movie), 96

Tsongas, Paul, 171

Twain, Mark, 10

Tweed, Boss, 10, 12

Unforgettable (music video), 96

Venardos, Lane, 41

Video cameras: documentary use of, 21; home use of, 17, 94–95

Video tape, and length of sound bites, 65–66, 67
Vietnam War, 54, 56, 124, 127; movie themes using, 141, 142, 144–45, 146–47, 152, 171, 174
Voight, Jon, 128, 145

Walken, Christopher, 146
Wallace, Chris, 49, 50–51
Wallace, De Witt, 77
Wallace, George, 24, 58, 171
Warhol, Andy, 15–16, 17, 18, 19–20, 98, 112–13, 115, 122, 172, 175
Wayne, John, 23, 124, 127, 137, 138, 149, 151, 152, 159, 174
Western movies, 127–28, 128–29, 130–31
"West 57th" (television program), 17
Wexler, Haskell, 100–1

Wheatley, Bill, 50, 61–62
Whig party, 71, 72
Whitaker, Bill, 51
White, Theodore, 42, 82
Willis, Bruce, 136
Willis, N. P., 10
Wilson, Woodrow, 78
Winner, Michael, 139
Winogrand, Garry, 19, 98, 107, 116–18, 119, 120–21, 128, 135
Wizard of Oz, The (movie), 91, 93
Wooten, Jim, 44, 45, 52, 60
"World News Tonight" (television program), 169

Zamyatin, Eugene, 77–78
Zinnemann, Fred, 128
Zirinsky, Susan, 32, 66, 89–90, 91, 92